T0093429

AI for Big Data-Based Engineering Applications from Security Perspectives

Artificial intelligence (AI), machine learning, and advanced electronic circuits involve learning from every data input and using those inputs to generate new rules for future business analytics. AI and machine learning are now giving us new opportunities to use big data that we already had, as well as unleash a whole lot of new use cases with new data types. With the increasing use of AI dealing with highly sensitive information such as healthcare, adequate security measures are required to securely store and transmit this information. This book provides broader coverage of the basic aspects of advanced circuits design and applications.

AI for Big Data-Based Engineering Applications from Security Perspectives is an integrated source that aims at understanding the basic concepts associated with the security of advanced circuits. The content includes theoretical frameworks and recent empirical findings in the field to understand the associated principles, key challenges, and recent real-time applications of advanced circuits, AI, and big data security. It illustrates the notions, models, and terminologies that are widely used in the area of Very Large Scale Integration (VLSI) circuits, security, identifies the existing security issues in the field, and evaluates the underlying factors that influence system security. This work emphasizes the idea of understanding the motivation behind advanced circuit design to establish the AI interface and to mitigate security attacks in a better way for big data. This book also outlines exciting areas of future research where already existing methodologies can be implemented. This material is suitable for students, researchers, and professionals with research interest in AI for big data-based engineering applications from security perspectives, faculty members across universities, and software developers.

AI for Big Data-Based Engineering Applications from Security Perspectives

Edited By

Balwinder Raj, Brij B. Gupta, Shingo Yamaguchi, and Sandeep Singh Gill

CRC Press
Taylor & Francis Group
Boca Raton London New York

CRC Press is an imprint of the
Taylor & Francis Group, an **informa** business

First edition published 2023
by CRC Press
6000 Broken Sound Parkway NW, Suite 300, Boca Raton, FL 33487-2742

and by CRC Press
4 Park Square, Milton Park, Abingdon, Oxon, OX14 4RN

CRC Press is an imprint of Taylor & Francis Group, LLC

Library of Congress Cataloging-in-Publication Data
Names: Raj, Balwinder, 1980- editor. | Gupta, Brij, 1982- editor. |
Yamaguchi, Shingo, 1969- editor. | Gill, Sandeep Singh, editor.
Title: AI for big data based engineering applications from the security
perspectives / edited by: Balwinder Raj, Brij B. Gupta, Shingo Yamaguchi
and Sandeep Singh Gill.
Description: First edition. | Boca Raton : CRC Press, 2023. |
Includes bibliographical references.
Identifiers: LCCN 2022060840 (print) | LCCN 2022060841 (ebook) |
ISBN 9781032136134 (hardback) | ISBN 9781032136141 (paperback) |
ISBN 9781003230113 (ebook)
Subjects: LCSH: Integrated circuits–Design and construction–
Data processing–Security measures. | Artificial intelligence–Industrial applications. |
Big data.
Classification: LCC TK7874.A356 2023 (print) | LCC TK7874 (ebook) |
DDC 005.75–dc23/eng/20230313
LC record available at https://lccn.loc.gov/2022060840
LC ebook record available at https://lccn.loc.gov/2022060841

ISBN: 9781032136134 (hbk)
ISBN: 9781032136141 (pbk)
ISBN: 9781003230113 (ebk)

DOI: 10.1201/9781003230113

Typeset in Minion
by codeMantra

Contents

Preface

Artificial intelligence (AI) is a new technical discipline that researches and develops theories, methods, technologies, and application systems for simulating the extension and expansion of human intelligence. The ability of AI to work well with data analytics is the primary reason why AI and big data are now seemingly inseparable. AI, machine learning, and deep learning are learning from every data input and using those inputs to generate new rules for future business analytics. AI and machine learning are now giving us new opportunities to use the big data that we already had, as well as unleash a whole lot of new use cases with new data types. In this book, we will provide an overview of the existing threats which violate privacy aspects and security issues inflicted by big data as a primary driving force within AI.

Chapter 1 deals with role of AI in 3D printing and additive manufacturing. 3D printing/rapid prototyping/additive manufacturing is defined as the process of developing three-dimensional objects from a computer model. Additive manufacturing along with tissue engineering is termed ad 3D bioprinting. It is a platform that brings together technocrats, medical professionals, and physicists to develop organ printing, which is believed to revolutionize the organ donation shortage scenario worldwide. It also overcomes the general problems of a receptor's immune response as the printed organ is seeded with the receptor's own stem cells. AI has relatedness with the terms machine learning and neural networks. AI in collaboration with 3D bioprinting is expected to increase performance at every step: preparation, bioprinting, postbioprinting by requiring less human intervention and being less error-prone, which improves the entire bioprinting workflow. AI in its present state has lucrative opportunities when combined with bioprinting, but current status still requires human intervention at almost every step, as AI is not fully incorporated with 3D bioprinting to date.

Chapter 2: In many industries, recent technological advancements and connectivity have resulted in the creation of internet of things (IoT) and AI applications. IoT offers a wide range of applications in every industry around the world, including engineering, medicine, banking, agriculture, power, and farming. Scientists, researchers, doctors, and technologists, etc. see a big future in IoT. Although AI is not a panacea, capturing patient data will lead to precision medicine, assist in detecting disease before it manifests, and enable independent living for the elderly, among many other things. However, there will be obstacles to this advancement, both ethically and in terms of privacy. In this vein, the effects of IoT and AI in healthcare are investigated. This chapter also identifies gaps and future research areas in technology design and adoption, data security and privacy regulations, and system efficacy and safety for the top application categories, which include communication protocols and sensor networks.

Chapter 3: Spintronics is one of the rising technologies with massive growth and the capability to rise in the coming years, especially in the industrial market for AI applications. In spintronics or spin electronics, data are accumulated by using the spin property of electrons. Due to this property of electrons, there is a huge shift in device functionality. A lot of research work is still ongoing to understand and enhance this property. Here, we explore and discuss the spin property, which can solve the biggest issue today's world is facing, that is, power consumption. With this new technology, there are many advantages like high speed, compact devices, less power consumption, reduced heat dissipation, and nonvolatility. The applications of the different types of spintronic-based devices include quantum computing, data storage, industrial motors, MRAM, current sensor, magnetic sensor, and many more. This chapter covers the basic idea of spintronics, the working principle of spintronics, the different types of material used for the fabrication of devices, and the challenges which researchers are facing. The different types of power-reducing techniques and devices are discussed along with the phenomena of spintronics like GMR, TMR, spin transfer torque, spin hall effect, etc. The main focus of writing this chapter is for readers to understand the basics of spintronics, moving into spintronic devices with its applications in AI.

Chapter 4: This chapter covers AI and IoT aspects in healthcare. Lack of resources and delays in diagnosis lead heart disease patients to a critical situation. Cardiovascular disease patients are increasing day by day due to arrhythmias. Cardiovascular diseases like cardiac arrest or silent heart attack deaths increased by 30% during the COVID-19 pandemic. With the advancement of the internet, it has become possible for doctors to remain in touch with patients remotely and carry out patient monitoring 24×7. This has become a reality due to revolution in the telecom sector, which made 4G, LTE, LTE-A, 5G, and 6G services available. The combination of these technologies with internet access came to be known as internet of medical things (IoMT). The techniques developed for measurement of vital signals like heart rate and respiration from multimodal physiological signals, namely, ECG, AB, PPG, EMG, EOG, EEG, etc. are reviewed in this chapter.

Chapter 5: Images captured under dense smog suffer from various problems such as distortion of spatial information and poor visibility. The majority of existing restoration models are for other variants of weather degradation techniques such as fog, haze, rain, and dust. It is challenging to create a restoration model for smoggy images as they affect machine vision systems such as aerial imaging and sensing imaging. In this chapter, a novel deep learning–based desmogging architecture is proposed. The transmission map and atmospheric veil are estimated using optimized dark channel prior (DCP). The result generated by DCP is satisfactory for images distorted due to foggy or hazy weather conditions, but the presence of black fumes due to smog gradients in the atmosphere makes it difficult to separate sky and nonsky regions. To overcome the disadvantage, the transmission map of the image obtained after computation using DCP is optimized by enhancing contrast and entropy of the image. Various performance metrics are calculated, and a comparative analysis of the proposed model with existing desmogging or dehazing algorithms is presented.

Chapter 6: In 2020, the COVID-19 virus became a major public health concern. Face recognition is quickly becoming a popular alternative due to its non-contact characteristics. Putting on a face mask is one of the most effective ways to stop the transmission of the COVID-19 virus. Wearing a face mask can reduce your risk of contracting the virus by as much as 70% or more. Due to the WHO's recommendation, those who gather in congested areas should wear masks. In certain places, incorrect usage of face masks has exacerbated the spread of disease. Mask-monitoring systems were deemed the best solution. AI and image processing capabilities may allow governments to mandate the wearing of face masks. Using machine learning, deep learning, and a variety of other approaches, this chapter tackles the problems of facial identification, helmet detection, and mask detection in depth. A disguise can be detected using any or all of the methods listed above. Detector masks must be made more effective immediately. The pros and cons of several methods of detecting a face mask are also presented.

Chapter 7: This chapter presents various types of emerging nonvolatile memories like FeFET-based memory, MRAM, STTRAM nanowire-based memory, etc. Nonvolatile memory devices have moved toward nanoscale size as a result of technological advancements and rising high-density demand. New products are urgently needed to overcome the present flash memory devices' high programming voltage and current leakage issues. Carbon nanotube and nanowire have now been determined for different nonvolatile memory applications to be among the most significant nano-materials, having exceptional mechanical and electrical characteristics. Comparisons of different nanowires on the basis of parameters such as diameter, length, mobility, and resistivity have been presented in this chapter. Furthermore, a comparative analysis of emerging nonvolatile memories (eNVM) devices has been carried out based on key performance metrics.

Chapter 8: This chapter describes the design analysis of intelligent irrigation systems with automatic watering for plants, temperature monitoring for the safety of plants, and energy saving based on intelligent controllers and the global-system-for-mobile-communication (GSM). The designed structure has been controlled remotely through wireless technology such as GSM by sending a short message service (SMS) as password to initialize the intelligent controller for the plants' watering and temperature monitoring. The system can automatically generate an alert message to the owner's handset and show the current status of plant watering through SMS. The switching of water pumps depends on the moisture level of the soil or plant area and the status of moisture level as shown through water level indicators. If the moisture level of the soil is higher or the plants are full of water, the microcontroller automatically stops the water pump, which saves electricity. On the other hand, if the environmental temperature is less than or more than the required temperature level, then the system will automatically send an alert message to the owner that intervention is required. The intelligence is performed by utilizing the auto switching of the water pump for plant watering, energy saving, safety of fields from undesired environment using temperature monitoring and remotely controlled atmosphere. The system consists of an intelligent microcontroller, GSM modem, temperature sensor, analog to digital converter, moisture sensor, relay driver unit, water pump, and display units. The circuit designing and simulation has been done in Proteous software, with designing in KEIL software followed by Flash Magic burning tools.

Chapter 9: Power dissipation is the key factor that is considered while designing low-power circuits. Complementary metal oxide semiconductor (CMOS) technology faces major challenges in nanoscaled circuits, where power dissipation increases by a large amount. Quantum Dot Cellular Automata (QCA) is a prominent nanotechnology for the evolution of nanostructure-based circuits. In QCA nanotechnology, large amounts of power dissipation are mitigated by the concept of reversible computing. Reversible gates provide one-to-one mapping, therefore dissipating much less power. Different reversible gates in QCA nanotechnology have different structures and characteristics. This chapter compares various notable reversible gates and their results, which are investigated at logical and cell levels. The reversible gate designs are different in terms of the number of QCA cells, occupied area, and time delays. Various comparisons are performed for the cell count, occupied area, and the applied number of clock zones. Different reversible gates are presented and compared for the use in complex designs. Reversible gates having a smaller number of garbage outputs are preferred. The reversible gates are simulated using the QCA designer.

Acknowledgments

This book is based on research carried out by a number of authors. Many people have contributed greatly to this book on AI for big data–based engineering applications from security perspectives. We are grateful to a number of friends and colleagues in encouraging us to start working on this book. We as the editors would like to acknowledge all of them for their valuable help and generous ideas in improving the quality of this book. With our feelings of gratitude, we would like to introduce them in turn. The first mention is the authors and reviewers of each chapter of this book. Without their outstanding expertise, constructive reviews, and devoted effort, this comprehensive book would not have its intended impact. The second mention is the CRC Press/Taylor and Francis Group staff for their constant encouragement, continuous assistance, and untiring support. Without their technical support, this book would not have been completed. The third mention is the editors' families for being the source of continuous love, unconditional support, and prayers not only for this work, but throughout the editors' lives. Last but far from least, we express our heartfelt thanks to the Almighty for bestowing us with the courage to face the complexities of life and complete this work.

Sep. 2022
Balwinder Raj
Brij B. Gupta
Shingo Yamaguchi
Sandeep Singh Gill

About the Editors

Dr. Balwinder Raj (MIEEE'2006) did his B.Tech., Electronics Engineering (PTU Jalandhar); M.Tech., Microelectronics (PU Chandigarh); and Ph.D., VLSI Design (IIT Roorkee), India in 2004, 2006, and 2010, respectively. For his postdoctoral research work, the European Commission awarded him "Erasmus Mundus" Mobility of life research fellowship based on his studies at the University of Rome, Tor Vergata, Italy in 2010–2011. Dr. Raj received the India4EU (India for European Commission) Fellowship and worked as a visiting researcher at KTH University, Stockholm, Sweden, October–November 2013. He also visited Aalto University, Finland, as a visiting researcher during June 2017. Currently, he is working as an Associate Professor at the Dr B. R. Ambedkar National Institute of Techology Jalandhar, India; previously, he worked at National Institute of Technical Teachers Training and Research Chandigarh, India. Dr. Raj has also worked as an Assistant Professor at ABV-IIITM Gwalior (An autonomous institute established by Ministry of HRD, Govt. of India) from July 2011 to April 2012. He has received the Best Teacher Award from Indian Society for Technical Education (ISTE) New Delhi on 26 July 2013. Dr. Raj received the Young Scientist Award from Punjab Academy of Sciences during the 18th Punjab Science Congress held on 9 February 2015. He has also received a research paper award in the International Conference on Electrical and Electronics Engineering held at Pattaya, Thailand, from 11 to 12 July 2015. Dr. Raj has authored/co-authored 5 books, 12 book chapters, and more than 100 research papers in peer-reviewed international/national journals and conferences. His areas of interest in research are classical/non-classical nanoscale semiconductor device modeling; nanoelectronics and their applications in hardware security, sensors and circuit design, FinFET-based memory design, low-power VLSI design, digital/analog VLSI design, and FPGA implementation.

Prof. Brij B. Gupta is working as the Director of International Center for AI and Cyber Security Research, Incubation and Innovations, and as a Full Professor with the Department of Computer Science and Information Engineering (CSIE), Asia University, Taiwan. In more than 17 years of professional experience, he has published over 500 papers in journals/ conferences including 35 books and 10 Patents with over 19,500 citations. He has received numerous national and international awards including the Canadian Commonwealth Scholarship (2009), Faculty Research Fellowship Award (2017), MeitY, GoI, IEEE GCCE outstanding and WIE paper awards and Best Faculty Award (2018 and 2019), NIT KKR, respectively. Prof. Gupta was recently selected for 2022 Clarivate Web of Science Highly Cited Researchers in Computer Science (He is the only researcher from Taiwan and India in Computer Science in this prestigious 2022 HCR List). He was also selected in the 2022, 2021, and 2020 Stanford University ranking of the world's top 2% scientists. He is also a Visiting/ Adjunct Professor with several universities worldwide. He is also an IEEE Senior Member (2017) and was selected as 2021 Distinguished Lecturer in IEEE CTSoc. Dr. Gupta is also serving as Member-in-Large, Board of Governors, IEEE Consumer Technology Society (2022–2024). He is also leading IJSWIS, IJSSCI, STE, and IJCAC as Editor-in-Chief. Moreover, he is also serving as Lead-Editor of a Book Series with CRC and IET Press. He also served as TPC Member in more than 150 international conferences and is also serving as Associate/Guest Editor of various journals and transactions. His research interests include information security, cyber physical systems, cloud computing, blockchain technologies, intrusion detection, AI, social media, and networking.

Dr. Shingo Yamaguchi is a Professor in the Graduate School of Sciences and Technology for Innovation, Yamaguchi University, Japan. He received the B.E., M.E., and D.E. degrees from Yamaguchi University, Japan, in 1992, 1994, and 2002, respectively. He was a Visiting Scholar of University of Illinois at Chicago, U.S., in 2007. He is currently the Director of the Center for Information and Data Science Education, Yamaguchi University. He also serves as the Editor-in-Chief of *International Journal of Internet of Things and Cyber-Assurance*. He was part of the Board of Governors of IEEE Consumer Electronics Society and served as the Editor-in-Chief of *IEEE Consumer Electronics Magazine*. He was also a Conference Chair of IEEE International Conferences, such as GCCE 2014 and ICCE 2021. He is a Senior Member of IEEE and IEICE.

Dr. Sandeep Singh Gill is currently Professor and Head in ECE Department NITTTR Chandigarh. He has more than 25 years of teaching and research experience. He has also held many administrative positions like Dean Academic, Dean Administration, Coordinator of TEQIP, Head of Department, and many more. Dr. Gill has guided 110 M.Tech. theses and many Ph.D. scholars. He has published more than 150 research papers in international/national journals and conferences and filed one patent. His research areas are VLSI design automation, soft computing, and CAD tools.

Contributors

Sharu Bansal
ECE Department
Sant Longowal Institute of
    Engineering and Technology
Longowal, Sangrur, India

Neha Bhardwaj
ECE Department
National Institute of Technical
    Teachers Training and Research
Chandigarh, India

Tarun Chaudhary
Department of ECE
Dr. B.R. Ambedkar National
    Institute of Technology
Jalandhar, Punjab, India

Meenakshi Devi
School of Engineering, Computing
    & Mathematics
University of Oxford Brookes
Oxford, United Kingdom

Sandeep Singh Gill
VLSI Design Lab, ECE Department
National Institute of Technical
    Teachers Training and Research
Chandigarh, India

Akshay Juneja
Department of Electrical and
    Instrumentation Engineering
Thapar Institute of Engineering
    and Technology
Punjab, India

Amod Kumar
Electronics and Communication
    Engineering Department
National Institute of Technical
    Teachers Training and Research
Chandigarh, India

Dilip Kumar
ECE Department
Sant Longowal Institute of
    Engineering and Technology
Longowal, Sangrur, India

Parveen Kumar
Department of Electronics and
    Communication Engineering
Dr. B.R. Ambedkar National
    Institute of Technology
Jalandhar, Punjab, India

Vijay Kumar
Information Technology
Dr. B.R. Ambedkar National
Institute of Technology
Jalandhar, India

Preetiyanka
Department of ECE
J.C. Boss University (YMCA)
Farridabad, Haryana, India

Pushparaj
Electronics and Communication
Engineering Department
National Institute of Technical
Teachers Training and Research
Chandigarh, India

Balwant Raj
Department of ECE
University Institute of Engineering
and Technology (UIET)
Panjab University SSG Regional
Centre
Hoshiarpur, India

Balwinder Raj
VLSI Design Lab, Department
of Electronics and
Communications Engineering
Dr. B.R. Ambedkar National
Institute of Technology
Jalandhar, India

Garima Saini
Electronics and Communication
Engineering Department
National Institute of Technical
Teachers Training and Research
Chandigarh, India

Parul Sharma
VLSI Design Lab, Department
of Electronics and
Communications Engineering
National Institute of Technical
Teachers Training and Research
Chandigarh, India

Sanjeev Kumar Sharma
Department of Electronics and
Communication Engineering
Dr. B.R. Ambedkar National
Institute of Technology
Jalandhar, Punjab, India

Vijay Kumar Sharma
School of Electronics and
Communication Engineering
Shri Mata Vaishno Devi University
Katra, Jammu and Kashmir, India

Mandeep Singh
Department of ECE
Dr. B.R. Ambedkar National
Institute of Technology
Jalandhar, Punjab, India

Sunil Kumar Singla
Department of Electrical and
Instrumentation Engineering
Thapar Institute of Engineering
and Technology
Punjab, India

Meenakshi Sood
CDC Department
National Institute of Technical
Teachers Training and Research
Chandigarh, India

CHAPTER 1

Artificial Intelligence-Empowered 3D Bioprinting

Neha Bhardwaj, Meenakshi Sood, and Sandeep Singh Gill

National Institute of Technical Teachers Training and Research

CONTENTS

DOI: 10.1201/9781003230113-1

1.1   INTRODUCTION

Additive Manufacturing is a process to design or develop an object in a layered manner by adding materials layer by layer from a CAD model. 3D printing, also known as Additive Manufacturing or Rapid Prototyping, is a process of creating a 3D object from a digital model created using a computer. Additive Manufacturing can be defined as "cut and stack" approach for creating a free-form object in layered manner [1,2].

3D printing has interesting applications in many fields like manufacturing, industrial, medical, sociocultural, jewelry, etc. [3–5]. Hull [6] first introduced the concept of 3D printing in the year 1986. He had expertise in stereolithographic process and Standard Tessellation Language (STL) file format, which till date is the most widely used file format in Additive Manufacturing. Pereira et al. [7] stated how Additive Manufacturing started as early as in the 1960s and since then has expanded applications in many fields like medicine, manufacturing, etc. [3,7]. The materials that can be deposited by the process of 3D printing are ceramics, grapheme-based materials, thermoplastics, etc. [4]. Application of 3D printing or Additive Manufacturing has substantially reduced the production cost and time. The main advantage lies in creating objects as per the need of consumer by employing this technique. 3D printing is nowadays widely used in the world in almost every domain. Open source designs can be created by the use of Additive Manufacturing in field of agriculture, medicine, aerospace, etc. [3,5,8]. Even though there are many advantages offered by Additive Manufacturing, there are still some disadvantages, e.g., being able to produce the desired object or organ makes it completely machine-driven with less human intervention, so it can raise concerns about employability of the people. At the same time, with the mere possession of blue prints or CAD models may lead to replication of products easily [9]. 3D printing technology has revolutionized almost every industry in terms of design, development and manufacturing.

1.2   APPLICATIONS OF 3D PRINTING

1.2.1   Aeronautics Industry

In aeronautics, 3D printing has proved its capability in developing lightweight parts, with improved and complex geometries, which has substantially reduced energy requirement and resources. Nickel-based alloys are employed to print 3D aerospace parts owing to its excellent tensile properties and resistance to climatic degradation [10–12].

1.2.2 Automobile Industry

In automotive industry, light and more compact structures can be created for cars, which have resistance to denting and degradation. Many leading manufacturers like BMW, Audi, etc. have already employed 3D printing in car spare parts manufacturing and prototyping [13,14].

1.2.3 Catering Industry

Food industry is also deploying 3D printing to create specific dietary meals for athletes, patients and pregnant women. Specific materials can be mixed and processed into various complicated structures and shapes to create special diets by using Additive Manufacturing. 3D food printing is a low-cost, robust, and ecofriendly process for food customization for specific requirements [15,16].

1.2.4 Health Care/Medical Industry

As there are many patients awaiting organ transplantation, 3D printing proves to be a boon in health industry as patient-specific organs and tissues can be printed. It finds application in skin printing, bone and cartilage, vascular grafts, etc. 3D-printed models are useful for surgeons and medical students for preoperative planning and hands-on medical training, as they are simulation of patients' real pathological condition [17–26].

1.2.5 Textile Industry

Customization of clothes, jewelry, accessories, etc. incorporating the latest fashion designs can be done using 3D printing, according to customer's size and personal preferences. Many leading manufacturers like Nike and Adidas are employing 3D printing technology in manufacturing shoes on a large scale [27,28].

1.2.6 Construction Industry

3D printing can be used to build entire building with complex geometries or can be utilized to develop mechanical components. This also helps in lessening the construction time and quickens the construction process. Recently IIT Madras in India has constructed a 600-square-feet house by employing 3D printing. Other examples of 3D-printed houses are Apis Cor Printed House in Russia and Canal House in Amsterdam [29,30].

1.2.7 Electronics Industry

3D printing finds applications in various structural electronic devices like active electronic materials, electrodes and adaptive design devices. 3D electrodes are being printed easily in less time and with more accuracy by using this technology. Furthermore, this process has high precision and high speed, such that almost eight electrodes can be 3D printed in less than half an hour [31].

1.3 3D BIOPRINTING

Additive Manufacturing in collaboration with tissue engineering is termed as 3D bioprinting. It has attracted the attention of many researchers owing to its easy fabrication, high accuracy and customized production [1]. This technique is diversified in terms of its applications and also how material is deposited layer by layer under computer control to create a 3D object. 3D bioprinting or organ printing can be defined as a multi-disciplinary field involving engineers, doctors and scientists working together to create biological substitutes to cater organ shortage worldwide.

Bioprinting is a broad term and involves modeling of tissue or organ on a software, preparation of bioinks, deposition of bioinks and finally the printing of computed model through a supportive 3D printer [32]. The choice of materials selection for 3D bioprinting is crucial as human tissues and organs have complex functionality and structure, so it is imperative to wisely select the biomaterial for tissue printing as it is almost impossible for a single material to mimic human tissue functionality. Also, the compatibility of the material selected for organ printing should be compatible with 3D printer and printing software [33]. With the advent of tissue engineering, doctors see printed organs as more effective and viable solution to organ transplant in comparison to organ donation from donors [34,35]. 3D bioprinting is a different process than 3D printing as it involves cells and biomaterials. 3D bioprinting of tissues/organs (in vitro and in situ) is very important as the donor availability is limited and receptor's immune and body response may not be conducive for donor organ, and this is the reason medical experts and engineers consider 3D bioprinting as a boon in the medical field [36,37]. This field of merging electronics and biology shall be a boon for bridging the gap between organ shortage and transplantation needs. 3D bioprinting has the ability to generate patient-specific bodily structures which can mimic the human organs. However, 3D bioprinting has major challenges like vascularization, cell proliferation, cytotoxicity, immune system response of patient, etc. Future research should take into account all these major challenges in addition to organ printing.

Mao et al. [33] have specifically mentioned the importance of compatibility of materials with printers and printing technology. 3D bioprinting or organ printing has many useful applications in the field of health care like personalized medical implants and devices, medical training, preoperative surgical planning, etc. [38,39]. Murphy and Atala [40,41] in their research have mentioned applications of 3D bioprinting in various domains: transplantation of several tissues, including multilayered skin, bone, vascular grafts, tracheal splints, heart tissue and cartilaginous structures. Ozbolat and Yu [35] described the difference between tissue engineering and 3D bioprinting as the former involves seeding of cells to create scaffolds and then cell proliferation and differentiation, whereas the latter is a computer-aided bioadditive manufacturing process in which hydrogel-based scaffolds and living cells are printed together for 3D organ fabrication. Bin Zhang et al. [42] demonstrated the recent developments in fabrication of various body parts and tissues. Furthermore, cytotoxicology and drug delivery for the same were also reviewed. The differences between 3D printing and 3D bioprinting were mentioned with a focus on the challenges faced.

3D printing is being used extensively in the field of medicine by medical professionals to make diagnostic assessments about the severity and spread of the disease, presurgical planning and surgical simulation [38]. 3D-printed models can serve as an excellent tool to carry out presurgical planning and post-surgery discussions. They can also help doctors to carry out surgery in a smooth manner [43]. Imaging techniques play a crucial role in designing of a model. The three main steps in 3D bioprinting phase are designing of model, selection of compatible bioinks and efficient deposition as illustrated in Figure 1.1. The flow of bioprinting is detailed stepwise in the following section.

Figure 1.1 illustrates 3D bioprinting of aorta, the largest vessel in human body that carries the blood from the heart to the rest of the organs. Zhang et al. [42] developed a patient-specific 3D-printed phantom of aorta with stent grafts in situ, and the developed phantom was then scanned with different computed tomography (CT) protocols to determine the optimal scanning parameters for post-treatment patients. The whole step-by-step process is illustrated in Figure 1.1.

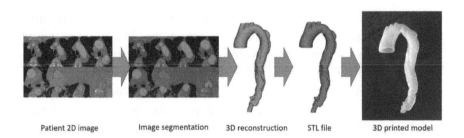

| Patient 2D image | Image segmentation | 3D reconstruction | STL file | 3D printed model |

FIGURE 1.1 A schematic representing various steps in the 3D bioprinting process [42].

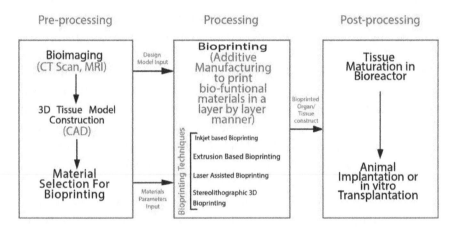

FIGURE 1.2 Flowchart for 3D bioprinting [44].

The 3D bioprinting has three main steps: bioimaging, processing and post-processing, which are illustrated in Figure 1.2. The detailed explanation of these steps is given in the following subsections.

1.3.1 Pre-Processing Phase

In the preprinting phase comes the imaging and model formulation of the selected organ/tissue as described in Figure 1.2. Medical imaging is a technique to acquire internal images of affected body parts or organs for better diagnosis and to assess the extent and severity of the disease. Many imaging modalities are available and are chosen depending upon many parameters like cost, ease of availability, resolution, etc. The data collected from various imaging techniques serve as database to point out the anomalies in normal and affected body parts.

Muller et al. [38], in their research article, showed that 3D-printed models are effective in understanding the anatomy, allowing presurgical simulation, accurate implant fabrication and medical trainees to enhance their knowledge. Medical imaging plays a pivotal role in 3D bioprinting as various Imaging techniques are employed to create realistic 3D models for doctors [39]. Papaioannou et al. [45], in their research, have reviewed the imaging modalities, biomaterials and cellular engineering which can successfully lead to the fabrication of patient-specific vascular tissue construct. Lau et al. [43,46], in their research, demonstrated the uses of 3D printed models for diagnostic assessment. A patient-specific 3D model of brain tumor was created. Magnetic Resonance Imaging (MRI) Modality was employed, and images obtained were then segmented and post-processed to point anomalies. The 3D model created provided realistic information and visualization of brain anatomy [43]. Thore M. BuÈcking et al et al. [46] investigated the accuracy of Congenital Heart Disease 3D Model by comparing the results with CT images and STL files. A quantitative analysis demonstrated the accuracy of the 3D printed model as there were only slight differences in CT and segmented STL images. Thore M. BuÈcking et al. [40,46] demonstrated the upgradation in image segmentation tools which are used to create patient-specific 3D models. The process by which imaging data obtained through CT reports is generally divided into three steps to create a 3D model: image segmentation, mesh refinement and finally 3D model. Zhang et al. [42] developed a patient-specific 3D model and the developed model was scanned with different CT protocols to calculate the best-suited scanning parameters for treating patients. It was observed that image quality can be obtained by decreasing tube voltage. Gerorge E. et al. [44] mentioned about the process of converting Digital Medical Imaging and Communication Data (DICOM) to 3D models and described the imaging, post-processing and equipment requirements to make a 3D printed model from standard radiologic images effectively.

Mamdouh et al. [47] presented a method for converting medical data from 2D to 3D using Mimics Software and editing them to give a best-suited representation of human anatomy.

Usman Akram et al. [48] demonstrated a technique employing CT images to divide and segment the liver using a global threshold in context to removing noise and clarity by exploiting supporting mathematical equations. The results show improvement with tools to retain the actual shape and size of the liver. Shi and Fahmi [49] suggested in his study that flex line model is the best way to calculate the proportion of distortions and weights in 3D Liver modeling. Nguyen et al. [50] performed a comparative analysis of the DICOM digital image conversion methods to analyze and construct the 3D model of human body parts. Thanh and Hai [51,52] in their research constructed a 3D image using MRI imaging data of the brain inside human cortex. Dataset comprising 44 2D MRI brain images of 256×192 pixels resolution was used in this research, and the medical database was provided by Binh Duong General Hospital, Vietnam. The multilevel Otsu method was employed for image segmentation, and it was suggested that imaging data to be collected from different angles to get a clear picture of brain for proper diagnosis.

1.3.2 Material Selection and Bioinks

Gungor-Ozkerim et al. [53] utilized bioink as a biomaterial or mixture of biomaterials in the form of hydrogels. Cell types are encapsulated in it for creation of various tissue constructs. In 3D bioprinting, a bioink is any natural or synthetic polymer selected for its favorable biocompatibility characteristics and good rheological properties. These characteristics are useful in supporting living cells to facilitate their adhesion, proliferation and differentiation during cell or tissue maturation.

The bioink selection is dependent on the specific application (e.g., target tissue), the type of cells and the bioprinter to be used [54–57]. An ideal bioink should have desirable mechanical, rheological, chemical and biological characteristics [58]. While bioprinting, few parameters are to be considered, like uniform filament diameter for suitable bioink deposition, bleeding of filaments at intersects, etc. Bioinks available can be categorized as natural, artificial and commercially used bioinks. Some of the commonly used bioinks are discussed in the following section.

i. Hydrogel-Based Bioinks

Hydrogels are biocompatible and biodegradable, which account for their widespread use as bioink. Some of the hydrogel materials are Alginate, Gelatin, Collagen, Fibrin, Gellan Gum, Hyaluronic Acid, Agarose, Chitosan, Silk, Decellularized Extracellular Matrix, Poly(Ethylene Glycol) (PEG) [58,59].

Recent research studies report that cells laden with hydrogels for the construction of 3D organ constructs lack immunogenicity as hydrogels are patient-specific [60].

ii. Protein-Based Bioinks

Collagen, the most important structural protein in the Extracellular Matrix (ECM) of cells has in vitro and in vivo compatibility along with tissue-matching physiochemical properties. Koch et al. [59] used collagen with encapsulated keratinocytes and fibroblasts to 3D bioprint skin tissue.

iii. Polysaccharides

Alginate is a natural polysaccharide found in ECM of human body. It has favorable biocompatibility and low cytotoxicity, and is a low-cost process, thus making it favorable for bioprinting [60]. At times, Alginate is blended with biomaterials in the process of 3D bioprinting. It is the most widely used bioink till date.

iv. Synthetic Polymer-Based Bioinks

The most commonly used polymer in synthetic-based polymer bioinks is PEG. The main advantages of this material are its non-cytotoxicity and non-immunogenicity [61,62].

Besides these, many other different kinds of bioinks exist like Composite bioinks. Bioinks with bioactive molecules are being used depending upon the application to ensure correct functionality and strength of biological 3D-printed construct.

1.3.3 Bioprinting Techniques

3D bioprinting marks the combination of cells, tissues, growth factors and biomaterials to create biocompatible tissues and organs. Bioprinting along with tissue engineering has the ability to create various tissues and organs like skin, cartilage, bones, etc. After creation of 3D model, a compatible bioprinter is used to print the synthetic tissue. Till date, three major bioprinting techniques are available: Inkjet, Laser-Assisted (LAB) and Extrusion bioprinting. Each printing technology has its own strengths and limitations [63].

i. Inkjet Printing

It is the first bioprinter to be used to print living cells and tissues together [64]. Encapsulating the cells in a highly hydrated polymer overcame the problem of cells becoming dead during the printing process [65]. The printable cells and biomaterials are given a desired pattern using droplets, emitted via thermal or piezoelectric process as illustrated in Figure 1.2. The main advantage of Inkjet printers is their low printing cost in comparison to the available commercial bioprinters. Also, these have high printing speed as printer head supports parallel work mode. They offer a high cell viability of 80%–90% as demonstrated experimentally by Cui et al. [66,67]. Some disadvantages are as follows: high cell density leads to high viscosity of bioinks, so when deposited through Ink jet printer, it can lead to clogging of the printer head. Oversettling effect is observed in Inkjet printers, i.e., when bioinks are loaded into the ink cartridge, they are mixed well. During the printing process, cells begin to settle in the cartridge, increasing the viscosity of the bioink which leads to the clogging of the printer head.

ii. Laser-Assisted Printing

Laser Direct write and Laser Induced transfer technologies gave rise to Laser-Assisted Printing [68]. These printers have donor-type layers that respond to laser stimulation as shown in Figure 1.3. The donor layer has a 'ribbon' structure which consists of an energy-absorbing layer (e.g., titanium or gold) on the top and a bioink solution layer at the bottom. During the process of printing, a focused laser pulse is applied to energize some area of the absorbing layer. This laser pulse vaporizes a portion of the donor layer, creating high-pressure bubble at the interface of the bioink layer and hence ejecting the suspended bioink. This technique offers high cell viabilities and a resolution between 10 and 50 micrometers. The main advantages offered are as follows: high-level accuracy can be achieved in printing multiple cell types [69,70]. High degree of precision and resolution are achievable through LAB. The main disadvantage is its high cost. Also, they

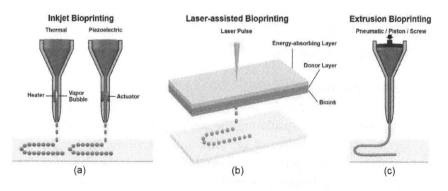

FIGURE 1.3   (a–c) Schematic illustrations of 3D bioprinters [73].

are huge and cumbersome to install in comparison to other available bioprinters [63]. Laser-Assisted Bioprinters have some unexplored parameters which may affect the droplet size and quality.

iii. Extrusion Printing

Extrusion Printing technique uses pressure techniques to dispense the bioink. With the application of continuous force, these printers can print direct lines rather than droplets. The main benefit is that they have good compatibility with hydrogels of varying viscosities [64]. High-density cells can be easily printed via Extrusion bioprinters [71,72]. These bioprinters expose the encapsulated cells to a large mechanical stress which may reduce cell viability [63]. Extrusion bioprinting is a promising bioprinting technique which can bioprint constructs and tissues at a clinically relevant size. At the same time, shear stress can affect the cells morphology and their metabolic activity [72].

Figure 1.3 represents the different types of bioprinters discussed above. The diagram demonstrates various parts of these printers in detail. Extrusion-based bioprinters are most widely used because these printers are versatile and comparatively cheaper in cost.

1.4 ARTIFICIAL INTELLIGENCE AND 3D BIOPRINTING

Machine learning is a method of data analysis for automating analytical model building. It is a subset of Artificial Intelligence (AI) that systems can learn from data, can make decisions, pattern recognition with less or no human intervention.

1.4.1 Machine Learning Methods

Supervised learning is a combination of machine learning and AI. It makes use of labeled datasets to train algorithms for data classification and predicting outcomes. As input data are fed into the model, the weights are adjusted until the model has been fitted appropriately; supervised learning finds applications in classification such as classifying spam in a different folder from the inbox. Unsupervised learning makes use of unlabeled data unlike supervised learning. From that data, patterns are discovered that helps in solving clustering or association problems. Clustering or cluster analysis is a machine learning technique to group unlabeled data. Besides these, reinforcement learning is there, in which the training data are fed into algorithms between unsupervised and supervised learning.

In this learning, only an indication of correct or incorrect action is provided unlike indicating correct output in supervised learning. In addition to the above learning methods, many new machine learning methods are also developed to incorporate in bioprinting for better response like Semi-Supervised Learning [74]. Deep learning in 3D bioprinting is seeding 3D scaffolds with living cells and biomaterials; growth factors are created from raw data collected from multiple processing layers of different models [75].

1.4.2 Deep Learning in 3D Bioprinting Workflow

Deep learning incorporated into 3D bioprinting will help to decrease the complexity and manufacturing cost. It will also decrease the human burden by providing generalized modeling of complex processes. A general 3D bioprinting workflow comprises preprinting phase, printing phase and lastly post-printing phase as shown in Figure 1.3.

A design map in bioprinting process is crucial to address various design factors in the process of material selection and bioprinting like shape and resolution, material heterogeneity, etc., as illustrated in Figure 1.4. In this map, 3D bioprinting process is explained diagrammatically stating biomaterials along with cells and growth factors as first step of bioprinting, followed by utilization of software tools to design a 3D model and thereafter selection of a suitable bioprinting technology to print the anatomical structure under consideration.

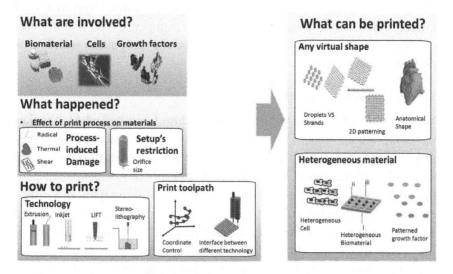

FIGURE 1.4   Design map illustrating various factors involved in the 3D bioprinting process [76].

1.4.3 Image Attainment and Segmentation

To 3D print a patient's personalized tissue/construct, image acquisition is the first step. Various imaging modalities like CT scan, MRI, and X-ray are used to acquire images of internal organ [48]. Multiple 2D image slices are used to reconstruct 3D images from the above-mentioned imaging techniques as illustrated in Figure 1.3. MRI techniques are commonly used to scan soft tissues, and CT scans are used for scanning hard tissues [1,3]. The use of higher tesla MRIs are usually not recommended as it may cause vertigo, dizziness and nausea in some patients. The potential gap between 3D image resolution (in range of mm) and printing resolution (in micrometers) can be reduced by application of deep learning algorithms in bioprinting. In generating high-resolution 3D images of cardiac tissues, deep learning has proved to be successful [4]. After getting 2D images, a 3D model is created of the particular tissue/organ by using available sophisticated software packages. Segmentation is used to identify region of interest to generate a 3D model of a particular anatomical structure. Supervised Machine plays an important role in organ segmentation by taking 3D images as training inputs and training labels being segmentation map annotated by medical experts. Such sophisticated package usage of deep learning in image acquisition and segmentation techniques can help in generating successful patient-generic 3D model. Roth et al. proposed two-stage segmentation inputs to improve the quality of 3D segmentation maps [77]. Medical image segmentation plays an important role in correct diagnosis and presurgical planning for doctors. Convolutional Neural Networks play a crucial role and remain the preferred choice till date for image analysis [78].

1.4.4 Material Selection and Cell Quality

Quality profile of involved cells and suitable materials for 3D bioprinting of selected tissue or organ is very crucial. Labeling of biomarkers is not required in accessing the cell status inputs. Deep learning in cell-based diagnostics is an efficient monitoring tool during the preprinting phase for cell quality assurance and control in 3D bioprinting processes. Contamination of cells is a big concern that has to be taken into account. Deep learning techniques are used to train the model to detect first signs of cell contamination by taking pictures of contaminated and uncontaminated cell structures and to train the model by using these real-time pictures so that contamination can be detected [79,80]. Extensive studies have to be carried out to study cells best suited for bioprinting [46]. Also, the stress cells can bear without getting damaged inside the receptor's body, and printing process is a major concern. Integrating AI algorithms in the forefront of bioprinter supporting software and relevant G Codescan perfectly determine the size of printer nozzle head. By incorporating AI along with fine-tuned bioprinter printing parameters, printing time and human intervention can be effectively reduced. Tootoni et al. compared various learning techniques in the context of predicting dimensional accuracy of 3D-printed parts [81].

1.4.5 Printing of Anatomical Structure

There are many printing technologies and related 3D bioprinters for 3D printing of the selected anatomical structure. Stereolithography-based, Inkjet, Extrusion-based, and Laser-Assisted bioprinting are the available 3D printing techniques. Among these, extrusion-based printing technique is the most widely used printing technique. Complex relationships between different parameters can be understood by applying deep learning algorithms on large datasets [69,75,82].

AI when incorporated in bioprinting can give suggestions on printing parameters of the best-suited printing material and printer for the desired anatomical structure bioprinting by analyzing data and applying algorithms, thus increasing the efficiency with less error and human intervention.

1.5 SUMMARY

AI with bioprinting offers remarkable exciting opportunities for AI experts, medicos and engineers to carry out interdisciplinary research combined on one platform. It is used mostly in drug research and as scaffolds to repair damaged tissues and ligaments. The future of organ printing can be revolutionized by collaborating bioprinting and AI together; however, generating big database to create models and G codes by application of AI algorithms is still a concern and extensive research is being carried out worldwide in this domain. Deep learning along with 3D bioprinting may help in calculating the diagnostic accuracy of 3D models created. 3D bioprinting has applications in delineating brain glioma, accurate diagnostic assessment of blockage in heart, etc. Deep learning with 3D bioprinting can help in creation of more accurate models, streamlining the entire work flow with less human intervention.

REFERENCES

1. B. K. Gu, D. J. Choi, S. J. Park, et al. "3-dimensional bioprinting for tissue engineering applications," *Biomaterials Research*, Vol. 20, p. 12, 2016. DOI: 10.1186/s40824-016-0058-2

2. D. L. Bourell, et al., "A Brief History of Additive Manufacturing and the 2009 Roadmap for Additive Manufacturing: Looking Back and Looking Ahead," *US – TURKEY Workshop on Rapid Technologies*, September 24–24, 2009.

3. N. Shahrubudin, T. C. Lee, & R. Ramlan, "An overview on 3D printing technology: Technological, materials, and applications," *Procedia Manufacturing*, Vol. 35, 2019, pp. 1286–1296. ISSN 2351-9789.

4. L. Ze-Xian, T.C. Yen, M. R. Ray, D. Mattia, I.S. Metcalfe, & D. A. Patterson, "Perspective on 3D printing of separation membranes and comparison to related unconventional fabrication techniques," *Journal of Membrane Science*, Vol. 523, No. 1, pp. 596–613, 2016.

5. Thomas, "3D printed jellyfish robots created to monitor fragile coral reefs," 3D Printer and 3D Printing News, 2018. [Online]. Available: http://www.3ders.org/articles/20181003-3d-printed-jellyfish-robots-created-to-monitor-fragile-coral-reefs.html.

6. C. W. Hull, Apparatus for production of three-dimensional objects by stereo lithography. US patent: 4,575,330. 1986.

7. T. Pereira, et al, "A comparison of traditional manufacturing vs. additive manufacturing, the best method for the job," 14th Global Congress on Manufacturing and Management (GCMM-2018) *Procedia Manufacturing*, Vol. 30, pp. 11–18, 2019.

8. O. Keles, C. W. Blevins, & K. J. Bowman, "Effect of build orientation on the mechanical reliability of 3D printed ABS," *Rapid Prototyping Journal*, Vol. 23, No.2, pp. 320–328, 2017.

9. A. Pirjan & D. M. Petrosanu, "The impact of 3D printing technology on the society and economy," *Journal of Information Systems & Operations Management*, Vol. 7, pp. 1–11, 2013.

10. S. C. Joshi, & A. A. Sheikh, "3D-printing in aerospace and its long-term sustainability," *Virtual and Physical Prototyping*, Vol. 10, No. 4, pp. 175–185, 2015.

11. W. Yu-Cheng, C. Toly, & Y. Yung-Lan, "Advanced 3D printing technologies for the aircraft industry: A fuzzy systematic approach for assessing the critical factors," *The International Journal of Advanced Manufacturing Technology*, Vol. 3, No. 3, pp. 1–10, 2018.

12. A. Uriondo, M. Esperon-Miguez, S. & Perinpanayagam, "The present and future of additive manufacturing in the aerospace sector: A review of important aspects," *Journal of Aerospace Engineering*, Vol. 229, No.11, pp. 1–14, 2015.

13. V. Sreehitha, "Impact of 3D printing in automotive industry," *International Journal of Mechanical and Production Engineering*, Vol. 5, No. 2, pp. 91–94, 2017.

14. M. Petch, "Audi gives update on use of SLM metal 3D printing for the automotive industry," *3D Printing Industry*, 2018.

15. L. Lili, M. Yuanyuan, C. Ke, & Z. Yang, "3D printing complex egg white protein objects: Properties and optimization," *Food and Bioprocess Technology*, Vol. 1, pp. 1–11, 2018.

16. Z. Liu, M. Zhang, B. Bhandari, & Y. Wang, "3D printing: Printing precision and application in food sector," *Trends in Food Science & Technology*, Vol. 2, No. 1, pp. 1–36, 2017.

17. J. Dogra, S. Jain, & M. Sood, Glioma extraction from MR images employing gradient based kernel selection graph cut technique. *Visual Computer*, Vol. 36, pp. 875–891, 2020. DOI: 10.1007/s00371-019-01698-3.

18. C. Bhardwaj, S. Jain, & M. Sood, "Two-tier grading system for NPDR severities of diabetic retinopathy in retinal fundus images," *Recent Patents on Engineering*, Vol. 15, No. 2, 2021. DOI: 10.2174/187221211466620010910 3922.

19. T. Xu, K. W. Binder, M. Z. Albanna, D. Dice, W. Zhao, J. J. Yoo, et al., "Hybrid printing of mechanically and biologically improved constructs for cartilage tissue engineering applications," *Bio Fabrication*, Vol. 5, No. 1, p. 015001, 2013.

20. Y. Wang, X. Li, C. Li, M. Yang, & Q. Wei, "Binder droplet impact mechanism on a hydroxyapatite microsphere surface in 3D printing of bone scaffolds," *Journal of Material Science*, Vol. 50, No. 14, pp. 5014–5023, 2015.

21. G. Brunello, S. Sivolella, R. Meneghello, L. Ferroni, C. Gardin, & A. Piattelli, et al., "Powder-based 3D printing for bone tissue engineering," *Biotechnology Advances*, Vol. 34, No. 5, pp. 740–753, 2016.

22. B. P. Hung, B. A. Naved, E. L. Nyberg, M. Dias, C. A. Holmes, J. H. Elisseeff, et al., "Three-dimensional printing of bone extracellular matrix for craniofacial regeneration," *ACS Biomaterials Science & Engineering*, Vol. 2, No. 10, pp. 1806–1816, 2016.

23. M. J. Sawkins, P. Mistry, B. N. Brown, K. M. Shakesheff, L. J. Bonassar, & J. Yang, "Cell and protein compatible 3D bio printing of mechanically strong constructs for bone repair," *Bio Fabrication*, Vol. 7, No. 3, p. 035004, 2015.

24. C. L. Ventola, "Medical application for 3D printing: Current and projected uses," *Medical Devices*, Vol. 39, No. 10, pp. 1–8, 2014.

25. Y. Qian, D. Hanhua, S. Jin, H. Jianhua, S. Bo, W. Qingsong, & S. Yusheng, "A review of 3D printing technology for medical applications," *Engineering*, Vol. 4, No. 5, pp. 729–742, 2018.

26. R. Bogue, "3D printing: The dawn of a new era in manufacturing," *Assembly Automation*, Vol. 33, No. 4, pp. 307–311, 2013.

27. S. Horaczek, "Nike hacked a 3D printer to make its new shoe for elite marathon runners," Popular Sciences, 2018. [Online]. Available: https://www.popsci.com/nike-3d-printed-sneakers.

28. A. Richardot, "3D printed fashion: Why is additive manufacturing interesting for fashion?" Sculpteo. 2018. [Online]. Available:https://www.sculpteo.com/blog/2018/01/24/3d-printed-fashion-why-is-additive-manufacturing-interesting-for-fashion/.

29. M. Sakin, & Y. C. Kiroglu, "3D printing of buildings: Construction of the sustainable houses of the future by BIM," *Energy Procedia*, Vol. 134, pp. 702–711, 2017.

30. I. Hager, A. Golonka, & R. Putanowicz, "3D printing of building components as the future of sustainable construction," *Procedia Engineering*, Vol. 151, pp. 292–299, 2016.

31. Y. F. Chuan, N. L. Hong, M. A. Mahdi, M. H. Wahid, & M. H. Nay, "Three-dimensional printed electrode and its novel applications in electronic devices," *Scientific Report*, Vol. 1, pp. 1–11, 2018.

32. C. Jamieson, P. Keenan, D. Kirkwood, S. Oji, C. Webster, K. A. Russell, & T. G. Koch, "A review of recent advances in 3D bio printing with an eye on future regenerative therapies in veterinary medicine," *Frontiers in Veterinary Science*. Vol. 7, p. 584193, 2021. DOI: 10.3389/fvets.2020.584193.

33. H. Mao, et al., "Recent advances and challenges in materials for 3D bio printing," *Elsevier Progress in Natural Science: Materials International*, Vol. 30, pp. 618–634, 2020.

34. https://microbenotes.com/3d-bioprinting.

35. I. T. Ozbolat, Y. Yu, "Bioprinting toward organ fabrication: challenges and future trends," *IEEE Transactions on Biomedical Engineering*, Vol. 60, No. 3, pp. 691–699, 2013. doi: 10.1109/TBME.2013.2243912.

36. G. M. Abouna, "Organ shortage crisis: Problems and possible solutions," *Transplantation Proceedings*, Vol. 40, No. 1, pp. 34–38, 2008.

37. B. Zhang, Y. Luo, L. Ma, L. Gao, Y. Li, Q. Xue, et al., "3D bio printing: An emerging technology full of opportunities and challenges," *Bio-Design and Manufacturing*, Vol. 1, No. 1, pp. 2–13, 2018.

38. A. Muller, et al., "The application of rapid prototyping techniques in cranial reconstruction and preoperative planning in neurosurgery," *Journal of Craniofacial Surgery*, Vol. 14, pp. 899–914, 2003.

39. A. Squelch, "3D printing and medical imaging," *Journal of Medical Radiation Sciences*, Vol. 65, No. 3, pp. 171–172, 2018. doi: 10.1002/jmrs.300

40. S. Murphy, & A. Atala, "3D bio printing of tissues and organs," *Nature of Biotechnology*, Vol. 32, pp. 773–785, 2014. DOI: 10.1038/nbt.2958.

41. C. Mandrycky, Z. Wang, K. Kim, & D. H. Kim, "3D bio printing for engineering complex tissues," *Biotechnology Advances*. Vol. 34, No. 4, pp. 422–434. 2016. DOI: 10.1016/j.biotechadv.2015.12.011. PMID: 26724184; PMCID: PMC4879088.

42. B. Zhang, et al. "3D bioprinting: A novel avenue for manufacturing tissues and organs," *Engineering*, Vol. 5, No. 4, pp. 777–794, 2019. DOI: 10.1016/j.eng.2019.03.009..

43. I. Lau, et al., "Patient specific 3D printed model in delineating brain glioma and surrounding structures in a pediatric patient," *Digital Medicine*, Vol. 3, pp. 86–92, 2017.

44. E. George, et al., "Measuring and establishing the accuracy and reproducibility of 3D printed medical models," *RadioGraphics*, Vol. 37, No. 5, pp. 1424–1450, 2017. DOI:10.1148/rg.2017160165.

45. T. G. Papaioannou, et al., "3D bio printing methods and techniques: Applications on artificial blood vessel fabrication," *Acta Cardiologica Sinica*, Vol. 35, pp. 284–289, 2019.

46. T. M. Bücking, E. R. Hill, J. L. Robertson, E. Maneas, A. A. Plumb, D. I. Nikitichev. "From medical imaging data to 3D printed anatomical models," *PLoS One*, Vol. 12, No. 5, e0178540, 2017. doi: 10.1371/journal.pone.0178540.

47. R. Mamdouh, et al., "Converting 2D-medical image files 'DICOM' into 3D-models, based on image processing, and analysing their results with Python programming," *WSEAS Transactions on Computers*, Vol. 19, pp. 10–20, 2020. DOI:10.37394/23205.2020.19.2.

48. M. Usman Akram, A. Khanum, & K. Iqbal, "An automated system for liver CT enhancement and segmentation," *ICGST-GVIP Journal*, Vol. 10, No. IV, pp. 17–22, 2010.

49. H. Shi, & R. Fahmi, "Energy Minimization within the F.E. Framework to Predict Liver Tissue deformation," in *GVIP 05 Conference*, Cairo, Egypt, December 2005.

50. V. S. Nguyen, M. H. Tran, & H. M. Q. Vu, "A Research on 3D Model Construction from 2D DICOM," in *International Conference on Advanced Computing and Applications (ACOMP)*, Can Tho, Vietnam, 2016.

51. C. Q. T. Thanh, & N. T. Hai, "Trilinear interpolation algorithm for reconstruction of 3D MRI brain image," *American Journal of Signal Processing*, Vol. 7, No. 1, pp. 1–11, 2017.

52. C. Kumar, & A. Kumari, "3D reconstruction of brain tumor from 2D MRI's using FCM and Marching cubes," *International Journal of Advanced Research in Electronics and Communication Engineering (IJARECE)*, Vol. 3, No. 9, pp. 46–51, 2014.

53. P. S. Gungor-Ozkerim, I. Inci, Y. S. Zhang, A. Khademhosseini, & M. R. Dokmeci, "Bio inks for 3D bio printing: An overview," *Biomaterials Science*, Vol. 6, No. 5, pp. 915–946, 2018. DOI: 10.1039/c7bm00765e. PMID: 29492503; PMCID: PMC6439477.

54. S. Wüst, R. Müller, S. Hofmann, "Controlled positioning of cells in biomaterials—approaches towards 3D tissue printing," *Journal of Functional Biomaterials*, Vol. 2, pp. 119–154, 2011. DOI:10.3390/jfb2030119.

55. A. B. Dababneh, & I. T. Ozbolat, "Bioprinting technology: a current state-of-the-art review." ASME *Journal of Manufacturing Science and Engineering*, Vol. 136, No. 6, 061016, 2014. DOI:10.1115/1.4028512.

56. S. Khalil, & W. Sun, "Bioprinting endothelial cells with alginate for 3D tissue constructs," *Journal of Biomechanical Engineering*, Vol. 131, No. 11, 111002, 2009. DOI: 10.1115/1.3128729.

57. Z. Wang, R. Abdulla, B. Parker, R. Samanipour, S. Ghosh, & K. Kim, "A simple and high-resolution stereolithography-based 3D bioprinting system using visible light crosslinkable bioinks," *Biofabrication*, Vol. 7, No. 4, p. 045009, 2015. DOI: 10.1088/1758-5090/7/4/045009.

58. P. Bajaj, R. M. Schweller, A. Khademhosseini, J. L. West, & R. Bashir, "3D biofabrication strategies for tissue engineering and regenerative medicine," *Annual Review of Biomedical Engineering*, Vol. 16, pp. 247–276, 2014. DOI: 10.1146/annurev-bioeng-071813-105155.

59. L. Koch, A. Deiwick, S. Schlie, S. Michael, M. Gruene, V. Coger, D. Zychlinski, A. Schambach, K. Reimers, P. M. Vogt, & B. Chichkov, "Skin tissue generation by laser cell printing," *Biotechnology and Bioengineering*, Vol. 109, pp. 1855–1863, 2012. DOI: 10.1002/bit.24455.

60. K. Y. Lee, & D. J. Mooney, "Alginate: properties and biomedical applications," *Progress in Polymer Science*, Vol. 37, No. 1, pp. 106–126, 2012.

61. C. Xu, W. Chai, Y. Huang, & R. R. Markwald, "Scaffold-free inkjet printing of three-dimensional zigzag cellular tubes," *Biotechnology and Bioengineering*, Vol. 109, No. 12, 3152–3160, 2012. DOI: 10.1002/bit.24591.

62. J. Zhu, "Bioactive modification of poly(ethylene glycol) hydrogels for tissue engineering," *Biomaterials*, Vol. 31, No.17, pp. 4639–4656, 2010. DOI: 10.1016/j.biomaterials.2010.02.044..

63. C. Mandrycky, Z. Wang, K. Kim, D. H. Kim, "3D bioprinting for engineering complex tissues," *Biotechnology Advances*, Vol. 34, No. 4, pp. 422–434, 2016. DOI: 10.1016/j.biotechadv.2015.12.011. PMID: 26724184; PMCID: PMC4879088.

64. S. V. Murphy, & A. Atala, "3D bioprinting of tissues and organs," *Nature of Biotechnology*, Vol. 32, pp. 773–785, 2014.

65. S. Iwanaga, K. Arai, & M. Nakamura, *Inkjet Bioprinting*; Elsevier Inc.: Amsterdam, the Netherlands, 2015; ISBN 9780128010150.

66. X. Cui, K. Breitenkamp, M. G. Finn, M. Lotz, & D. D. D'Lima, "Direct human cartilage repair using three-dimensional bioprinting technology," *Tissue Engineering Part A*, Vol., 18, No. 11–12, pp. 1304–1312, 2012. DOI: 10.1089/ten.TEA.2011.0543.

67. X. Cui, K. Breitenkamp, M. Lotz, & D. D. D'Lima, "Synergistic action of fibroblast growth factor-2 and transforming growth factor-beta1 enhances bioprinted human neocartilage formation," *Biotechnology and Bioengineering*, Vol. 109, No. 9, pp. 2357–2368, 2012.

68. M. Duocastella, M. Colina, J. M. Fernández-Pradas, P. Serra, J. L. Morenza, "Study of the laser-induced forward transfer of liquids for laser bioprinting," *Applied Surface Science*, Vol. 253, No. 19, pp. 7855–7859, 2007.

69. A. Kosik-Kozioł, M. Costantini, T. Bolek, K. Szöke, A. Barbetta, J. Brinchmann, W. ʹSwi̧eszkowski, "PLA short sub-micron fiber reinforcement of 3D bioprinted alginate constructs for cartilage regeneration," *Biofabrication*, Vol. 9, p. 044105, 2017.

70. J. A. Barron, P. Wu, H. D. Ladouceur, B. R. Ringeisen, "Biological laser printing: A novel technique for creating heterogeneous 3-dimensional cell patterns," *Biomedical Microdevices*, Vol. 6, pp. 139–147, 2004.

71. J. M. Ameer, G. A. He, & T. C. Reid, "R.R.3-d bioprinting technologies in tissue engineering and regenerative medicine: Current and future trends," *Genes & Diseases*, Vol. 4, pp. 185–195, 2017.

72. P. Falguni, J. Jinah, J. W. Lee, & C. Dong-Woo, Extrusion bioprinting. In *Essentials of 3D Biofabrication and Translation*; Elsevier: Amsterdam, the Netherlands, 2015; pp. 123–152. DOI:10.1016/b978-0-12-800972-7.00007-4.

73. F. Ulucan-Karnak, "3D bioprinting in medicine," *Global Journal of Biotechnology and Biomaterial Science*, Vol. 7, No. 1, pp. 001–005, 2021. DOI: 10.17352/gjbbs.000015.

74. M. I. Jordan, & T. M. Mitchell, "Machine learning: Trends, perspectives, and prospects. *Science*, Vol. 349, pp. 255–260, 2015.
75. C. Yu, & J. Jiang, "A perspective on using machine learning in 3D bioprinting," *International Journal of Bioprinting*, Vol. 6, No. 1, p. 253, 2020. DOI: 10.18063/ijb.v6i1.253.
76. J. M. Lee, & W. Y. Yeong, "Design and printing strategies in 3D bioprinting of cell-hydrogels: A review. *Advanced Healthcare Materials*, Vol. 5, No. 22, pp. 2856–2865, 2016. DOI: 10.1002/adhm.201600435.
77. H. R. Roth, L. Lu, N. Lay, A. P. Harrison, A. Farag, A. Sohn, & R. M. Summers, "Spatial aggregation of holistically-nested convolutional neural networks for automated pancreas localization and segmentation," *Medical Image Analysis*, Vol. 45, pp. 94–107, 2018.
78. S. Niyas, et al. "Medical Image Segmentation using 3D Convolutional Neural Networks: A Review." arXiv preprint arXiv: 2108.08467 (2021).
79. C. M. Hamel, D. J. Roach, & K. N. Long, et al., "Machine-learning based design of active composite structures for 4D printing," *Smart Materials and Structures*, Vol. 28, p. 065005, 2019. DOI: 10.1088/1361-665X/ab1439.
80. Z. Li, Z. Zhang, J. Shi, et al., "Prediction of surface roughness in extrusion-based additive manufacturing with machine learning," *Robotics and Computer-Integrated Manufacturing*, Vol. 57, pp. 488–495, 2019.
81. M. S. Tootooni, A. Dsouza, & R. Donovan, P. Rao, Z. Kong, P. Borgesen, Classifying the Dimensional Variation in Additive Manufactured Parts from Laser-Scanned Three-Dimensional Point Cloud Data. *Journal of Manufacturing Science and* Engineering, 2017.
82. A. N. Leberfinger, D. J. Ravnic, A. Dhawan, & I. T. Ozbolat, "Concise review: Bioprinting of stem cells for transplantable tissue fabrication," *Stem Cells Translational Medicine*, Vol. 6, pp. 1940–1948, 2017.

CHAPTER 2

AI and IoT in Smart Healthcare

Sharu Bansal and Dilip Kumar

Sant Longowal Institute of Engineering and Technology

CONTENTS

2.1 INTRODUCTION

In this era of research and technology, Internet of things (IoT) and artificial intelligence (AI) are big buzz words. IoT means inter-network of devices, machines, objects, and users called things, which are uniquely identified and connected through various communication networks and the Internet, thus forming IoT. IoT is not just one technology. Neither is it restricted to one domain. It is getting used in each and every profession and uses all the global technologies [1,2].

DOI: 10.1201/9781003230113-2

Every day, individuals across the world desire to be more interconnected. An era has come where each person has a lot of electronic devices. With this advancement, everyone's life is dependent on these devices. Earlier, devices were not much connected to a network [3]. As technology is growing, IoT came into picture and has become one of the most prominent technologies. Entities in IoT are devices, machines, platform, virtual devices, etc. With research in the existing technology and the urge to become more connected to everything, technology took a step ahead by connecting devices to the Internet making it a global network of things [4,5].

It's only the beginning, and IoT and AI have a long way to go. Achieving tasks that were once major challenges now appear to be simple. IoT and AI are causing a global explosion. In terms of IoT and AI, new devices, operating systems, architectures, platforms, security, communication protocols, and many other things are emerging. As more research is completed, numerous new issues will emerge. As a result, every day, a new taxonomy is added to the concept of IoT and AI [6]. It will take some time for the boundary to become stable. Both progress and obstacles are increasing at the same time.The chapter's contribution is summarized below:

1. The chapter outlines the major roadblocks to IoT expansion and how Internet and upcoming technologies can help solve some of these issues.

2. This chapter analyzes numerous communication protocols to assist in understanding and selecting the right one for the purpose.

3. The message format and structural model of constrained application protocol (CoAP) are also detailed in this chapter.

4. It also provides an overview of wearable sensor technology.

5. Finally, it illustrates the smart healthcare system by using IoT and AI technologies.

2.1.1 Emerging Technologies

There are the technologies like AI and big data, which act as companions of IoT.

1. AI in IoT: AI is a set of computer programs which use some mechanisms to learn and use the learned knowledge to write the code according to the application [7,8]. As the IoT applications are growing exponentially, the problem of data congestion and data storage is also

increasing. To solve these problems, AI is a kind of algorithm used to manage and control the data by reducing the storage space. There are four fundamentals on which AI works: (a) learning and modes of learning, which can be supervised (task-driven), unsupervised (data-driven), and reinforcement (learns to react on environment); (b) cognitive and sensory abilities (abilities to see, hear, and comprehend); (c) aggregation and managing the data [9]; and (d) interpretation of data to find data is structured or unstructured [10]. IoT collects data from devices like sensors and actuators, and AI analyzes, decides, understands the patterns from the data, and learns the behavior of the IoT application. The combination of IoT and AI technologies has various applications which gives a lot of opportunities to work in this field. One of the examples is the self-driving car, which is run by Tesla Motors. This car consists of a large number of sensors, which act as an IoT device, and AI predicts the behavior of the car and the surroundings [11].

2. Big Data and IoT: The amount of data produced from connected nodes is expanding all the time. The term "big data," which refers to the size of the data set, is used to describe it. It is a technique for locating and analyzing data to find patterns and relationships. Storage, data security challenges, big data analysis, and influence on daily life are the four fundamentals of big data. Data come in a variety of sizes and formats, including numerical, text, audio, video, and figures. Structured, unstructured, and semi-structured data are all possible. The one and only way to organize data is to employ big data. There is still a lot of data following filtering out all the data duplication [12]. Managing this type of information is critical. Big data is a technique for handling massive amounts of data and delivering it to an analytics tool. The data is then transferred to a data center. Big data storage has challenges such as digital encryption, secure communication mining, secure screening, and secure analytics. Volume, diversity, and velocity are the three aspects of big data analytics. Volume is the measurement of the size of data streams. Big data diversity refers to a wide range of data types such as audio, video, and text. The rate at which data can be processed is referred to as velocity. Several big data and IoT applications have a significant impact in the society, like smart watches that regularly monitor a person's quality of life through storing information and transmitting

a message to a specialist if the individual gets ill or has other problems. Big data analytics is the process of analyzing a large amount of data in order to draw conclusions [13]. To improve decision-making, a mix of IoT and big data is used. The amount of data gathered from "connected devices" is substantial. As a result, big data analytics is required, which manages data through reports, queries, training data, and analytical tools.

2.1.2 Architecture of IoT

The architecture is a diagram that shows the key individual parts, their operational layout, and the principles that are highlighted [14]. As indicated in Figure 2.1, IoT is divided into five layers: physical layer, transport layer, storage layer, processing layer, and application layer.

1. The first layer is the physical layer, which really is located at the ground. This layer's sensor measures and collects data based on physical and environmental factors such as X-Y-Z coordinates. Sensors send the acquired data to the next level. In addition, this layer preprocesses the input to remove any undesired information [15].

2. Transport layer—This layer oversees transporting preprocessed data from the interaction channel to the storage layer and vice versa. Node-to-node interaction is indeed handled by this layer. Wireless, 3G, local area network (LAN), bluetooth, radio frequency identification (RFID), and near field communication are some of the communication protocols used.

3. Storage layer—The information collected from different sensors and nodes is organized, managed, and stored by this layer [16].

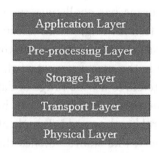

FIGURE 2.1   Five-layered architecture.

4. Processing layer—This layer oversees performing various strategic and critical procedures on the data storage, as well as processing the data into meaningful information utilizing facts and figures. These useful data are then used to generate numerous analytics and observations, considering all possible permutations and computations. Datasets, cloud technology, and big data processing are all used at this tier.

5. Application layer—This layer is responsible for delivering an application to give various services to users based on the analytics and observations from the processed data. It defines a variety of IoT applications, such as smart buildings, transport systems, and smart healthcare, among others. A user might utilize this layer to execute an action and then send a signal to the actuators in the physical layer to perform the action [17].

2.1.3 IoT Ecosystem

IoT ecosystem is a network that is produced by bringing together all of the productive heterogeneous devices of IoT in a controlled manner to create a system that is efficient so that it helps to take up existing problems and challenges, and tries to solve them. A big IoT ecosystem is connecting trillions of devices across the globe in a single ecosystem and a small IoT ecosystem can be connecting all devices owned by a single person (Figure 2.2).

The sensors and actuators interface with the gateway using a variety of communication protocols. The sensors, also known as preceptors, receive and transmit all data in the form of environmental parameters to the gateway. The actuator is responsive to its surroundings and receives commands from the gateway. The gateway can control and handle hundreds of thousands of sensing devices. It also controls data flow between devices. Filtering and structuring of data collected from sensors are performed by it. The controller oversees hundreds of gateways and performs high-level data processing such as identification, processing, and transformation of data into useful information. After that, the controller interacts with middleware. The middleware contains procedures like storing all information to a central server, analyzing data, producing reports, regulating, and coordinating the system that is present beneath it, and all data could be kept by the middleware's cloud. Middleware provides services and analytical data to all applications, including smart buildings and homes. These services can be accessed using an application programming interface (API). The user is then given a proper IoT view by the application.

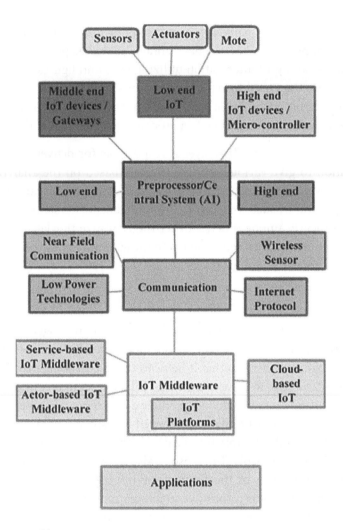

FIGURE 2.2   IoT ecosystem.

2.2 COMMUNICATION PROTOCOL

Two or more machines or devices talk to each other in the form of a language. A communication protocol is a set of guidelines that enables the transmission of information between two or more entities of a communications system using any modification of a physical quantity [18].

2.2.1 Transport Control Protocol (TCP)/IP Stack

It controls the data transfer between the machines. Three handshake procedures are to be followed: (1) The sender will send messages in a synchronized way to the receiver; (2) the receiver sends the acknowledgment

(ACK) of receiving the message; and (3) the sender sends the message to get the ACK message. It is slow because of its verification procedure. User datagram protocol (UDP) is fast by cutting down the ACK procedure. UDP is less reliable than TCP, but it is fast due to low overhead and small header [19,20].

2.2.2 CoAP

CoAP is an IoT protocol. The most popular protocol is hyper-text transfer protocol (HTTP) over Internet. HTTP is mostly used in browser-based web pages. It runs on client–server model. But, HTTP is complex and has a large overhead. HTTP uses TCP but CoAP uses UDP. CoAP supports multicast communication, but HTTP doesn't support it. HTTP works on the client–server model while CoAP can use both client–server and publish–subscribe models. CoAP can do asynchronous communication, but HTTP does synchronous communication [21,22]. HTTP is not efficient for sending a single piece of information. CoAP will be lighter and faster than HTTP for IoT applications. The IETF's constrained RESTful environment (CoRE) group is responsible for defining the CoAP protocol. CoAP is mostly employed in lossy low-power networks. CoAP is not an HTTP compression protocol; rather, it is a RESTful design style that operates in a limited environment and utilizes HTTP functionalities [23]. It's a specific web transfer protocol for IoT [24] that is designed to work with restricted nodes and networks. Nodes with an 8-bit microprocessor and limited ROM and RAM will be supported by CoAP. It is based on client–server interaction between the endpoints of application and supported by universal resource identifier (URI). CoAP uses UDP instead of TCP in the transport layer [25,26] (Table 2.1).

Although UDP has some disadvantages, it works better than TCP in case of a constrained environment. UDP gives low overhead, which leads to small header, and it offers service of high quality [27,28].

CoAP has a control layer where the architecture of CoAP is divided into two layers—one for RESTful interaction called request–response sublayer used for mapping the requests to response and the other for de-duplication or for reliability called the message layer. Each communication has a unique message ID that can be used to identify duplication and provide optional dependability [29,30] (Figure 2.3).

The message layer of CoAP protocol is used to control the exchange of messages between two endpoints—the message format in both cases of request and response [28]. Message ID (MID) is used to avoid duplication and both request and response have same the MID. There are four types of messages—CON, NON-CON, ACK, and reset (RST) [29].

TABLE 2.1   Comparison of Various Protocols

Criteria	MQTT	CoAP	AMQP	HTTP
Architecture	Client/Broker	Client/Broker or Client/Server	Client/Server	Client/Server
Abstraction	Publish/Subscribe	Request/Response or Publish/Subscribe	Publish/Subscribe or Request/Response	Request/Response
RESTful	No	Yes	No	Yes
Semantics/ Methods	Connect, Disconnect, Publish, Subscribe, Unsubscribe, Close	Get, Post, Put, Delete	Consume, Deliver, Publish, Get, Select, ACK, Delete, Recover, Reject, Open, Close	Get, Post, Put, Options, Connect, Delete
Quality of Service (QoS)	QoS 0- At most once (Fire-and-Forget), QoS 1- At least once, QoS 2- Exactly once	Confirmable Message (similar to Atmost once) or Non-confirmable Message (similar to At least once)	Settle Format (similar to Atmost once) or Unsettle Format (similar to At least once)	Limited (via Transport Protocol—TCP)
Encoding Format	Binary	Binary	Binary	Text
Licensing Model	Open Source	Open Source	Open Source	Free
Transport	TCP	UDP	TCP	TCP

In CON, message can be retransmitted till the receiver gives ACK of receiving the message. If ACK message is not received, message can be retransmitted up to four times. After each resend of message, this retransmission timeout (RTO) t_{init} gets doubled and max retransmission can up to four times [30,31]. This message type gives reliable transmission. The message can be resend after time out occurs. This time out can be represented by initial RTO t_{init}. The time interval bounds can be defined by $T_o = 2$ s.

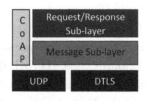

FIGURE 2.3   CoAP structural model.

$$C_{rand} = 1.5$$

$$T_o \leq t_{init} \leq T_o C_{rand}$$

$$2s \leq t_{init} \leq 3s$$

ACK is the reception of the CON message, which gives the signal of receiving the message by using the same MID which is used by the CON message [32,33]. Sometimes there are empty ACKs that give the signal to close the transmission and this type of ACK message has 4-byte base header, zero code, no options, and no payload. In NON (nonconfirmable), no ACK message is received while transmitting the message. It means loss of message is acceptable. RST can be used when some error occurs due to some context missing of NON or CON messages. RST message also uses the same MID as that of NON or CON messages. RST for NON message is optional. RST shows that the reliable transmission is closed with some failure [34,35].

CoAP messages carry request–response semantics, which may be of method code and response code. CoAP options carry URI in the form of request–response information and payload content type. Token can be used for matching responses to request for a particular message. Sometimes, CoAP messages may not arrive on time because of nonreliability. So, there is the need for reliable transmission in form of (1) multicast support, (2) detection of duplication, and (3) reliability with exponential back-off. The reliability mainly concerns with confirmable messages. When a sender and client or server sends the message, the receiver may accept with an ACK or may reject it with RST. The sender sends the message within RTO interval by the procedure of exponential back-off [36,37].

In CoAP, requests come in the form of CON and NON-CON messages. CoAP supports the fundamental HTTP methods of GET, POST, PUT, and DELETE, which can be readily translated to different devices or server-client interactions [38,39]. These methods are same as of HTTP. The GET corresponds to retrieve and it is safe among all; it means it only retrieves the resources and no other action is taken. POST and PUT corresponds to update and create, respectively. PUT and DELETE are idempotent in nature. But POST is not idempotent. It uses for processing of data [40–42].

Response can be of any type in piggybacked, separate response and nonconfirmable. Piggybacked can be of CON messages [43,44]. The server or client received an immediate answer to a request in the form of a confirmable message, which was followed by an ACK message [45,46]. The client sends the request to the server with message ID, code GET, and token to get the temperature information as shown in Figure 2.4. The client receives ACK message with the same token, same message ID, response code of GET 2.05, and temperature information [47].

If the server is unable to react promptly to a request carried in a CON message, it will send a separate response [48,49]. On a CoAP server, the state of a resource can change over time [50,51]. CoAP used to have a capability that allowed clients to "observe" resources. The purpose of observing is to get the representation of a resource and have the server keep that representation updated over time. The value of observe can be increasing by one whenever there is a change in temperature as shown in Figure 2.4. In whole communication, the token and message ID remain same [52,53]. The server updates the client with ACK message whenever changes occur.

In Response after a while, the client sends the request to the server. The server simply sends the response ACK with no information as the server doesn't receive any value from the sensor as shown in Figure 2.4. After some time, when the server gets the temperature value, it sends the message to client with new message ID but token remains the same [54]. The client sends the ACK message to the server for receiving the value. The client sends the request to server with /.wellknown/core in Resource Recovery as shown in Figure 2.5. It means that all the resources that a server receives is required by the client as response [55,56].

2.3 WEARABLE SENSORS

WBANs are already regarded a critical part of an Internet-based health service, and the development of precise detectors with a compact form factor will be critical in the future [57]. A lot of study has gone into figuring out the best ways to detect pulse. Recent studies [58] have created, used, and investigated pressure, sonar, and radio wave sensors.

Pulse is a key signal, which can be used to identify a range of crisis situations, such as cardiogenic shock, increased heart rate, and hypotension syncope. Pulse sensors have been intensively researched for medical and fitness applications [59]. Pulse can be felt in a variety of places, including the chest, wrist, earlobe, and fingertip. Even though earlobe and fingertip readings are quite accurate, they are not wearable [60]. Although a shoulder gadget is wearable, wristband sensors are regarded to be the most practical for long-term use [61].

Respiratory Sensor—Because breathing is so important, several previous studies have created sensors to measure respiratory rate. Several types of respiration rate sensors emerge from the earlier works [62,63]. The first is a thermistor-based nasal sensor. The air expelled is warmer than the

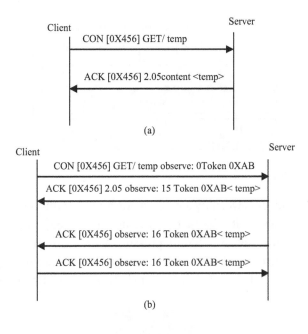

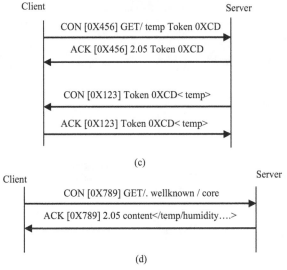

FIGURE 2.4 (a) Piggybacked response, (b) separate response, (c) response after a while, and (d) resource recovery.

ambient temperature, which is the basis for these sensors. As a result, the sensor refers to the number of breaths taken by measuring temperature changes [64]. This has been shown to operate well, although precision might well be compromised through other forms of temperature variations, such

4-byte CoAP Base Header				
Ver	Type	Tok-len	Code	Message ID (MID)

0-8 Bytes Token

Options

Marker OxFF	Payload

FIGURE 2.5   Message format.

as when the gadget is worn by a cook inside a restaurant. It's also inconvenient to wear because it's distracting and noticeable [65] (Figure 2.6).

Blood Pressure Sensor—Blood pressure (BP) is routinely monitored alongside the three vital signs, even though it is not a vital sign in and of itself. High blood pressure (hypertension) is indeed a major risk factor

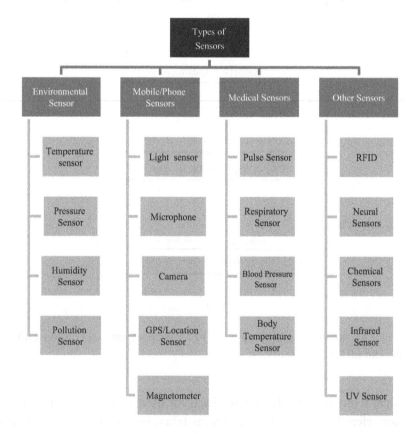

FIGURE 2.6   Various types of sensors.

for cardiovascular disease and stroke. Creating a connecting element for constantly and quasi sensing blood pressure is still a challenge in the realm of healthcare IoT [66]. Many researches [67,68] have attempted to quantify pulse transit time (PTT), which would be the time required for a heartbeat to move from the heart to another location, such as the earlobe or the radial artery [69]. Another study [70] sought to compute this characteristic between the head and the finger of a palm, whereas another [71] attempted to measure it between the ear and the wrist. PTT is inversely related to systolic blood pressure (SBP) and is often measured using an ECG on the chest and a PPG sensor on the ear, wrist, or elsewhere [72].

2.4 SMART HEALTHCARE SYSTEM

This chapter proposes real-life smart healthcare system. The independent applications are clubbed together to end up in an IoT ecosystem. Figure 2.7 shows that each node is a distributed system across the town and is connected over a WSN. This shows how an IoT ecosystem converts an independent system into a scalable and highly capable system.

2.4.1 Prerequisites

1. A car is installed with sensors like impact sensors, speed sensors, accelerometer, positioning sensors, etc.

2. The person who drives the car has a lot of sensors in the form of wearable devices.

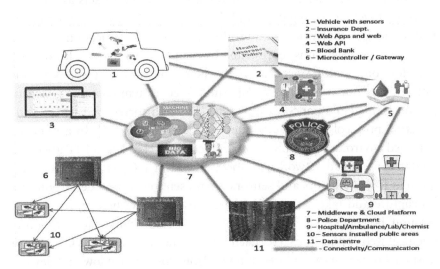

FIGURE 2.7 Smart healthcare.

3. The mobile/vehicle intelligence system is connected to car sensors and wearable devices.

4. Different kinds of medical sensors are installed across the town for analyzing the parameters like temperature, humidity, poisonous gases, insects, etc.

5. Blood banks are installed with sensors like quantity, weight to identify blood stock of different groups across the town.

6. Health insurance policy departments and the online medical web are connected to the central system for fully updated information of people residing in the town.

7. All nodes representing a domain are connected to form a robust and reliable ecosystem.

8. All vehicles, home, people, areas, and devices should be uniquely identified and connected to middleware. They should be registered on the cloud platform.

IoT middleware has cloud IoT platform. It enables a visual platform to virtually map all the nodes, devices, and systems into a single system [73,74]. Technically, it decouples and optimizes the logical and arithmetic complexity, thus simplifying it as a single integrated flawless system. IT platform not only helps to manage the network but also acts as a bridge to bring together AI, big data, and data centers [75]. The ecosystem provides role-specific services like admin and user, web application, and web API. Communication is represented by each connecting line. It not only enables communication between the nodes but also is responsible for interring device connectivity [76]. The IoT ecosystem contains a variety of constrained and nonconstrained devices, with corresponding communication protocols available to support these devices [77]. In a nonconstrained environment, application protocols like HTTP and FTP are used, and in constrained networks, protocols like MQTT, CoAP, and AMQP are present [78]. Actuators and sensors are present on each node responsible to capture and take actions. They are present everywhere starting from ground, hospitals, cars, mobiles, ambulance, blood bank, chemist, online medical web applications, etc. Each node of the ecosystem has OS. OS are installed based on capabilities of nodes from constrained low-end devices to a supercomputer for IoT middleware [79,80].

2.4.2 Benefits of Smart Healthcare Ecosystem

1. Vehicle Accident—In case of accidents, impact sensor sends signal, GPS sends location, wearable devices send heart rate and blood pressure, accelerometer sends the speed, and emergency calls are triggered to the family. Sending isolated information is of limited use. Here mobile/vehicle intelligence system acts as a gateway. All sensors are interconnected, so the gateway sends consolidated information. Alarm is triggered to the central system and a system makes an automated call to the registered contact number of persons to understand the situation. The central system triggers multiple calls in parallel [81,82].

   a. Finds the nearest multispecialty hospital, ambulance, lab.

   b. Triggers call to the insurance department.

   c. Analyzes the situation of an accident. If there is no medical emergency, the call is redirected to other departments. If the victim or any other person at the accident spot replies to the call as a critical situation, emergency steps are taken.

   d. Auto FIR is registered and sent to hospital.

      In case of emergency, the central system further makes parallel calls to the police, hospital, lab, ambulance, and insurance department. The ambulance moves the victim to the hospital. While the patient is on the way to the hospital, the central system auto-registers the patient in the hospital. Blood bank is notified for blood group [83]. The lab assistant is readily available for collecting blood samples. The hospital connects to the insurance department for cashless procedures and the doctors are available for treatment of the patient. This is really a life saver system [84].

2. The medical sensors are installed smartly in the town; the sensors give information about an outbreak of an epidemic to the central node of the ecosystem. The information is passed to the government, hospitals, public, Internet web, and media. This is a big alarm to control the epidemic in time [85].

3. The health insurance departments keep on posting messages to clients for upgrading the policies depending on the past and current medical history of every individual. Moreover, health departments give information to people about health awareness camps, health clubs, and yoga centers [86].

4. The blood banks keep notice of the blood availability in all centers. All blood banks are connected to each other. In case the blood stock is low, the sensors send signals to the central system. The central system further sends signal to the actuator to transport blood from other centers to complete emergency blood collection [87,88].

5. The central system maintains a whole history of data centers. The technologies like AI and big data keep on sending updates and information to people about their check-up status, insurance status, etc. [89].

So, smart healthcare ecosystem rightly justifies that IoT ecosystem is a revolution. The ideas that were restricted due to isolated system got a boost through IoT. It introduces and uses parallelism to a high extend [90,91].

2.5 CONCLUSION

In this chapter, the future of IoT-based healthcare systems that can be used for either generic or disease-monitoring systems is discussed. Furthermore, for every element of the model, there is comprehensive and systematic review of the most recent articles. Several nonintrusive wearable sensors, with a concentration on those that measure pulse rate, heart rate, and oxygen levels, were demonstrated, and reviewed. The communication protocol CoAP's usefulness for healthcare applications was discussed. Based on our study of state-of-the-art technology in the fields of wearable sensors and communications standards, we identified several important topics for future research. Researchers who want to make significant progress in the field of IoT-based healthcare should concentrate on AI and the creation of a safe environment. Overall, there is no edge system that uses all the elements in our proposed model: wearable sensors, communications, and AI, for general or specific purposes. Developing such a system would be a huge step forward in IoT-based healthcare, and it is the true aim of experts in this field.

REFERENCES

1. A. Čolaković, and M. Hadžialić, "Internet of Things (IoT): A Review of Enabling Technologies, Challenges, and Open Research Issues", *Computer Networks*, Vol. 144, pp. 17–39, 2018.
2. I. Mashal, O. Alsaryrah, T. Y. Chung, C. Z. Yang, W. H. Kuo, and D. P. Agrawal, "Choices for Interaction with Things on Internet and Underlying Issues", *Ad Hoc Networks*, Vol. 28, pp. 68–90, 2015.
3. P. P. Ray, "A Survey on Internet of Things Architectures", *Journal of King Saud University-Computer and Information Sciences*, Vol. 30, No. 3, pp. 291–319, 2018.

4. I. Lee, and K. Lee, "The Internet of Things (IoT): Applications, Investments, and Challenges for Enterprises", *Business Horizons*, Vol. 58, No. 4, pp. 431–440, 2015.

5. A. Whitmore, A. Agarwal, and L. Da Xu, "The Internet of Things—A Survey of Topics and Trends", *Information Systems Frontiers*, Vol. 17, No. 2, pp. 261–274, 2015.

6. S. D. T. Kelly, N. K. Suryadevara, and S. C. Mukhopadhyay, "Towards the Implementation of IoT for Environmental Condition Monitoring in Homes", *IEEE Sensors Journal*, Vol. 13, No. 10, pp. 3846–3853, 2013.

7. A. Al-Fuqaha, M. Guizani, M. Mohammadi, M. Aledhari, and M. Ayyash, "Internet of Things: A Survey on Enabling Technologies, Protocols, and Applications", *IEEE Communications Surveys & Tutorials*, Vol. 17, No. 4, pp. 2347–2376, 2015.

8. E. Ahmed, I. Yaqoob, A. Gani, M. Imran, and M. Guizani, "Internet-of-Things-Based Smart Environments: State of the Art, Taxonomy, and Open Research Challenges", *IEEE Wireless Communications*, Vol. 23, No. 5, pp. 10–16, 2016.

9. J.P. Lemayian, and F. Al-Turjman, 2019. "Intelligent IoT communication in smart environments: an overview". *Artificial intelligence in IoT*, pp. 207–221.

10. A. A. Osuwa, E. B. Ekhoragbon, and L. T. Fat, 2017. Application of artificial intelligence in Internet of Things. In *2017 9th International Conference on Computational Intelligence and Communication Networks (CICN)*, Girne, Northern Cyprus (pp. 169–173). IEEE.

11. A. Bhardwaj, P. Kumar, B. Raj, and S. Anand, "Design and Performance Optimization of Doping-Less Vertical Nanowire TFET Using Gate Stack Technique," *Journal of Electronic Materials (JEMS)*, Springer, Vol. 41, No. 7, pp. 4005–4013, 2022.

12. J. Singh, and B. Raj, "Tunnel Current Model of Asymmetric MIM Structure Levying Various Image Forces to Analyze the Characteristics of Filamentary Memristor", *Applied Physics A*, Springer, Vol. 125, No. 3, pp. 203.1 to 203.11, 2019.

13. C. Goyal, J. S. Ubhi, and B. Raj, "Low Leakage Zero Ground Noise Nanoscale Full Adder Using Source Biasing Technique", *Journal of Nanoelectronics and Optoelectronics*, American Scientific Publishers, Vol. 14, pp. 360–370, 2019.

14. G. Singh, R. K. Sarin, and B. Raj, "A Novel Robust Exclusive-OR Function Implementation in QCA Nanotechnology with Energy Dissipation Analysis", *Journal of Computational Electronics*, Springer, Vol. 15, No. 2, pp. 455–465, 2016.

15. T. Wadhera, D. Kakkar, G. Wadhwa, and B. Raj, " Recent Advances and Progress in Development of the Field Effect Transistor Biosensor: A Review" *Journal of Electronic Materials*, Springer, Vol. 48, No. 12, pp. 7635–7646, 2019.

16. G. Wadhwa, P. Kamboj, and B. Raj, "Design Optimisation of Junctionless TFET Biosensor for High Sensitivity", *Advances in Natural Sciences: Nanoscience and Nanotechnology*, Vol. 10, No. 7, p. 045001, 2019.

17. P. Bansal, and B. Raj, "Memristor Modeling and Analysis for Linear Dopant Drift Kinetics", *Journal of Nanoengineering and Nanomanufacturing*, American Scientific Publishers, Vol. 6, pp. 1–7, 2016.
18. A. Singh, M. Khosla, and B. Raj, "Circuit Compatible Model for Electrostatic Doped Schottky Barrier CNTFET," *Journal of Electronic Materials*, Springer, Vol. 45, No. 12, pp. 4825–4835, 2016.
19. Ashima, D. Vaithiyanathan, and B. Raj, "Performance Analysis of Charge Plasma Induced Graded Channel Si Nanotube", *Journal of Engineering Research (JER)*, EMSME Special Issue, pp. 146–154, 2021.
20. A. S. Tomar, V. K. Magraiya, and B. Raj, "Scaling of Access and Data Transistor for High Performance DRAM Cell Design", *Quantum Matter*, Vol. 2, pp. 412–416, 2013.
21. N. Jain, and B. Raj, "Parasitic Capacitance and Resistance Model Development and Optimization of Raised Source/Drain SOI FinFET Structure for Analog Circuit Applications", *Journal of Nanoelectronics and Optoelectronins*, ASP, USA, Vol. 13, pp. 531–539, 2018.
22. S. Singh, S. K. Vishvakarma, and B. Raj, "Analytical Modeling of Split-Gate Junction-Less Transistor for a Biosensor Application", *Sensing and Bio-Sensing*, Elsevier, Vol. 18, pp. 31–36, 2018.
23. M. Gopal, and B. Raj, "Low Power 8T SRAM Cell Design for High Stability Video Applications", *ITSI Transaction on Electrical and Electronics Engineering*, Vol. 1, No. 5, pp. 91–97, 2013.
24. B. Raj, J. Mitra, D. K. Bihani, V. Rangharajan, A. K. Saxena, and S. Dasgupta, "Analysis of Noise Margin, Power and Process Variation for 32 nm FinFET Based 6T SRAM Cell", *Journal of Computer (JCP)*, Academy Publisher, FINLAND, Vol. 5, No. 6, pp. 43–56, 2010.
25. D. Sharma, R. Mehra, and B. Raj, "Comparative Analysis of Photovoltaic Technologies for High Efficiency Solar Cell Design", *Superlattices and Microstructures*, Elsevier, Vol. 153, pp. 106861, 2021.
26. P. Kaur, A. S. Buttar, and B. Raj, "A Comprehensive Analysis of Nanoscale Transistor Based Biosensor: A Review", *Indian Journal of Pure and Applied Physics*, Vol. 59, pp. 304–318, 2021.
27. D. Yadav, B. Raj, and B. Raj, "Design and Simulation of Low Power Microcontroller for IoT Applications", *Journal of Sensor Letters*, ASP, Vol. 18, pp. 401–409, 2020.
28. S. Singh, and B. Raj, "A 2-D Analytical Surface Potential and Drain current Modeling of Double-Gate Vertical t-shaped Tunnel FET", *Journal of Computational Electronics*, Springer, Vol. 19, pp. 1154–1163, 2020.
29. J. Singh, and B. Raj, "An Accurate and Generic Window Function for Non-linear Memristor Model" *Journal of Computational Electronics*, Springer, Vol. 18, No. 2, pp. 640–647, 2019.
30. M. Kaur, N. Gupta, S. Kumar, B. Raj, and A. K. Singh, "Comparative RF and Crosstalk Analysis of Carbon Based Nano Interconnects", *IET Circuits, Devices & Systems*, Vol. 15, No. 6, pp. 493–503, 2021.
31. N. Kandasamy, F. Ahmad, D. Ajitha, B. Raj, and N. Telagam, "Quantum Dot Cellular Automata Based Scan Flip Flop and Boundary Scan Register", *IETE Journal of Research*, Vol. 69, pp. 535–548, 2020.

32. S. K. Sharma, B. Raj, and M. Khosla, "Enhanced Photosensivity of Highly Spectrum Selective Cylindrical Gate $In_{1-x}Ga_xAs$ Nanowire MOSFET Photodetector", *Modern Physics Letter-B*, Vol. 33, No. 12, p. 1950144, 2019.

33. J. Singh, and B. Raj, "Design and Investigation of 7T2M NVSARM with Enhanced Stability and Temperature Impact on Store/Restore Energy", *IEEE Transactions on Very Large Scale Integration Systems*, Vol. 27, No. 6, pp. 1322–1328, 2019.

34. A. K. Bhardwaj, S. Gupta, B. Raj, and A. Singh, "Impact of Double Gate Geometry on the Performance of Carbon Nanotube Field Effect Transistor Structures for Low Power Digital Design", *Computational and Theoretical Nanoscience*, ASP, Vol. 16, pp. 1813–1820, 2019.

35. N. Jain, and B. Raj, "Thermal Stability Analysis and Performance Exploration of Asymmetrical Dual-k Underlap Spacer (ADKUS) SOI FinFET for Security and Privacy Applications", *Indian Journal of Pure & Applied Physics (IJPAP)*, Vol. 57, pp. 352–360, 2019.

36. A. Singh, M. Khosla, and B. Raj, "Design and Analysis of Dynamically Configurable Electrostatic Doped Carbon Nanotube Tunnel FET", *Microelectronics Journal*, Elesvier, Vol. 85, pp. 17–24, 2019.

37. N. Jain, and B. Raj, "Dual-k Spacer Region Variation at the Drain Side of Asymmetric SOI FinFET Structure: Performance Analysis towards the Analog/RF Design Applications", *Journal of Nanoelectronics and Optoelectronics*, American Scientific Publishers, Vol. 14, pp. 349–359, 2019.

38. J. Singh, S. Sharma, B. Raj, and M. Khosla, "Analysis of Barrier Layer Thickness on Performance of $In_{1-x}Ga_xAs$ Based Gate Stack Cylindrical Gate Nanowire MOSFET", *JNO*, ASP, Vol. 13, pp. 1473–1477, 2018.

39. N. Jain, and B. Raj, "Analysis and Performance Exploration of High-k SOI FinFETs over the Conventional Low-k SOI FinFET toward Analog/RF Design", *Journal of Semiconductors (JoS)*, IOP Science, Vol. 39, No. 12, pp. 124002-1-7, 2018.

40. C. Goyal, J. S. Ubhi, and B. Raj, "A Reliable Leakage Reduction Technique for Approximate Full Adder with Reduced Ground Bounce Noise", *Journal of Mathematical Problems in Engineering*, Hindawi, Vol. 2018, Article ID 3501041, 16 pages, 2018.

41. Anuradha, J. Singh, B. Raj, and M. Khosla, "Design and Performance Analysis of Nano-scale Memristor-Based Nonvolatile SRAM", *Journal of Sensor Letter*, American Scientific Publishers, Vol. 16, pp. 798–805, 2018.

42. G. Wadhwa, and B. Raj, "Parametric Variation Analysis of Charge-Plasma-Based Dielectric Modulated JLTFET for Biosensor Application", *IEEE Sensor Journal*, Vol. 18, No. 15, pp. 6070–6077, 2018.

43. J. Singh, and B. Raj, "Comparative Analysis of Memristor Models for Memories Design", *JoS*, IoP, Vol. 39, No. 7, pp. 074006-1-12, 2018.

44. D. Yadav, S. S. Chouhan, S. K. Vishvakarma, and B. Raj, "Application Specific Microcontroller Design for IoT Based WSN", *Sensor Letter*, ASP, Vol. 16, pp. 374–385, 2018.

45. G. Singh, R. K. Sarin, and B. Raj, "Fault-Tolerant Design and Analysis of Quantum-Dot Cellular Automata Based Circuits", *IEEE/IET Circuits, Devices & Systems*, Vol. 12, pp. 638–664, 2018.

46. J. Singh, and B. Raj, "Modeling of Mean Barrier Height Levying Various Image Forces of Metal Insulator Metal Structure to Enhance the Performance of Conductive Filament Based Memristor Model", *IEEE Nanotechnology*, Vol. 17, No. 2, pp. 268–275, 2018.

47. A. Jain, S. Sharma, and B. Raj, "Analysis of Triple Metal Surrounding Gate (TM-SG) III-V Nanowire MOSFET for Photosensing Application", *Opto-Electronics Journal*, Elsevier, Vol. 26, No. 2, pp. 141–148, 2018.

48. A. Jain, S. Sharma, and B. Raj, "Design and Analysis of High Sensitivity Photosensor Using Cylindrical Surrounding Gate MOSFET for Low Power Sensor Applications", *Engineering Science and Technology, an International Journal*, Elsevier's, Vol. 19, No. 4, pp. 1864–1870, 2016.

49. A. Singh, M. Khosla, and B. Raj, "Analysis of Electrostatic Doped Schottky Barrier Carbon Nanotube FET for Low Power Applications," *Journal of Materials Science: Materials in Electronics*, Springer, Vol. 28, pp. 1762–1768, 2017.

50. G. Saiphani Kumar, A. Singh, B. Raj, "Design and Analysis of Gate All around CNTFET Based SRAM cell Design", *Journal of Computational Electronics*, Springer, Vol. 17, No.1, pp. 138–145, 2018.

51. G. P. Singh, B. S. Sohi, and B. Raj, "Material Properties Analysis of Graphene Base Transistor (GBT) for VLSI Analog Circuits", *Indian Journal of Pure & Applied Physics (IJPAP)*, Vol. 55, pp. 896–902, 2017

52. S. Kumar and B. Raj, "Estimation of Stability and Performance Metric for Inward Access Transistor Based 6T SRAM Cell Design Using n-type/p-type DMDG-GDOV TFET", *IEEE VLSI Circuits and Systems Letter*, Vol. 3, No. 2, pp. 25–39, 2017.

53. S. Sharma, A. Kumar, M. Pattanaik, and B. Raj, "Forward Body Biased Multimode Multi-Threshold CMOS Technique for Ground Bounce Noise Reduction in Static CMOS Adders", *International Journal of Information and Electronics Engineering*, Vol. 3, No. 3, pp. 567–572, 2013.

54. H. Singh, P. Kumar, and B. Raj, "Performance Analysis of Majority Gate SET Based 1-bit Full Adder", *International Journal of Computer and Communication Engineering (IJCCE)*, IACSIT Press Singapore, ISSN: 2010-3743, Vol. 2, No. 4, 2013.

55. A. K. Bhardwaj, S. Gupta, and B. Raj, "Investigation of Parameters for Schottky Barrier (SB) Height for Schottky Barrier Based Carbon Nanotube Field Effect Transistor Device", *Journal of Nanoelectronics and Optoelectronics*, ASP, Vol. 15, pp. 783–791, 2020.

56. P. Bansal, and B. Raj, "Memristor: A Versatile Nonlinear Model for Dopant Drift and Boundary Issues", *JCTN*, American Scientific Publishers, Vol. 14, No. 5, pp. 2319–2325, 2017.

57. N. Jain, and B. Raj, "An Analog and Digital Design Perspective Comprehensive Approach on Fin-FET (Fin-Field Effect transistor) Technology - A Review", *Reviews in Advanced Sciences and Engineering (RASE)*, ASP, Vol. 5, pp. 1–14, 2016.

58. S. Sharma, B. Raj, and M. Khosla, "Subthreshold Performance of $In_{1-x}Ga_xAs$ Based Dual Metal with Gate Stack Cylindrical/Surrounding Gate Nanowire MOSFET for Low Power Analog Applications", *Journal of Nanoelectronics and Optoelectronics*, American Scientific Publishers, USA, Vol. 12, pp. 171–176, 2017.

59. B. Raj, A. K. Saxena, and S. Dasgupta, "Analytical Modeling for the Estimation of Leakage Current and Subthreshold Swing Factor of Nanoscale Double Gate FinFET Device" *Microelectronics International, UK*, Vol. 26, pp. 53–63, 2009.

60. S. S. Soniya, G. Wadhwa, and B. Raj, "An Analytical Modeling for Dual Source Vertical Tunnel Field Effect Transistor", *International Journal of Recent Technology and Engineering (IJRTE)*, Vol. 8, No. 2, pp. 603–608, 2019.

61. K. Hartke, 2015. Observing resources in the constrained application protocol (CoAP) (No. RFC 7641).

62. K. Mekki, E. Bajic, F. Chaxel, and F. Meyer, "A Comparative Study of LPWAN Technologies for Large-Scale IoT Deployment", *ICT Express*, Vol. 5, No. 1, pp. 1–7, 2019.

63. S. Persia, C. Carciofi, and M. Faccioli, 2017, NB-IoT and LoRA connectivity analysis for M2M/IoT smart grids applications. In *2017 AEIT International Annual Conference*, Cagliari, Italy (pp. 1–6). IEEE.

64. W. Ayoub, A. E. Samhat, F. Nouvel, M. Mroue, and J. C. Prévotet, "Internet of Mobile Things: Overview of LoRaWAN, DASH7, and NB-IoT in LPWANs Standards and Supported Mobility", *IEEE Communications Surveys & Tutorials*, Vol. 21, pp. 1561–1581, 2018.

65. A. H. Ngu, M. Gutierrez, V. Metsis, S. Nepal, and Q. Z. Sheng, 2017. "IoT Middleware: A Survey on Issues and Enabling Technologies", *IEEE Internet of Things Journal*, Vol. 4, No. 1, pp. 1–20.

66. M. A. da Cruz, J. J. Rodrigues, A. K. Sangaiah, J. Al-Muhtadi, and V. Korotaev, "Performance Evaluation of IoT Middleware", *Journal of Network and Computer Applications*, Vol. 109, pp. 53–65, 2018.

67. S. Bandyopadhyay, M. Sengupta, S. Maiti, and S. Dutta, "Role of Middleware for Internet of Things: A Study", *International Journal of Computer Science and Engineering Survey*, Vol. 2, No. 3, pp. 94–105, 2011.

68. A. Palade, C. Cabrera, F. Li, G. White, M. A. Razzaque, and S. Clarke, "Middleware for Internet of Things: An Evaluation in a Small-Scale IoT Environment", *Journal of Reliable Intelligent Environments*, Vol. 4, No. 1, pp. 3–23, 2018.

69. C. Pereira, J. Cardoso, A. Aguiar, and R. Morla, "Benchmarking Pub/Sub IoT Middleware Platforms for Smart Services", *Journal of Reliable Intelligent Environments*, Vol. 4, No. 1, pp. 25–37, 2018.

70. A. Ranganathan, J. Al-Muhtadi, S. Chetan, R. Campbell, and M. D. Mickunas, 2004, October. Middlewhere: a middleware for location awareness in ubiquitous computing applications. In *ACM/IFIP/USENIX International Conference on Distributed Systems Platforms and Open Distributed Processing*, Berlin, Heidelberg (pp. 397–416). Springer, Berlin, Heidelberg.

71. G. Kokkonis, A. Chatzimparmpas, and S. Kontogiannis, 2018, September. Middleware IoT protocols performance evaluation for carrying out clustered data. In *2018 South-Eastern European Design Automation, Computer Engineering, Computer Networks and Society Media Conference (SEEDA_CECNSM)*, Kastoria, Greece (pp. 1–5). IEEE.

72. H. Hejazi, H. Rajab, T. Cinkler, and L. Lengyel, 2018, January. Survey of platforms for massive IoT. In *2018 IEEE International Conference on Future IoT Technologies (Future IoT)*, Eger, Hungary (pp. 1–8). IEEE.

73. J. Kim, J. Yun, S. C. Choi, D. N. Seed, G. Lu, M. Bauer, A. Al-Hezmi, K. Campowsky, and J. Song, "Standard-Based IoT Platforms Interworking: Implementation, Experiences, and Lessons Learned", *IEEE Communications Magazine*, Vol. 54, No. 7, pp. 48–54, 2016.

74. A. Bröring, S. Schmid, C. K. Schindhelm, A. Khelil, S. Käbisch, D. Kramer, D. Le Phuoc, J. Mitic, D. Anicic, and E. Teniente, "Enabling IoT Ecosystems through Platform Interoperability", *IEEE Software*, Vol. 34, No. 1, pp. 54–61, 2017.

75. G. Keramidas, N. Voros, and M. Hübner, 2016. *Components and Services for IoT Platforms*. Springer International Pu, Cham.

76. G. Fortino, C. Savaglio, C. E. Palau, J. S. de Puga, M. Ganzha, M. Paprzycki, M. Montesinos, A. Liotta, and M. Llop, 2018. Towards multi-layer interoperability of heterogeneous IoT platforms: The INTER-IoT approach. In Gravina, R., Palau, C., Manso, M., Liotta, A., Fortino, G. (eds), *Integration, Interconnection, and Interoperability of IoT Systems*. Springer, Cham. https://doi.org/10.1007/978-3-319-61300-0_10

77. F. Y. Okay, and S. Ozdemir, "Routing in Fog-Enabled IoT Platforms: A Survey and an SDN-Based Solution", *IEEE Internet of Things Journal*, Vol. 5, No. 6, pp. 4871–4889, 2018.

78. T. Jell, C. Baumgartner, A. Bröring, and J. Mitic, 2018. BIG IoT: Interconnecting IoT platforms from different domains—First success story. In Latifi, S. (ed), *Information Technology - New Generations. Advances in Intelligent Systems and Computing* (Vol. 738). Springer, Cham. https://doi.org/10.1007/978-3-319-77028-4_91

79. A. Sehgal, V. Perelman, S. Kuryla, and J. Schonwalder, "Management of Resource Constrained Devices in the Internet of Things", *IEEE Communications Magazine*, Vol. 50, No. 12, pp. 144–149, 2012.

80. Z. K. Zhang, M. C. Y. Cho, C. W. Wang, C. W. Hsu, C. K. Chen, and S. Shieh, 2014, November. IoT security: ongoing challenges and research opportunities. In *2014 IEEE 7th International Conference on Service-Oriented Computing and Applications*, Matsue, Japan (pp. 230–234). IEEE.

81. A. Dorri, S. S. Kanhere, R. Jurdak, and P. Gauravaram, 2017, March. Blockchain for IoT security and privacy: The case study of a smart home. In *2017 IEEE International Conference on Pervasive Computing and Communications Workshops (PerCom Workshops)*, Kona, HI (pp. 618–623). IEEE.

82. B. Guo, D. Zhang, Z. Wang, Z. Yu, and X. Zhou, "Opportunistic IoT: Exploring the Harmonious Interaction between Human and the Internet of Things", *Journal of Network and Computer Applications*, Vol. 36, No. 6, pp. 1531–1539, 2013.

83. I. Yaqoob, I. A. T. Hashem, A. Ahmed, S. A. Kazmi, and C. S. Hong, "Internet of Things Forensics: Recent Advances, Taxonomy, Requirements, and Open Challenges", *Future Generation Computer Systems*, Vol. 92, pp. 265–275, 2019.

84. A. A. Mutlag, M. K. A. Ghani, N. A. Arunkumar, M. A. Mohamed, and O. Mohd, "Enabling Technologies for Fog Computing in Healthcare IoT Systems", *Future Generation Computer Systems*, Vol. 90, pp. 62–78, 2019.

85. L. Catarinucci, D. De Donno, L. Mainetti, L. Palano, L. Patrono, M. L. Stefanizzi, and L. Tarricone, "An IoT-Aware Architecture for Smart Healthcare Systems", *IEEE Internet of Things Journal*, Vol. 2, No. 6, pp. 515–526, 2015.

86. F. Fernandez, and G. C. Pallis, 2014, November. Opportunities and challenges of the Internet of Things for healthcare: Systems engineering perspective. In *2014 4th International Conference on Wireless Mobile Communication and Healthcare-Transforming Healthcare Through Innovations in Mobile and Wireless Technologies (MOBIHEALTH)*, Athens, Greece (pp. 263–266). IEEE.

87. A. Iyengar, A. Kundu, and G. Pallis, "Healthcare Informatics and Privacy", *IEEE Internet Computing*, Vol. 22, No. 2, pp. 29–31, 2018.

88. R. Zgheib, E. Conchon, and R. Bastide, 2019. Semantic middleware architectures for IoT healthcare applications. In Ganchev, I., Garcia, N., Dobre, C., Mavromoustakis, C., and Goleva, R. (eds), *Enhanced Living Environments. Lecture Notes in Computer Science*, Springer, Cham (Vol 11369). https://doi.org/10.1007/978-3-030-10752-9_11

89. S. B. Baker, W. Xiang, and I. Atkinson, "Internet of Things for Smart Healthcare: Technologies, Challenges, and Opportunities", *IEEE Access*, Vol. 5, pp. 26521–26544, 2017.

90. D. A. Gandhi, and M. Ghosal, 2018, April. Intelligent healthcare using IoT: A extensive survey. In *2018 Second International Conference on Inventive Communication and Computational Technologies (ICICCT)*, Coimbatore, India (pp. 800–802). IEEE.

91. N. Deshai, S. Venkataramana, B. V. D. S. Sekhar, K. Srinivas, and G. P. S. Varma, 2019. A study on IOT tools, protocols, applications, opportunities and challenges. In Satapathy, S., Bhateja, V., Somanah, R., Yang, X. S., and Senkerik, R. (eds), *Information Systems Design and Intelligent Applications. Advances in Intelligent Systems and Computing* (Vol. 862). Springer, Singapore. https://doi.org/10.1007/978-981-13-3329-3_34

CHAPTER 3

Spintronic Technology Applications for Artificial Intelligence

Parul Sharma and Sandeep Singh Gill

National Institute of Technical Teachers Training and Research

Balwinder Raj

National Institute of Technical Teachers Training and Research
Dr. B.R. Ambedkar National Institute of Technology

CONTENTS

DOI: 10.1201/9781003230113-3

3.1 INTRODUCTION

Spintronics is an innovative area of electronics that refines the spin of electrons in addition to its charge for device performance. Spintronics is also called spin electronics, where the spin property of an electron is supervised by the exterior magnetic field and centralizes the electrons [1]. These polarized electrons are used to manage the electric current. All spintronic gadgets behave in line with the straightforward scheme: (a) Data are saved (written) into spins as exact in spin direction (up or down), (b) all spins, be added to moveable electrons, hold the data alongside a wire, and (c) The data are examined at the end [2]. The spin direction of conducting electron holds on for a long time in comparison with conventional electronic devices, which makes spintronic devices more fascinated pro magnetic memory, magnetic sensor, and quantum computing where electron spin would act as a bit called a qubit of information [2] (Figure 3.1).

From the definition, it's crystal clear that the branch of spintronics is dependent on the direction of the spin of electrons rather than their charge (positive or negative). The spin-polarized electrons can be considered to have two states; spin-up and spin-down (with its spin either +1/2 or −1/2), which act as an on-state and off-state, respectively (Figure 3.2).

In other words, we can say that the electron will rotate clockwise or anti-clockwise around its axis with sustained frequency, and in logical

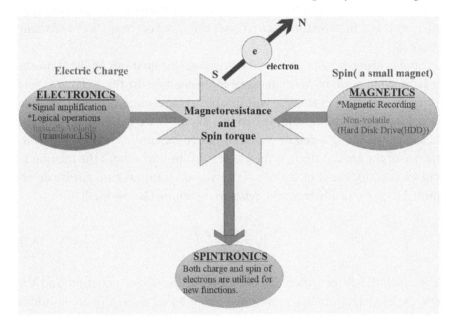

FIGURE 3.1   Spintronic composition.

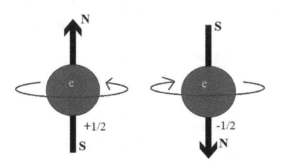

FIGURE 3.2   Spin-up and spin-down.

operations, the spin state is represented as logic "0" and logic "1." In a traditional semiconductor, the use of electron is in a simple binary proportion, i.e., electrons state represent only in "0" or "1," and every number is represented as a set of eight bits (between 0 and 255), where spintronic technology makes use of quantum bits, called qubits, which utilize the spin-up and spin downstate as a superposition of 0 and 1, and also has the potential to represent every number between 0 and 255 simultaneously. There are a lot of advantages to using the spin over a charge of an electron: (1) spin can be controlled by the external magnetic field, (2) protects consistency for a relatively long time in electronic material, (3) helps to make a compact device and improves the performance with low power consumption, and (4) is nonvolatile and increases the speed of the devices and many more [3].

Spin is differed from charge, is a bogus vector quantity and that means it have sable scale of $h/4\pi$ changeable divergence. In the magnetic field when the electron is sited, it will be able to have many states other than two; however, in digital simply two bits (0 and 1) are determined and rest of the values are ignored or not used [4]. To be familiar with the performance of the charge atom in metal, we need to understand the relation of power and thickness of metal's state. The division of spin can be determined hypothetically from the relation mentioned below [5,6]:

$$P_n = \frac{n\uparrow - n\downarrow}{n\uparrow - n\downarrow} \tag{3.1}$$

These are the three different conditions of the above equation and the energy level diagram are mentioned Table 3.1 of these three conditions [7,8] and see Figure 3.3.

The energy level diagrams are drawn by using the Stoner–Wohlfarth (SW) model of ferromagnet. After some time by utilizing this easy SW Model, researchers did variation to identify the science to catch the

TABLE 3.1 Conditions and Corresponding Outputs

Condition	Output
$n\downarrow = 0; P_{n=1}$	Merely majority spins are present and we get 100% spin polarization. Ferromagnetic half metal or Heusler alloys, etc.; material with 100% spin polarization.
$n\uparrow = 0; P_n = -1$	LSMO substance gives a pointed change from metal to insulator with a change in temperature.
$n\downarrow = n\uparrow; P_n = 0$	Only for common metals and paramagnetic metals.

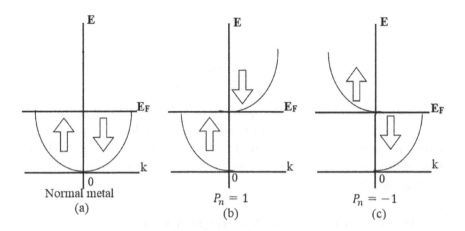

FIGURE 3.3 Energy level diagram using SW Model [6,9]. (a) Represents the spin-up and spin-down, both of which are equal in normal metal, (b) If $n_\downarrow=0$, then $n_\uparrow$ is 100% spin polarized and has $P_n=1$, and (c) when $n_\uparrow=0$ and $n_\downarrow=100\%$ spin polarized has $p_n=-1$.

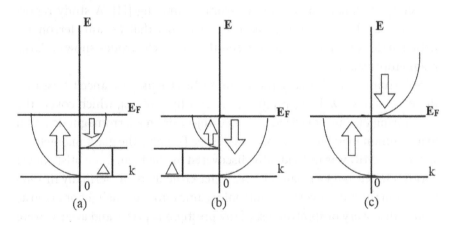

FIGURE 3.4 Energy level graph for half ferromagnetic metal at 0 K [5,9] (a) and (b) contain spin-up and spin-down and in (c) represents energy level graph for half ferromagnet metal at absolute 0 K below level E_F; the energy level or area is occupied by the spin-up while the above area is engaged by spin-down only.

attention of digital magnetic devices for collecting like floppy disk, hard drive and magnetic tapes and see Figure 3.4. Equation (3.2) or (3.3) is used to calculated the spin related energy (up and down [5,10]).

$$E_\uparrow = \frac{h^2}{4\pi^2 m_0}k \qquad (3.2)$$

or

$$E_\downarrow = \frac{h^2}{4\pi^2 m_0} K^2 + \Delta \tag{3.3}$$

where Δ = movement in the energy level of either spin-up or spin-down. The Fermi level of all abovementioned energy level diagram is above the base of both sub-bands. Boltzmann figure is only swap by the Fermi–Dirac Figure only and only when the Fermi level is properly beneath the base of the both sub-bands.

3.2 HISTORY OF SPINTRONIC TECHNOLOGY

Spintronics came to light due to discoveries in the 1980s covering spin-dependent electron transport wonders in solid-state devices. In the late 1960s, a group at IBM led by Japanese physicist Leo Esaki coined the term spintronics, and later he was awarded the Noble prize in 1973 for detecting the phenomenon of electronic tunneling [11]. A study report prepared by Leo Esaki and his team explains that an anti-ferromagnetic barrier of EuSe placed between the metal electrodes shows a large magnetoresistance.

Spintronics was initially the name for a Defense Advanced Research Project Agency (DARPA) program oversaw by Wolf [2], which covers the monitoring of spin-polarized electrons injection in a ferromagnetic metal to a common metal by Johnson and Silsbee [71] plus the giant magnetoresistance (GMR) was individually discovered by the French scientist Albert Fert in France and German scientist Peter Gruenberg in Germany in 1988 [12]. From these discoveries, spintronics came into the limelight or taken as a birth discovery of spintronics. Many prestigious prizes and awards were given to these two physicists for their discovery and for coming up with the best research work in the field of spintronics. They were also awarded the 2007 Noble prize in physics. The root of spintronics can be followed to the ferromagnet/superconductor tunneling experiment introduced by Meservey and Tedrow and earliest experiments on magnetic tunnel junction in the 1970s by scientist Julliere (Figure 3.5).

The utilization of semiconductors for spintronics started with the conceptual approach of a spin-FET by Datta and Das in 1990 and the idea of the electric dipole spin resonance given by Rashba in 1960 [14]. From that point onward, fast advancement has kept on upgrading both the purpose and capability of spintronics.

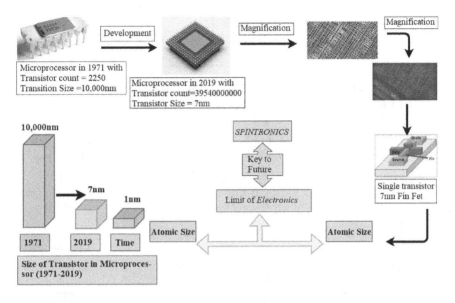

FIGURE 3.5 The number of transistors and the size of microprocessor in 1971 and the number of transistors and size of microprocessor in 2019 present the limitation of electronics. Moreover, while scaling down, one may face many problems. Spintronics is the answer to overcome all those problems [13].

3.3 THEORY

With the advancement in technology, day by day the devices are getting smaller in size; hence, a reduction in the channel length circuit or device. The predictable gate length in outlook is 5nm due to this, off leakage current will be more for the complete chip [15,16]. But there is a limit till which we can reduce the channel length. Also, engineers face other challenges like fabrication of the device, leakage of current, designing, etc. [17]. Through, there are numerous practices to diminish the off-chip energy and those show potentials are Double Gate-Metal Oxide Semiconductor Field Effect Transistor (DG-MOSFET), Fin Field Effect Transistor (Fin-FET) [18], and Si-Nanowire MOSFET [19,20]. Gate MOSFET surrounded with duo material is one more method to get better carrier moving competence and trim the short cannel effect [21]. Carbon Nanotube Field Effect Transistor (CNT FET) [22] is a further possible nano-device analogous in construction of Complementary Metal Oxide Semiconductor (CMOS) technology [23]. It has superior performance, transconductance, and less energy utilization. Many logics have been built utilizing these techniques. The glitch with over declared logics is "Volatility". Spin logics is the uprising one, which

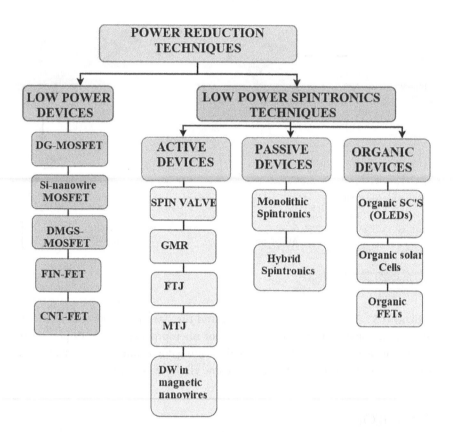

FIGURE 3.6   Spintronic power reduction techniques [19].

can solve the battery lifetime related problem. This increases the life of the battery by utilizing less energy from transportable gadgets to huge information centers and nonvolatile features (Figure 3.6).

Spin logic or spintronics is one of the most promising fields in applied science which have absolute the Moore's law and manufacturers are struggling to plant more than Moore's. If there is any mechanism which can compete with electronics which can trim any one of the functions like area, power utilization and speediness etc. of the very large-scale integration (VLSI) [24]. Luckily, spintronics can increase the speed of a device with a decrease in power dissipation. To toggle on logic "0" to logic "1," the scale of the charge required to switch in the active region of the charge-based device due to which the current run from source to drain. It's not achievable to reduce the power or heat dissipation with charge-based electronic gadgets because charge only possesses the direction (scalar quantity) and gives logic 1 in the presence of charge, otherwise logic 0 [25].

3.3.1 Main Spintronic Effects

3.3.1.1 Giant Magnetoresistance Effect

When resistance change is noticed in the metallic material or device when it comes under the effect of magnetic field, it is called magnetoresistance, and a very huge magnetoresistance effect is known as giant magnetoresistance. It was detected by the scientist "Albert Fert" and "Peter Grunberg" individually in 1988 [26] in ferromagnetic material films which are detached by an insulator or nonmagnetic film. Their effort was appreciated by honoring with Nobel prize in 2007. The electrical resistance of the multilayer is chosen by the magnetic state. Precisely, when the spins in the ferromagnetic layer are anti-parallel, the resistance will be high and in the case of parallel the resistance is low. The variation of the resistance in the hetero-structure is the result of variation in the direction of spin and is named as GMR [27]. This figure depicts the spin in the ferromagnetic material. The GMR was the first discovery and has many applications in different areas like sensors [28], medical field [29], magnetic imaging, galvanic isolators, and many others [30,31].

As per the tendency of spin action in the hetero-structure, GMR is split up in two ways (see Figures 3.7 and 3.8): (1) CIP GMR (Current in the Plane) and (2) CPP-GMR (Current Perpendicular to the Plane). The distinction between CIP-GMR and CPP-GMR was examined by utilizing "Single band tight-binding model" [33].

3.3.1.2 CIP GMR

The CIP-GMR was first noticed in the Fe/Cr/Fe hetero-structure and as the name indicates, the current is parallel to the layered structure plane. When no magnetic field is applied, the spin in the ferromagnetic material is not aligned and the strong magnetic field to the structure provides the

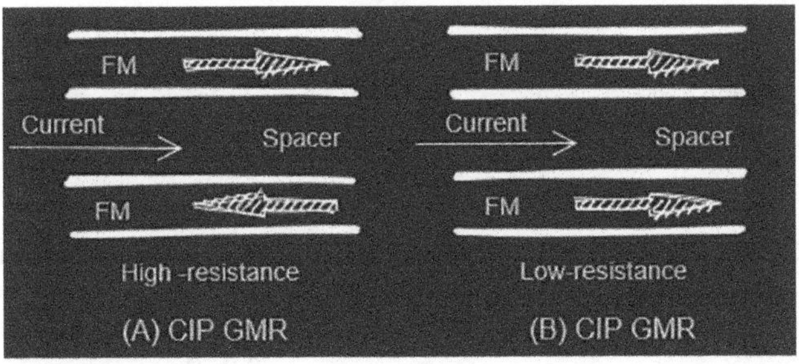

FIGURE 3.7   CIP-GMR [32].

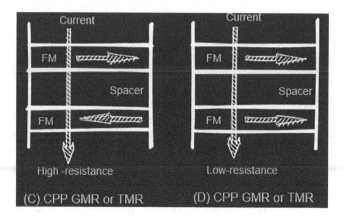

FIGURE 3.8   CCP-GMR [32].

spin alignment as output result. This shows the variation of the spin in the plane of electrical resistance. If spins are aligned in one state (either up- or down-spin) of the ferromagnetic layer automatically, there will be the same spin state in the second layer and this condition is proved for the spin-down state too. With parallel spin, the dispersion is weak for electrons in the ferromagnetic material and strong with opposed spins.

The majority current polarization' (α) of FM layer is calculated by [34]:

$$\alpha = \frac{\sigma_+ - \sigma_-}{\sigma_+ + \sigma_-} \tag{3.4}$$

where

$\sigma\pm =$ conductivity of electron's spin

and

$$\sigma\pm = e^2 g_{\pm} v_{\pm}^2 \tau_{\pm} \tag{3.5}$$

$g_{\pm}$ = density of electron
$v_{\pm}$ = Fermi velocity of electron
$\tau_{\pm}$ = Momentum relaxation time.

With the help of resistance model, we calculate the resistance of the hetero-structure and GMR depicted in Figure 3.9.

• Parallel resistance $R_P = \dfrac{2R_{\uparrow}R_{\downarrow}}{R_{\uparrow} + R_{\downarrow}}$ $\qquad$ (3.6)

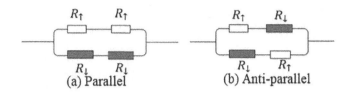

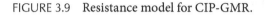
(a) Parallel   (b) Anti-parallel

FIGURE 3.9   Resistance model for CIP-GMR.

- Anti-Parallel resistance $R_{AP} = \dfrac{R_\uparrow + R_\downarrow}{2}$ (3.7)

Conductance across every arrangement specified below:

- Parallel Conductance $G_P = \dfrac{1}{R_P} = \dfrac{1}{2R_\uparrow} + \dfrac{1}{2R_\downarrow}$ (3.8)

- Anti-Parallel Conductance $G_{AP} = \dfrac{1}{R_{AP}} = \dfrac{2}{R_\uparrow + R_\downarrow}$ (3.9)

Thus, GMR is calculated from the equation

$$GMR = \left(\frac{G_P - G_{AP}}{G_{AP}} \right)$$ (3.10)

3.3.1.3 CPP-GMR

In 1991, the presence of CPP-GMR was hypothetically anticipated by Zhang and Levy [72] and afterward tentatively affirmed the equivalent in the Ag/Co layer [33]. In this arrangement, the electrons head out opposite to the attractive layers. The resistance of the hetero-structure is typically small over its width, and thus, it is exceptionally hard to evaluate. This issue can be amended by utilizing superconducting leads.

A limited polarization which develops in the nonattractive material is because of spin aggregation. CPP-GMR relies upon spin rest time. Various concentrations of spin-up and spin-down charge transporters at the locator interface are because of spin aggregation. It is characterized as the electrochemical potentiality distinction between spin-up and spin-down transporters. With the help of the resistance model, we calculate the resistance of the hetero-structure and GMR depicted in Figure 3.10:

$$R_P = \frac{\left(2R_\uparrow + R_{NM}\right)\left(2R_\downarrow + R_{NM}\right)}{2\left(R_\uparrow + R_\downarrow + R_{NM}\right)}$$ (3.11)

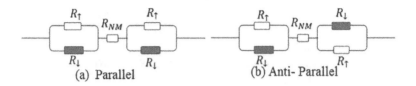

FIGURE 3.10   Resistance model for CPP-GMR.

$$R_{AP} = \frac{R_\uparrow + R_\downarrow + R_{NM}}{2} \tag{3.12}$$

The behavior of GMR across each arrangement is given as:

$$G_P = \frac{1}{R_P} = \frac{2\left(R_\downarrow + R_\uparrow + R_{NM}\right)}{\left(2R_\uparrow + R_{NM}\right)\left(2R_\downarrow + R_{NM}\right)} \tag{3.13}$$

$$G_{AP} = \frac{1}{R_{AP}} = \frac{2}{R_\uparrow + R_\downarrow + R_{NM}} \tag{3.14}$$

3.3.2 Tunnel Magnetoresistance Effect

When the magnetic field is applied to the magnetic material, which is divided by the semiconductor material or an insulator, the variation in resistance noticed due to the applied magnetic field is known as tunnel magnetoresistance. The result was first determined by "Michel Julliere," in France, in 1975, who examined the 14% variation of resistance in Fe/Ge-O/Co-intersection at 4.2 K temperature [33]. After this, many researches have done this and a few are mentioned in Table 3.1. Tunnel magnetoresistance is a magneto-resistive cause which happens in a magnetic tunnel junction (Figure 3.11).

The Magnetic Tunnel Junction (MTJ) consists of two ferromagnetic layers that are split by a thin layer of insulator material. The tunneling process is basically the traveling of electrons from one ferromagnetic layer to another ferromagnetic layer only and only if the thickness of the insulating layer is very thin, usually a few nanometers. In traditional physics, this practice was banned but Tunnel Magnetoresistance (TMR) is completely a quantum mechanical occurrence. In MTJ, the joints of the different layers are set by the process of photolithography.

When the exterior magnetic field is applied, the path of magnetization of ferromagnetic layers can be controlled independently. If the magnetization in the layer is parallel in direction than the electrons will channel through the insulating layer then both are in reverse direction (Figure 3.12).

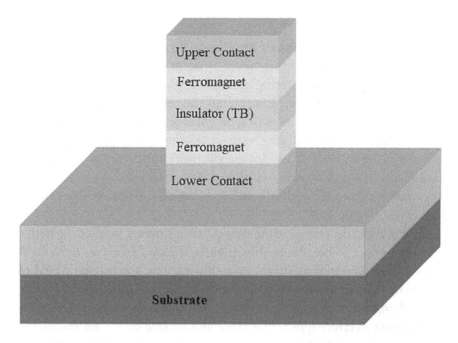

FIGURE 3.11   Magnetic tunnel junction.

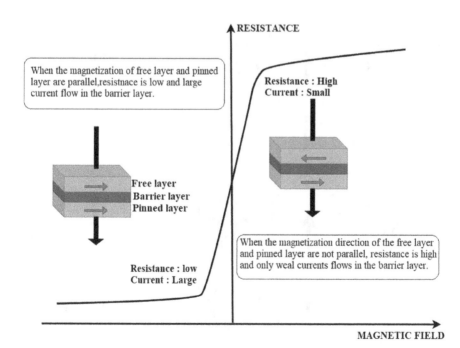

FIGURE 3.12   TMR shows great resistance when there is a minor quantity of current.

3.3.3 Spin Transfer Torque (STT)

STT develops when the movement of spin angular energy in a model is not stable, except sink or sources. This occur, when the current (spin) produced from the spin filtering method via passing it through one magnetic slim film of different moment and the same current is strained by the other magnetic slim film with different moment. Because the moment of both layers is not collinear with each other, some part of the spin angular energy which is held by the electron's spin is taken by the second magnet film. Moreover, when spin-polarized electrons exceed over the magnetic-domain wall or some space-based unequal magnetization dispersion (Figure 3.13).

In this cycle, the charge of the spin electron revolves to track the native magnetic area and because of this, angular energy spin vector movement varies as a function of position. In both situations, the magnetic field of the metal (ferromagnet) transforms the movement of spin angular energy by applying the torque on the moving spin to redirect it and as a result the moving electron applies the same and reverse torque on the metal. Now this torque, which is enforced by imbalance of electron conduction

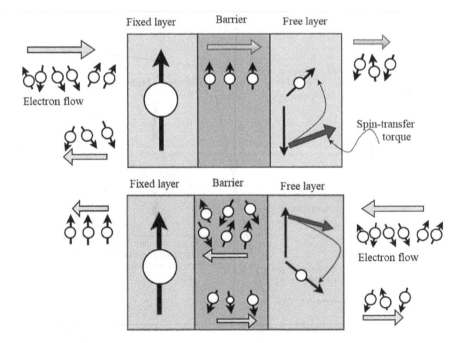

FIGURE 3.13   Spin transfer torque effect.

on metal, is termed as spin transfer torque. The intensity of torque can be estimated in two ways, that is, by directly considering the common precession of the spin and magnetic significance during the time of interaction (suggested by Jain and Raj) or by taking the complete variation in the spin's current before and after the interaction [35].

3.3.4 Spin Hall Effect (SHE)

In 1971, the Russian physicists "Mikhail I. Dyakonov and Vladimir I. Perel" calculated the transport phenomenon named as SHE. This transport phenomenon includes the spin collection on the tangential plane of the model-bearing electric current. The resisting plane boundaries will have spin with reverse sign. It is similar to the traditional hall effect, in which the charge of reverse sign comes out on the resisting tangential surface in an electric current-bearing model in the magnetic area. In traditional hall effect, because of the magnetic area, the charge develop at the edges is in pay for the "Lorentz power" following up on the charge carriers in the model. It is purely a spin-based phenomenon, so there is no need of a magnetic field. The SHE is associated with a similar family of the traditional hall effect. The SHE is caused by (1) irregularity in scattering of electrons and (2) band arrangements [33]. The spin-dependent Mott scattering and distortion are the two main reasons that led to SHE. When a strong magnetic field is applied, the spin nearly compresses the magnetic field, but when the field is enforced at right angle of the spin direction, then the SHE will vanish and this is characterized as Inverse SHE [36] (Figure 3.14).

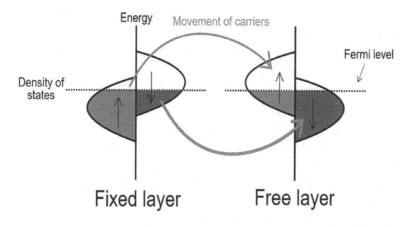

FIGURE 3.14   Spin hall effect.

3.3.5 Spin Seebeck Effect

The spin Seebeck effect is the creation of a spin voltage produced in a metal like ferromagnet by increasing the temperature in it. The phenomenon was noticed by Adachi et al. [74] in the metal/nonmagnetic metal hetero-structure when it is positioned beneath the temperature gradient as a result of which the electrons will reorganize themselves in accordance to their spin. This reorganization of electron spin will not create any unwanted heat, whereas traditional electron movement creates unwanted heat. Basically, this effect depends upon the temperature difference which means that when the difference is large then the Seebeck effect–based devices will produce a few mill volts. This effect will help to produce the smaller size devices with great functionality and more energy-proficient microchips [37].

3.4 LOW POWER SPINTRONIC TECHNOLOGIES

3.4.1 Active Devices

The devices which come under this section are spin valve, GMR effect–based devices, MTJ basically a TMR-based device, Front Tunnel Junction (FTJ), and DW in magnetic nanowires, and we will discuss every device under this area.

3.4.1.1 Spin Valve

It was introduced in the year 1991 and soon it became famous in the industrial market and completely modified the market related to magnetic sensors, Magnetoresistive Random Access Memory (MRAMs), etc. Spin valve construction is almost similar to the GMR. Basically, we can notice the effect of GMR in the spin valve device. In GMR, both the FM layers are exchanged by the source and drain and nonmagnetic layer is exchanged with the channel. The device fabrication is possible in both ways, either horizontally or vertically [1] (Figure 3.15).

From Figure 3.15 it is clear that it carries four different layers and each layer plays a different role during operation. The top layer is called the free layer made of ferromagnetic material and the second layer is called the spacer layer made of nonmagnetic material. The top layer is separated from the third layer by the second layer. The third layer is called the pinned layer and is made of magnetic material. The last layer or the fourth layer is called the AF pinned layer and is made of anti-ferromagnet material and it sets up the magnetic direction of the third layer [19].

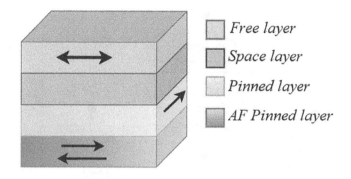

Free layer

Space layer

Pinned layer

AF Pinned layer

FIGURE 3.15   Representation of simple four-layered spin valve.

3.4.1.2 Magnetic Tunnel Junction

Tunnel junction, which is utilized for the logical and memory-based application, where electronic field and magnetic field comes together and provide great read and write speed, Nonvolatile, etc. and many more is named as magnetic tunnel junction. This is a very assuring device and also pays attention to its basic effects like tunneling, magnetoresistance, and STT. Its nanopillar is a very essential gadget in spin electronics. It contains an insulating film (aluminum oxide) approximately 1 nm, which is sandwiched between two magnetic metal films (like cobalt-iron). When the voltage is applied, the insulated film is so slim that electrons will move over the barrier. The tunneling current, which can be managed by the operating magnetic field, depends upon the relation between the direction of magnetization of both metal films. This event is termed as TMR effect [38] (Figure 3.16).

It is not easy to fabricate the MTJ with great service, and it includes various difficult steps. There are many methods to develop various layers of MTJ like technique of deposition are Molecular Beam Epitaxial, RF sputtering, Ion beam sputtering and E-beam evaporation. The devices of very small size like nanometers are developed by the process of lithography [4]. At present, there are many techniques to get better MTJ devices by making the right selection of material, dimensions, area, power efficiency, consistency, and low power consumption. Many methodologies such as Thermal Assisted Switching (TAS) and STT are examined, but they face problems with power usage and consistency. The benefit of MTJ is that it can be simply combined with CMOS circuitry, and devices like NV logic and NV memories [39] are built on hybrid grouping of MTJ and CMOS [19].

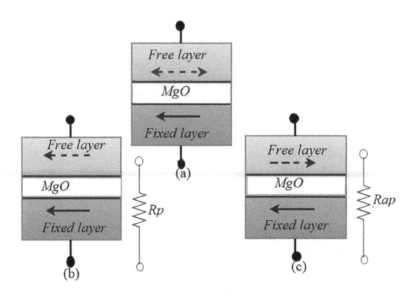

FIGURE 3.16   MTJ structure with parallel and anti-parallel.

3.4.1.3 Ferroelectric Tunnel Junction (FTJ)

The theory of FTJ was given by Esaki initially in 1971; however, the production is done newly. There are lots of problems faced by engineers during construction, especially to hold steady ferroelectric polarization on very narrow films prepared of few cell units [40]. It is a tunnel junction consisting of a very narrow film, which separates two distinctive metal electrodes. Because of the quick advancement in nano-manufacture, the basic thickness of ferroelectric slim film has dropped to 2 nm. It is a voltage-controlled gadget. Furthermore, the electrical obstruction of FTJ clearly relies upon the direction of the electric polarization. At the point when the electric field is applied over the slim ferroelectric layer, unconstrained ferroelectric polarization happens that offers ascent to two rationale states (high or low) with polarization indicating either up or down. Exchanging the ferroelectric polarization gives an adjustment in passage opposition, and this marvel is termed as tunneling electro resistance (TER) (It is a relation of high to low resistance). To control the direction of polarization of ferroelectric barrier, more exterior voltage is applied than threshold voltage [41].

3.4.1.4 DW in Magnetic Nanowires

The logical gates like NOT gate, AND gate, and magnetic shift register are built up using DW motion in magnetic nanowires. The great benefit of this

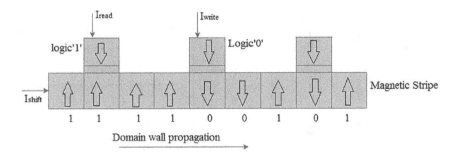

FIGURE 3.17   Demonstration of DW motion.

is that while calculating the result, it utilizes zero supply and hence is non-volatile in nature. The main trouble is that its working speed is very low (<100 kHz) and when the device starts working after some time, it starts producing the magnetic field in the CMOS circuits, which creates trouble within the circuit [42]. It operates on the basic principle of MTJ nanopillars of CoFeB/MgO/CoFeB. When the current generates DW which own two read and write heads MTJ0 and MTJ1 and a magnetic nanostripe. The insertion of the bits in magnetic bar utilizing different techniques of the STT or TAS methodology is done by Iwrite; Ishift will produce DW motion next to the magnetic bar; and spotting of magnetization path complete by TMR effect is done by Iread [4,19] (Figure 3.17).

3.4.2 Passive Devices

These are categorized as hybrid and monolithic spintronics, as explained in Figure 3.5.

3.4.2.1 Monolithic Spintronics

The monolithic spintronic is the one which trade with those gadgets, in which the spin logic solitary manage data collection and data transmission processes. The device falls under the category monolithic spintronics and is called spin single logic (SSL), in which storing and transmitting of data for communication is done by spin only [5]. It is a different kind of processor technology, introduced in 1994, and which became famous due to bistability of spin states of electrons in quantum dots. This method is applied to form SSL utilizing the magnetic field, electrons, and quantum dots generally. SSL gained fame because of the electron's spin constant state and the flow of the current is controlled by the spin not by the charge [19]. Spin is the vector quantity, and it has both magnitude and

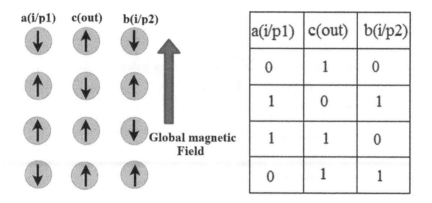

a(i/p1)	c(out)	b(i/p2)
0	1	0
1	0	1
1	1	0
0	1	1

FIGURE 3.18 Array of three spin-polarized single electron and each kept in a quantum dot and attain the NAND gate when the complete array is placed in a static magnetic field and permitted to relax to the thermodynamic ground state and with this the truth table is given.

magnetic division. The bistability of polarization is achieved by inserting the electrons in the DC magnetic field and after that permits the structure break to the thermodynamics ground state.

To understand the concept of monolithic spintronics, let us take the example of SSL of NAND GATE (2 I/P). Using this, one can understand the other combinational and sequential logics. From the figure (a), (b), and (c) are the linear array of an electron which hold the quantum dots. Wave function is the overlapping of the closest array of (a), (c) and (b), (c); hence, swapping of interface coupling will be done. Here (a), (b) are the inputs and (c) is the output (spin) of the NAND Gate. Logic (1) is written, whereas the polarization is parallel to the applied magnetic field and logic (0) when its polarization is anti-parallel to the field [4] (Figure 3.18).

The spin polarization represents the (c) output always when the spin polarization of (a), (b) inputs are ready to accept the requested input bits and structure is permitted to relax toward the ground state. With the use of clock pad, input signal can move to a separate node. The main advantage of employing this interface is one-way dispatch of signal, which builds the structured pipeline to attain the great speed along with the expense of clock bit rate.

3.4.2.2 Hybrid Spintronics

The original spin-based polarized transistor, identified as spin-FET transistor idea, was given by Datta Das in 1990 [75]. It employed the proposal of the spin transistor [43] (Figure 3.19).

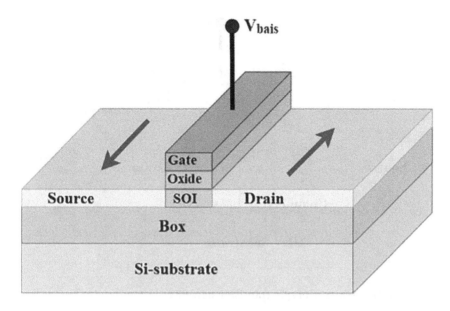

FIGURE 3.19   Structure of spin transistor spin-MOSFET.

This is also entitled as "Electro-Optic Modulator." Basically, the hybrid technique is different from monolithic. Data are stored and manipulated by spin logic, but hybrid spin does not exactly deal with data storage and information practice (either holes or electrons). Charge still plays a vital role in hybrid and spin has a secondary role, but its impact is increased by the existence of spin [4].

The initial spin-FET [44] of Datta Das was not manufactured fully; however, it is hypothetically verified and has outstanding utilization of spintronics' revolution. After there is wide range of spin-based transistor, each with their own working standards have been registered. Spin-FET transistor construction is almost similar with the classic MOSFET design [5]. It also has three terminal devices (snubbing bulk) with drain, source, and gate contacts. The channel, which is sandwiched between the source and the drain, is managed by the gate. When the voltage is applied at the gate, the gate electrodes manage the spin movement between both the layers of the ferromagnetic [45,46].

In spin-FET and devices related to it, the source and the drain have an analogous spin layout. The switching movement of on/off can be achieved by Spin antecedence of the Spin-polarized carrier impart in the channel diagonally spin orbit transmission [19,47,48] as presented in (Figure 3.20).

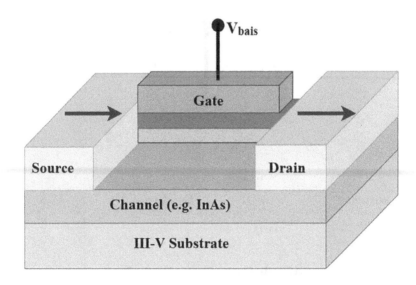

FIGURE 3.20 Structure of spin transistor spin-FET.

3.4.3 Organic Spintronics

There is immense transformation in the area of data stockpiling since the revelation of the giant magnetoresistance impact and the advancement of spintronics in the past 30 years [4]. Organic semiconductors (OSCs) made out of weightless components have powerless spin circle coupling (SOC) association and accordingly long spin unwinding time with the second level. As per the current investigations, it has been demonstrated that there is an extraordinary capability of magnificent spin transport normal for OSCs at room temperature [49]. Furthermore, the plentiful purposes of OSCs and coupling properties between ferromagnetic anodes and OSCs have additionally expanded the application methods of OSCs in spintronics, which have pulled in wide consideration in the territories of science, materials, and material science [50].

The material used in organic semiconductor is mainly hydrocarbon with π interconnect arrangement with irregular single or dual bonds. Organic semiconductor is divided into two wide groups: (1) Low Molecular Weight and (2) Long Chain Polymers. These materials gain popularity in the electronics market because of their smart properties like being natural arrangement elasticity, accessibility of inexpensive bulkiness processing methods, amalgamating with inorganic substance, and potential of chemical change of the particle arrangement to acquire modified ended optical and with thrilling properties [51]. These materials are used to construct

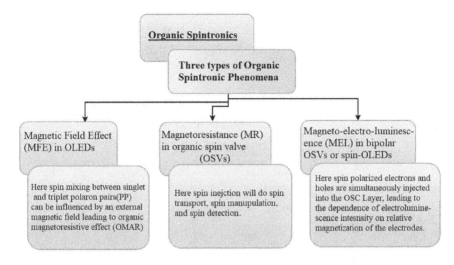

FIGURE 3.21   Categorization of organic spintronics based on organic spintronics phenomena.

large number devices such as OLEDs, photovoltaic cells, FETs, flash memories, etc. The division of organic spintronics on the bases of organic spintronic occurrence (Figure 3.21):

3.5 WHY IS SPINTRONICS BETTER THAN ELECTRONICS?

The reasons to go for spintronics over conventional electronics are:

1. Due to spintronics, the complex devices can manufacture easily, so it overcomes Moore's law.

2. To control the current through transistors, a special semiconductor material is required but in spintronics, spin can be appraised in metal like aluminum or copper.

3. Reduce heat draining.

4. Smaller devices in size.

5. To maintain the electron charge in the gadget, more power or current is required but in spintronics, due to the spin property of the electron, no additional power is required.

6. Spin can be controlled by the exterior magnetic field than charge, which increases the reading and writing speed of the device.

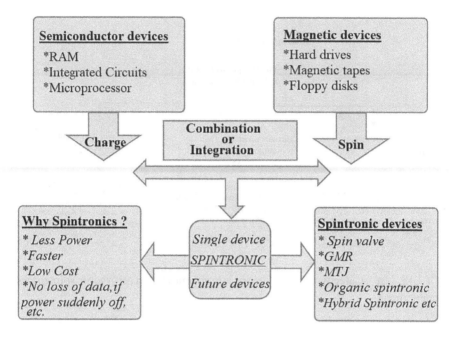

FIGURE 3.22   Electronics to spintronics.

7. Data transfer is fast in spintronics because spin states take less time to settle, which means spin is not energy dependent. It is nonvolatile which means that data transfer using spin resist secure after the power loss (Figure 3.22).

Variation from traditional electronics to spintronic technology opens a new door to manufacture devices with high speed, small power consumption, a speedy operation, which should be low price and robust.

3.6 WORKING PRINCIPLE OF SPINTRONIC DEVICES

In conventional electronic gadgets, data are kept and transferred by the progression of power in the form of negatively charged subatomic atoms called electrons. In the data processor, the binary code zeroes and ones are expressed by the existing or nonappearance of electrons in the semiconductor or other material. In spintronics, data are kept and transferred by utilizing the additional property of an electron called "spin" [3]. Spin is the inherent angular energy of the electron, where every electron behaves like a mini magnet bar or as a magnetic needle that represents the direction of the electron's spin like up or down (Figure 3.23).

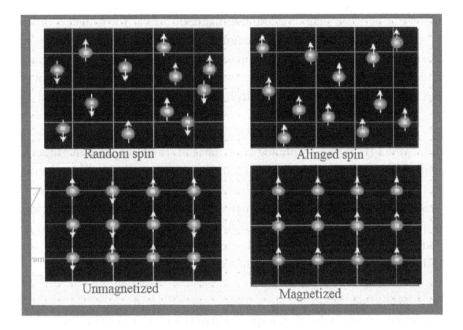

FIGURE 3.23 Understanding different spin configurations is essential for spin electronic gadgets. The upper left image explains that spin can arrange itself in a random way indicating in each possible direction and placed anywhere in the material. Upper right image explains that unsystematically arranged spins can indicate a particular direction and is termed as spin alignment. Lower left image explains that in solid-state material, the spins may be arranged in an order on a lattice crystal which forms a nonmagnetic material. Lower right spin might be arranged in a proper order in a magnetic material [52].

The working principle of spintronics-based devices depends upon any two adjacent electrons, which are in the reverse direction and only adjacent cells can interconnect with each other. Any two adjacent electrons of the series with an upward direction will be grasped as logic "1" and if it is downwarded, then as logic "0." If one adjacent electron's direction is up and the other's direction is downward, it is called a quantum dot [53]. The electrons that travel through a nonmagnetic material typically have an irregular spin, so the net impact is zero (0). The spin's direction can be controlled by the exterior magnetic field. So when the magnetic field is applied in any material, all the spins are aligned in one direction either all up or all down. This provides us a new method to keep the paired information as 1's (all spins up) and 0's (all spins down) [52]. The consequence was first to find in a gadget made of different layers of electrically directing materials: between magnetic and nonmagnetic layers. The gadget is called a "spin valve"; therefore, when a magnetic field is applied to the device, all the electron's spin turns from all up to all down and changes its resistance and behaves as a valve, which increment and decrement the movement of electric current known as "spin valve."

3.7 ISSUES IN SPINTRONICS

Spintronics is the new technology in science in which we use spin property with the charge of electrons, which increases the working of the device. Lots of work is being done by the scientists. It is a fast-developing technology and has a great impact on electronics. Since it is a new area, lots of research is still ongoing and scientists and researchers are facing some problems and issues in this field. Here, we are discussing some of the difficulties or issues facing spintronic devices.

3.7.1 Spin Injection

To be economically helpful, a spin electronics gadget needs to be tasked at ambient temperature and should be viable with the present semiconductor-designed hardware. Pretty much each believable spintronic gadget ought to possess methods for spin injection, control, and identification. The most popular wellsprings of spin-polarized electrons are made of ferromagnetic material [54]. The magnetite area of the ferromagnetic material cooperates with the spin of electrons; thus, most electrons were in the position to like and extended spins are lined up along the neighborhood charge. The spin's centralized current injection was accomplished from ferromagnetic material into superconductors, from ferromagnetic material into common metals, in the middle of ferromagnetic material isolated next to slim insulating film, from an ordinary metal utilizing attractive semiconductor, which is lined up into nonmagnetic semiconductors and injected holes from the p-type ferromagnetic material into nonmagnetic semiconductors [53].

3.7.2 Tunnel Injection

Introduction of a tunnel junction (T) at the ferromagnetic to ordinary conductor, answer of the conductivity crisscross problem. Two potential setups considered were ferromagnetic material-T-semiconductor and Schottky diode. The 2% ambient temperature burrowing spin infusion was accomplished from Fe into GaAs in the Schottky diode arrangements. Calculation of spin division of the current conduction over a ferromagnetic material insulator -2DEG intersection yield 40% with little reliance over the reach 4 K to 295 K[49]. A 30% infusion proficiency was accomplished from a Fe contact into a semiconductor light-producing diode structure ($T = 4.5$ K) and endured to nearly room temperature (4% at $T = 240$ K). The Schottky obstruction framed at the Fe/GaAs interface gives a normal tunnel obstacle for infusing spin spellbound electrons under opposite inclination. Passage infusion of "hot" (A lot of energy more than E_F) electrons into a ferromagnetic material can be utilized to make spin captivated flows. Since inflexibility means freeways for greater and minority electrons vary essentially, hot electron entry through a 3-nm Co layer can bring about 90% spin-centralized currents. The profoundly energized current at that point can be utilized for additional infusion into the semiconductor. The inconvenience of hot electron infusion is that the general proficiency is short [55].

3.7.3 Electrical Injection

The best electrical infusion (framing an ohmic contact) from FM into semiconductors answered to date [paper reference] appeared at 4.5% at $T < 10$ K. The finest ambient temperature for electrical infusion from ferromagnetic material into a semiconductor was accounted for by 'Datta et al' [75]. However, it isn't clear if test information decisively sets up electrical infusion into the semiconductor. The fundamental obstruction to the successful electrical infusion is the conductivity befuddle between the FM cathode and the semiconductor. The adequacy of the spin infusion relies upon the proportion of the (spin-dependent) conductivity of the ferromagnetic material and nonferromagnetic terminals, σ_F and σ_N, separately. At the point when $\sigma_F = \sigma_N$ as on account of a normal metal, at that point effective and generous spin infusion, can happen; yet when the Non-Ferromagnetic (NFM) cathode is a semiconductor, $\sigma_F \gg \sigma_N$ and the turn infusion effectiveness will be reduced. At most, the ferromagnetic material in which the power of electrons is 100% spin spellbound can proficiently spin infusion be normal in a diffused vehicle.

3.8 SPINTRONIC MATERIAL

Spin electronics or spintronics is the most encouraging and upcoming creation which utilizes the spinning of electrons to carry information, increasing storage capability, reduce heat dissipation, use of less power, etc. Still spintronics faces a lot of challenges like spin generation and injection, long interval spin transport, and control and identification of spin inclination.

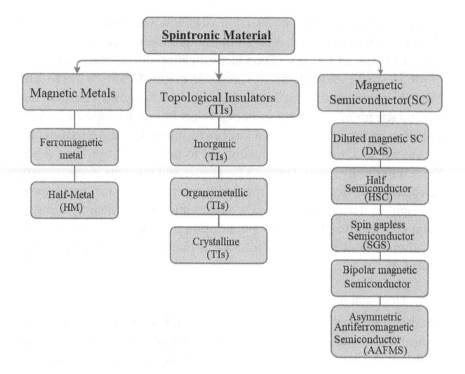

FIGURE 3.24   Flowchart of spintronic material.

The solution for these issues develops new concepts and study of different spintronic material. Classification of spintronic material is done on the basis's material electrical and magnetic features. The spintronic material is categorized as half metal, spin nonstop semiconductors, and bipolar magnetic semiconductors (BMSs) [56] (Figure 3.24).

Each material plays a different role in spintronic circuits such as the magnetic metals and topological insulators operate as source and drain, where the inner area is formed of magnetic semiconductors. Because of these three modules, the spin influence and identification can be executed individually built on the coupling outcome among the light and spin, electric field, or magnetic field (Figure 3.25).

3.8.1 Magnetic Metals

3.8.1.1 Ferromagnetic Metals

Metals like Fe, Ni, and Co come under ferromagnetic metals and are the earliest materials which were utilized in the assembly of MTJs and spin valves. All the abovementioned materials are present in nature in good

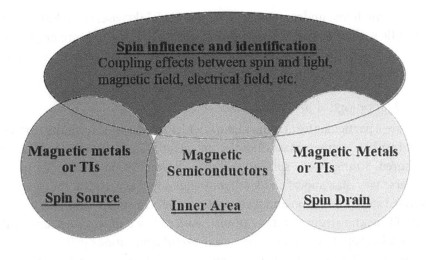

FIGURE3.25 Spintronic circuit composition of different spintronic materials.

amount, inexpensive, and easy to manage [32]. Because of low degree of spin polarization, material provide limited spin-polarized carrier is the main reason to study other metals than this.

3.8.1.2 Half-Metallic Ferromagnets (HMFs)

"de Groot and Mueller" suggest the HMFs material [57], CrO_2 [58,59], and Fe_3O_4 [60,61] lie under HMFs. The basic quality lies in the band structure, wherein one side of the spin network is occupied by metallic conduction and the other side by insulator or semiconductor. So in HMFs 100% spin polarization is attained because it naturally provides solo spin control electron. It is employed for real spin generation and insertion. To form a real-life spintronic device with HMFs, as well as high point Curie temperature of ferromagnetic material, the gap in the half-metallic needs to be ample enough to powerfully avoid the thermic disturbed spin-turnover transfer and protect half-metallicity at ambient temperature [62].

3.8.1.3 Half-Metallic Anti-Ferromagnets

It is a unique variety of half metals, which supply 100% spin polarization named as half-metallic anti-ferromagnets (HMAFMs) with no naturally visible polarization. The essential thought of HMAFMs for a half metal with stoichiometric creation, the spin charge for each cell entity must be a numeral in parts of Bohr's magneton and these zero digits can be zero after a cautious plan. Due to net zero charge, half-metallicity of HMAFMs will be unaltered under an outer attractive field. Likewise, HMAFMs won't meddle with others attractively. Along with this, HMAFMs are helpful in a certain particular circumstance, for example, making the tip of spin-polarized scanning tunneling magnifying instrument [14].

3.8.2 Topological Insulators (TIs)

TIs are a particular form of insulators, which are metallic from the surface but insulated in their mass. Besides, the metallic surface states are balance ensured. Strangely, the spin-up and spin-down electrons proliferate in an inverse way on a superficial level. Subsequently, TIs are ideal for unadulterated spin production and transportation, lacking of any charge current. All TIs acknowledged so far can just work at low temperatures, and still have a long approach to go before their useful applications [63].

In 2005, TIs existed only hypothetically in 2-D material but later based on these premises, they have been expanded to the 3-D state. Now, a non-stop spin situation is required to be developed at the border for 2-D or on top of the surface of 3-D, where a reverse spin current runs in the reverse path *i.e.,* helical condition. In support of 2D TIs, to form a spin nonstop condition, the valence and conduction bands are joined by the transverse-shape edge bands over the Fermi level. In 3D, a strong TI can be grown by the Dirac cone (intrinsic spin nonstop band) and by loading the 2D TI, a weak 3D TI can be developed [56]. Different trails were done for 2D material and 3D material and on the bases of this due to conductance measurement property of material of 2D have been widely discussed and in case of 3D material $Bi_{1-x}Sb_x$ (alloy) [64] have been selected as TI with the plane.

3.8.3 Magnetic Semiconductors

Attractive semiconductors, brushing the properties also, focal points of the two magnets and semiconductors, structure the reason for spintronics. Attractive semiconductors can be applied for turn age and infusion, and turn control and identification. Contrasted with different spintronics materials, attractive semiconductors can be effectively executed in gadgets by using semiconductor innovation. Unfortunately, generally attractive semiconductors experience the ill effects of low attractive requesting temperatures, obstructing their functional applications. When all is said in and done, attractive semiconductors can be partitioned into two classifications: weakened attractive semiconductors (DMSs) and natural attractive semiconductors. Besides, in view of various electronic and attractive properties, natural attractive semiconductors can be partitioned into half semiconductors (HSCs), turn gapless semiconductors (SGSs), bipolar magnetic semiconductors (BMSs), and awry anti-ferromagnetic semiconductors (AAFMSs).

3.9 SPINTRONIC DEVICES AND INSTRUMENTS

Due to vast advantages of spintronic technology, it is developing day by day specially in industrial market and the devices which are fabricated or developed using spintronic is the main motive for the nonstop research and study of hetero-structure. This portion gives short opening of different spintronic gadgets and appliances [63,65] (Figure 3.26).

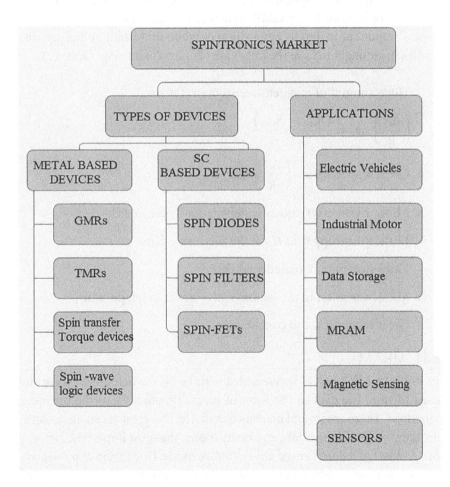

FIGURE 3.26 Spintronic devices with their applications.

TABLE 3.2   Performance Comparison [67]

Sr. No.	Advantages	GMR Sensor	AMR Sensor	Hall Sensor
1	Physical size	Small	Huge	Small
2	Cost	Less	High	Less
3	Power consumption	Less	High	Less
4	Sensitivity	High	High	Less
5	Signal level	Huge	Medium	Small
6	Temperature stability	High	Medium	Low

3.10   SENSORS

The basic working principle of all spintronic sensors is the GMR effect. GMR sensors are quite a complicated method, thus a variety of factors manipulate their operation. Every GMR structure's arrangement is different and depends upon the material composition or width of the film. A high-quality GMR sensor ought to have the following characteristics [66] (Table 3.2):

i. Huge amount of magneto-resistivity ratio, i.e.,

$$\left(\frac{\Delta R}{R}\right)\max = \frac{\left(R_{\max} - R_{\min}\right)}{R_{\max}}$$

ii. Great sensitivity $S = \left(\dfrac{\Delta R}{R}\right)\max / H_s$.

iii. Minor hysteresis frequently depicted by coercive field H_c.

iv. Little anisotropy field H_K of the unpinned film.

v. Huge swapping of biased field Hex.

vi. Minor variation in the factors with respect to temperature

vii. Great reiteration and consistency.

3.11   MRAM

In 1991, the MRAM [68] was revealed with Fe-Ni-Co hetero-structure and used to store the data in the form of magnetic quantity in the magnetic junctions. There are several benefits of MRAM like great speed, nonvolatility, reduced heat dissipation, and many more. The most important factor of MRAM is that it doesn't need any revitalize mode. Due to nonstop research, the access time is reduced up to 2 ns, nanoseconds, for read and write and −40 to −150 degree is attained in case of working temperature. Still there are certain disputes like thermal stability and critical current density [69].

3.12 UNIPOLAR SPIN DIODE

On account of the typical p-n diode, there are three regions named as P-type regions, N-type regions, and one depletion region. The P-type consists of holes in majority carrier and electrons in minority carrier and vice versa in N-type. Both these regions are separated by the depletion region. In unipolar spin diode, both the regions consist of reverse majority carriers and again both regions are divided by depletion region which doesn't carry any charge. In normal p-n diode, the current which flows forward biased is called as charge current and the same current is known as spin current in case of unipolar spin diode and is in reverse path when the component is joined in the forward biased. When it is joined in the inverse biased, they are in same path. The potential difference is V and the spin current density is J_s and we can calculate the J_s from the given expression:

$$J_s = 2hJ_o \sinh^2\left(\frac{qV}{2KT}\right) \tag{3.15}$$

$$\text{Where } J_o = \frac{D\rho}{L} \tag{3.16}$$

D = Diffusion Constant
ρ = Carrier Density of Minority Carrier
L = Minority carrier spin diffusion length

3.13 SPIN SOLAR CELL

In the manufacturing of spin solar cell, two types of material are used for two regions, i.e., P- region is fabricated using ferromagnetic SC like Ga and Mn, and for n-type negatively doped SC. The current which solar cells produce is called as spin-polarized current. The input is applied in the form of incident light to the cell and the input is converted into not only voltage but also spin cumulating. The I-V characteristics of spin solar cell are almost similar or behave as the Esaki diode.

3.14 SPIN LEDs

The polarized beam is the outcome of the spin-polarized carrier's emission recombination. This means that in active regions of the device where unpolarized charge carrier is already residing and from outside polarized spin carriers are inserted into this active region, where both recombine with each other and then with the discharge of electromagnetic radiation. The produced discharge ought to circularly polarized light either right or left. There are different types of spin LEDs like top-emitting LED, side-emitting LEDs, oblique geometry LED, etc. [70].

3.15 SUMMARY AND FUTURE SCOPE

In the electronic world, spintronics technology will be the future. At present, a lot of companies are working on the devices developed through spintronic technology. Due to its vast advantages, spintronics will develop in the next 10 years. The devices based on GMR will have a very bright future in the market because of hi-tech growth in the sector and this will boost the acceptance of GMR effect in Hard Disk Drive (HDD). The engineers have developed a better HDD based on the tunnel-magneto-resistive effect, which further has improvement in the GMR and increases the demand of the devices based on the GMR effect. Then in sector of SCs-based device the spin diode demand will also increase in the market as it the connected to the GMR. Basically, the GMR was first to develop and different done with different material combination and at different temperature. so, there is a lot research can be done on the new material like organic material, 2d material and devices like quantum computer, sensors etc. are the fields which can be explored. Moreover, there are some problems which engineers are still facing like spin injection, tunnel injection, or further development in spin relaxation and spin transport. In industrial areas, the demand for electrical vehicles is also growing, which increases the uptake of GMR to the next level. With the increase in electric vehicle automatically the spin diode a SC-based device demand also increase and hence increase the use of GMR and AMR. For future purposes, there are many areas in spintronics which need to be searched further like spintronics with artificial intelligence and artificial neurons for neuromorphic computing, enhancement in quantum computing with low temperature, etc. Spintronic technology–based devices can be used in different applications such as magnetic tunnel junction–based TRNG (true random number generator), spintronics-based sensor used in AI applications, etc.

REFERENCES

1. S. A. Wolf, D. D. Awschalom, R. A. Buhrman, J. M. Daughton, S. von Molna'r, M. L. Roukes, A. Y. Chtchelkanova, D. M. Treger, "Spintronics: A Spin-Based Electronics Vision for the Future", *Science*, Vol. 294, No. 5546, pp. 1488–1495, 2001.
2. K. N. Chopra, "Introduction to spintronics", in *Spintronic -Theoretical Analysis and Designing of Devices Based on Giant Magnetoresistance*, edited by K. N. Chopra, DRDO, New Delhi, 2019, pp. 1–6.

3. M. D. Amipara, "Nano Technology - Spintronics", *IOSR Journal of Electronics and Communication Engineering (IOSR-JECE)*, Vol. 9, pp. 14–18, 2014.
4. V. K. Joshi, "Spintronics- A Contemporary Review of Emerging Electronics Devices", *Engineering Science and Technology, an International Journal*, Vol. 19, No. 3, pp. 1503–1513, 2016.
5. S. Bandyopadhyay, M. Cahay, *Introduction to Spintronics*, Taylor and Francis, Boca Raton, FL, 2008.
6. G. A. Prinz, "Magnetoelectronics", *Science*, Vol. 282, No. 5394, pp. 1660–1663, 1998.
7. W. E. Pickett, J. S. Moodera, "Half Metallic Magnets", *Physics Today*, Vol. 54, No. 5, pp. 39–44, 2001.
8. E. C. Stoner, E. P. Wohlfarth, "A Mechanism of Magnetic Hysteresis in Hetergeneous Alloys", *Philosophical Transactions of the Royal Society of London. Series A, Mathematical and Physical Sciences*, Vol. 240, pp. 599–642, 1948.
9. R. Srinivasan, "Spintronics, Part -I Principles", *Resonance – Journal of Science Education*, Vol. 10, No. 9, pp. 53–62, 2005.
10. H. Iwai, "Road Map for 22 nm and beyond", *Microelectronic Engineering*, Vol. 86, No. 7–9, pp. 1520–1528, 2009.
11. G. P. Singh, B. S. Sohi, and B. Raj, "Material Properties Analysis of Graphene Base Transistor (GBT) for VLSI Analog Circuits", *Indian Journal of Pure & Applied Physics (IJPAP)*, Vol. 55, pp. 896–902, 2017
12. S. Kumar and B. Raj, "Estimation of Stability and Performance metric for Inward Access Transistor Based 6T SRAM Cell Design Using n-type/p-type DMDG-GDOV TFET", *IEEE VLSI Circuits and Systems Letter*, Vol. 3, No. 2, pp. 25–39, 2017.
13. S. Sharma, A. Kumar, M. Pattanaik, and B. Raj, "Forward Body Biased Multimode Multi-Threshold CMOS Technique for Ground Bounce Noise Reduction in Static CMOS Adders", *International Journal of Information and Electronics Engineering*, Vol. 3, No. 3, pp. 567–572, 2013.
14. H. Singh, P. Kumar, and B. Raj, "Performance Analysis of Majority Gate SET Based 1-bit Full Adder", *International Journal of Computer and Communication Engineering (IJCCE)*, IACSIT Press Singapore, ISSN: 2010-3743, Vol. 2, No. 4, pp. 1–8, 2013.
15. A. K. Bhardwaj, S. Gupta, and B. Raj, "Investigation of Parameters for Schottky Barrier (SB) Height for Schottky Barrier Based Carbon Nanotube Field Effect Transistor Device", *Journal of Nanoelectronics and Optoelectronics*, ASP, Vol. 15, pp. 783–791, 2020.
16. P. Bansal, and B. Raj, "Memristor: A Versatile Nonlinear Model for Dopant Drift and Boundary Issues", *JCTN*, American Scientific Publishers, Vol. 14, No. 5, pp. 2319–2325, 2017.
17. N. Jain, and B. Raj, "An Analog and Digital Design Perspective Comprehensive Approach on Fin-FET (Fin-Field Effect Transistor) Technology - A Review", *Reviews in Advanced Sciences and Engineering (RASE)*, ASP, Vol. 5, pp. 1–14, 2016.

18. S. Sharma, B. Raj, and M. Khosla, "Subthreshold Performance of $In_{1-x}Ga_xAs$ Based Dual Metal with Gate Stack Cylindrical/Surrounding Gate Nanowire MOSFET for Low Power Analog Applications", *Journal of Nanoelectronics and Optoelectronics*, American Scientific Publishers, USA, Vol. 12, pp. 171–176, 2017.

19. B. Raj, A. K. Saxena, and S. Dasgupta, "Analytical Modeling for the Estimation of Leakage Current and Subthreshold Swing Factor of Nanoscale Double Gate FinFET Device" *Microelectronics International, UK*, Vol. 26, pp. 53–63, 2009.

20. S. S. Soniya, G. Wadhwa, and B. Raj, "An Analytical Modeling for Dual Source Vertical Tunnel Field Effect Transistor", *International Journal of Recent Technology and Engineering (IJRTE)*, Vol. 8, No. 2, pp.603–608, 2019.

21. S. Singh, and B. Raj, "Design and Analysis of Hetrojunction Vertical T-Shaped Tunnel Field Effect Transistor", *Journal of Electronics Material*, Springer, Vol. 48, No. 10, pp. 6253–6260, 2019.

22. C. Goyal, J. S. Ubhi, and B. Raj, "A Low Leakage CNTFET Based Inexact Full Adder for Low Power Image Processing Applications", *International Journal of Circuit Theory and Applications*, Wiley, Vol. 47, No. 9, pp. 1446–1458, 2019.

23. B. Raj, A. K. Saxena, and S. Dasgupta, "A Compact Drain Current and Threshold Voltage Quantum Mechanical Analytical Modeling for FinFETs", *Journal of Nanoelectronics and Optoelectronics (JNO), USA*, Vol. 3, No. 2, pp. 163–170, 2008.

24. G. Wadhwa, and B. Raj, "An Analytical Modeling of Charge Plasma Based Tunnel Field Effect Transistor with Impacts of Gate Underlap Region", *Superlattices and Microstructures*, Elsevier, Vol. 142, p. 106512, 2020.

25. S. Singh, and B. Raj, "Modeling and Simulation Analysis of SiGe Hetrojunction Double GateVertical t-Shaped Tunnel FET", *Superlattices and Microstructures*, Elsevier, Vol. 142, p. 106496, 2020.

26. A. Singh, D. K. Saini, D. Agarwal, S. Aggarwal, M. Khosla, and B. Raj, "Modeling and Simulation of Carbon Nanotube Field Effect Transistor and Its Circuit Application", *Journal of Semiconductors (JoS)*, IOP Science, Vol. 37, pp. 074001–074006, 2016.

27. N. Jain, and B. Raj, "Device and Circuit Co-Design Perspective Comprehensive Approach on FinFET Technology - A Review", *Journal of Electron Devices*, Vol. 23, No. 1, pp. 1890–1901, 2016.

28. S. Kumar and B. Raj, "Analysis of I_{ON} and Ambipolar Current for Dual-Material Gate-Drain Overlapped DG-TFET", *Journal of Nanoelectronics and Optoelectronics*, American Scientific Publishers, USA, Vol. 11, pp. 323–333, 2016.

29. N. Anjum, T. Bali, and B. Raj, "Design and Simulation of Handwritten Multiscript Character Recognition", *International Journal of Advanced Research in Computer and Communication Engineering*, Vol. 2, No. 7, pp. 2544–2549, 2013.

30. S. Sharma, B. Raj, and M. Khosla, "A Gaussian Approach for Analytical Subthreshold Current Model of Cylindrical Nanowire FET with Quantum Mechanical Effects", *Microelectronics Journal*, Elsevier, Vol. 53, pp. 65–72, 2016.

31. K. Singh, and B. Raj, "Performance and Analysis of Temperature Dependent Multi-Walled Carbon Nanotubes as Global Interconnects at Different Technology Nodes," *Journal of Computational Electronics*, Springer, Vol. 14, No. 2, pp. 469–476, 2015.

32. S. Kumar and B. Raj, "Compact Channel Potential Analytical Modeling of DG-TFET Based on Evanescent–Mode Approach", *Journal of Computational Electronics*, Springer, Vol. 14, No. 2, pp. 820–827, 2015.

33. K. Singh, and B. Raj, "Temperature Dependent Modeling and Performance Evaluation of Multi-Walled CNT and Single-Walled CNT as Global Interconnects", *Journal of Electronic Materials*, Springer, Vol. 44, No. 12, pp. 4825–4835, 2015.

34. V. K. Sharma, M. Pattanaik, and B. Raj, "INDEP Approach for Leakage Reduction in Nanoscale CMOS Circuits", *International Journal of Electronics*, Taylor & Francis, Vol. 102, No. 2, pp. 200–215, 2014.

35. K. Singh, and B. Raj, "Influence of Temperature on MWCNT Bundle, SWCNT Bundle and Copper Interconnects for Nanoscaled Technology Nodes", *Journal of Materials Science: Materials in Electronics*, Springer, Vol. 26, No. 8, pp. 6134–6142, 2015.

36. N. Anjum, T. Bali, and B. Raj, "Design and Simulation of Handwritten Gurumukhi and Devanagri Numerical Recognition", *International Journal of Computer Applications*, Published by Foundation of Computer Science, New York, USA, Vol. 73, No. 12, pp. 16–21, 2013.

37. S. Khandelwal, V. Gupta, B. Raj, and R. D. Gupta, "Process Variability Aware Low Leakage Reliable Nano Scale DG-FinFET SRAM Cell Design Technique", *Journal of Nanoelectronics and Optoelectronics*, Vol. 10, No. 6, pp. 810–817, 2015.

38. V. K. Sharma, M. Pattanaik, and B. Raj, "ONOFIC Approach: Low Power High Speed Nanoscale VLSI Circuits Design", *International Journal of Electronics*, Taylor & Francis, Vol. 101, No. 1, pp. 61–73, 2014.

39. S. Khandelwal, B. Raj, and R. D. Gupta, "FinFET Based 6T SRAM Cell Design: Analysis of Performance Metric, Process Variation and Temperature Effect", *Journal of Computational and Theoretical Nanoscience*, ASP, USA, Vol. 12, pp. 2500–2506, 2015.

40. S. Singh, Y. Shekhar, R. Jagdeep, S. Anurag, and B. Raj, "Impact of HfO$_2$ in Graded Channel Dual Insulator Double Gate MOSFET", *Journal of Computational and Theoretical Nanoscience*, American Scientific Publishers, Vol. 12, No. 6, pp. 950–953, 2015.

41. V. K. Sharma, M. Pattanaik, and B. Raj, "PVT Variations Aware Low Leakage INDEP Approach for Nanoscale CMOS Circuits", *Microelectronics Reliability*, Elsevier, Vol. 54, pp. 90–99, 2014.

42. B. Raj, A. K. Saxena and S. Dasgupta, "Quantum Mechanical Analytical Modeling of Nanoscale DG FinFET: Evaluation of Potential, Threshold Voltage and Source/Drain Resistance", *Elsevier's Journal of Material Science in Semiconductor Processing*, Elsevier, Vol. 16, No. 4, pp. 1131–1137, 2013.

43. M. Gopal, S. S. D. Prasad, and B. Raj, "8T SRAM Cell Design for Dynamic and Leakage Power Reduction", *International Journal of Computer Applications*, Published by Foundation of Computer Science, New York, USA, Vol. 71, No. 9, pp. 43–48, 2013.

44. M. Pattanaik, B. Raj, S. Sharma, and A. Kumar, "Diode Based Trimode Multi-Threshold CMOS Technique for Ground Bounce Noise Reduction in Static CMOS Adders", *Advanced Materials Research*, Trans Tech Publications, Switzerland, Vol. 548, pp. 885–889, 2012.

45. B. Raj, A. K. Saxena, and S. Dasgupta, "Nanoscale FinFET Based SRAM Cell Design: Analysis of Performance Metric, Process Variation, Underlapped FinFET and Temperature Effect", *IEEE Circuits and System Magazine*, Vol. 11, No. 2, pp. 38–50, 2011.

46. V. K. Sharma, M. Pattanaik, and B. Raj, "Leakage Current ONOFIC Approach for Deep Submicron VLSI Circuit Design", *International Journal of Electrical, Computer, Electronics and Communication Engineering*, World Academy of Sciences, Engineering and Technology, Vol. 7, No. 4, pp. 239–244, 2013.

47. T. Chawla, M. Khosla, and B. Raj, "Design and Simulation of Triple Metal Double-Gate Germanium on Insulator Vertical Tunnel Field Effect Transistor", *Microelectronics Journal*, Elsevier, Vol. 114, pp. 105125, 2021.

48. P. Kaur, S. S. Gill, and B. Raj, "Comparative Analysis of OFETs Materials and Devices for Sensor Applications", *Journal of Silicon*, Springer, Vol. 14, pp. 4463–4471, 2022.

49. S. K. Sharma, P. Kumar, B. Raj, and B. Raj, "$In_{1-x}Ga_xAs$ Double Metal Gate-Stacking Cylindrical Nanowire MOSFET for Highly Sensitive Photo detector", *Journal of Silicon*, Springer, Vol. 14, pp. 3535–3541, 2022.

50. B. Raj, A. K. Saxena, and S. Dasgupta, "Analytical Modeling of Quasi Planar Nanoscale Double Gate FinFET with Source/Drain Resistance and Field Dependent Carrier Mobility: A Quantum Mechanical Study", *Journal of Computer (JCP)*, Academy Publisher, FINLAND, Vol. 4, No. 9, pp.1–6, 2009.

51. S. Bhushan, S. Khandelwal, and B. Raj, "Analyzing Different Mode FinFET Based Memory Cell at Different Power Supply for Leakage Reduction", Seventh International Conference on Bio-Inspired Computing: Theories and Application, (BIC-TA 2012), *Advances in Intelligent Systems and Computing*, Vol. 202, pp. 89–100, 2013.

52. J. Singh, and B. Raj, "Temperature Dependent Analytical Modeling and Simulations of Nanoscale Memristor", *Engineering Science and Technology, an International Journal*, Elsevier's, Vol. 21, pp. 862–868, 2018.

53. S. Singh, S. Bala, B. Raj, and B. Raj, "Improved Sensitivity of Dielectric Modulated Junctionless Transistor for Nanoscale Biosensor Design", *Sensor Letter*, ASP, Vol. 18, pp. 328–333, 2020.

54. V. Kumar, S. K. Vishvakarma, and B. Raj, "Design and Performance Analysis of ASIC for IoT Applications", *Sensor Letter*, ASP, Vol. 18, pp. 31–38, 2020.

55. A. Jaiswal, R. K. Sarin, B. Raj, and S. Sukhija, "A Novel Circular Slotted Microstrip-fed Patch Antenna with Three Triangle Shape Defected Ground Structure for Multiband Applications", *Advanced Electromagnetic (AEM)*, Vol. 7, No. 3, pp. 56–63, 2018.

56. G. Wadhwa, and B Raj, "Label Free Detection of Biomolecules using Charge-Plasma-Based Gate Underlap Dielectric Modulated Junctionless TFET", *Journal of Electronic Materials (JEMS)*, Springer, Vol. 47, No. 8, pp. 4683–4693, 2018.

57. G. Singh, R. K. Sarin, and B. Raj, "Design and Performance Analysis of a New Efficient Coplanar Quantum-Dot Cellular Automata Adder", *Indian Journal of Pure & Applied Physics (IJPAP)*, Vol. 55, pp. 97–103, 2017.

58. A. Singh, M. Khosla, and B. Raj, "Design and Analysis of Electrostatic Doped Schottky Barrier CNTFET Based Low Power SRAM", *International Journal of Electronics and Communications, (AEÜ)*, Elsevier, Vol. 80, pp. 67–72, 2017.

59. P. Kaur, V. Pandey, and B. Raj, "Comparative Study of Efficient Design, Control and Monitoring of Solar Power Using IoT", *Sensor Letter*, ASP, Vol. 18, pp. 419–426, 2020.

60. G. Wadhwa, P. Kamboj, J. Singh, B. Raj, "Design and Investigation of Junctionless DGTFET for Biological Molecule Recognition", *Transactions on Electrical and Electronic Materials*, Springer, Vol. 22, pp. 282–289, 2020.

61. T. Chawla, M. Khosla, and B. Raj, "Optimization of Double-Gate Dual Material GeOI-Vertical TFET for VLSI Circuit Design", *IEEE VLSI Circuits and Systems Letter*, Vol. 6, No. 2, pp. 13–25, 2020.

62. S. K. Verma, S. Singh, G. Wadhwa and B. Raj, "Detection of Biomolecules Using Charge-Plasma Based Gate Underlap Dielectric Modulated Dopingless TFET", *Transactions on Electrical and Electronic Materials (TEEM)*, Springer, Vol. 21, pp. 528–535, 2020.

63. N. Jain, and B. Raj, "Impact of Underlap Spacer Region Variation on Electrostatic and Analog/RF Performance of Symmetrical High-k SOI FinFET at 20 nm Channel Length", *Journal of Semiconductors (JoS)*, IOP Science, Vol. 38, No. 12, p. 122002, 2017.

64. S. Singh, and B. Raj, "Analytical Modeling and Simulation Analysis of T-Shaped III-V Heterojunction Vertical T-FET", *Superlattices and Microstructures*, Elsevier, Vol. 147, pp. 106717, 2020.

65. G. Singh, R. K. Sarin, and B. Raj, "Design and Analysis of Area Efficient QCA Based Reversible Logic Gates", *Journal of Microprocessors and Microsystems*, Elsevier, Vol. 52, pp. 59–68, 2017.

66. A. Singh, M. Khosla, and B. Raj, "Compact Model for Ballistic Single Wall CNTFET under Quantum Capacitance Limit", *Journal of Semiconductors (JoS)*, IOP Science, Vol. 37, pp. 104001–104008, 2016.

67. S. Singh, M. Khosla, G. Wadhwa, and B. Raj, "Design and Analysis of Double-Gate Junctionless Vertical TFET for Gas Sensing Applications", *Applied Physics A*, Springer, Vol. 127, No. 16, pp. 725–732, 2021.

68. I. Singh, B. Raj, M. Khosla, and B. K. Kaushik, "Potential MRAM Technologies for Low Power SoCs", *SPIN World Scientific Publisher, SCIE*; Vol. 10, No. 04, p. 2050027, 2020.
69. S. Singh, and B. Raj, "Parametric Variation Analysis on Hetero-Junction Vertical t-Shape TFET for Supressing Ambipolar Conduction", *Indian Journal of Pure and Applied Physics*, Vol. 58, pp. 478–485, 2020.
70. S. S. Soniya, G. Wadhwa, and B. Raj, "Design and Analysis of Dual Source Vertical Tunnel Field Effect Transistor for High Performance", *Transactions on Electrical and Electronics Materials*, Springer, Vol. 21, pp. 74–82, 2019.
71. M. Johnson, and R. H. Silsbee, "Interfacial charge-spin coupling: Injection and detection of spin magnetization in metals", *Physical Review Letters* Vol. 55, No. 17, pp. 1790–1793, 1985.
72. S.F. Zhang, and P.M. Levy, "Conductivity perpendicular to the plane of multilayered structures," *Journal of Applied Physics*, Vol. 69, No. 8, pp. 4786–4788, 1991.
73. Asano, Y., A. Oguri, and S. Maekawa., "Parallel and perpendicular transport in multilayered structures," *Physical Review B* , vol. 48.9, p. 6192, 1993.
74. H. Adachi, K. Uchida, E. Saitoh and S. Maekawa, "Theory of spin seebeck effect," *Reports on Progress in Physics,* vol. 76, No. 3, p. 036501(20), February 2013.
75. S. Datta and B. Das, "Electronic analog of electro-optic modulator," *Applied Physics Letter,* vol. 56, no. 7, pp. 665–667, 1995.

CHAPTER 4

AI-Based ECG Signal Monitoring System for Arrhythmia Detection Using IoMT

Pushparaj, Amod Kumar, and Garima Saini

National Institute of Technical Teachers Training and Research

CONTENTS

4.1 INTRODUCTION

Every year, around 17 million people die from cardiovascular diseases (CVDs) worldwide. Hypertension, sudden cardiac arrest, arrhythmia/rhythm disturbance, stroke, peripheral artery disease, and other conditions come under CVD. Shortness of breath, dizziness, abrupt weakness, fluttering in the chest, lightheadedness, and fainting are all symptoms of a heart that isn't working properly.

Arrhythmias are a serious condition in which the heart beats excessively fast, too slowly, or in an irregular manner (Thakur and Patel, 2021). Arrhythmia can cause stroke, heart attack, or even death (Huang et al., 2014). Cardiovascular signals like electrocardiography (ECG) (Kumar and Saini, 2021), arterial blood pressure, and photoplethysmogram (PPG) are regularly used to identify heartbeats since they are directly related to cardiac function. One of the most essential health indicators is heart rate, which may be determined with merely an ECG. It is an electrophysiology (EP) study in the form of a non-invasive test (Bandodkar et al., 2014) that measures the electrical activity of the heart. The ECG waveform deviates from its normal shape and size as a result of arrhythmias, and therefore, it is an effective way to examine and detect precise location and the type of arrhythmias in the heart (Ali et al., 2021).

4.1.1 IoT-Enabled Healthcare System

In the traditional healthcare practices, patients are unable to see doctors on a regular basis, and communication is restricted to visits, teleconferences, and text messages. There was no means for doctors or hospitals (Shukla et al., 2019) to constantly monitor their patients' health and make appropriate suggestions. As the number of elderly people and patients suffering from chronic diseases is growing rapidly, drawbacks of traditional healthcare services are becoming more visible. Multiple physical signs (Chen et al., 2014) should be sampled at different frequencies to satisfy the medical requirements, while transmitting them separately at their own sample frequencies will lead to huge amount of data and a great burden to the remote server (Anuradha et al., 2018). The monitoring of blood fat and glucose is not continuous as the test of these indicators needs intervention from patients.

Advent of Internet of Things (IoT) in the last decade has changed the scenario completely. The IoT is employed in a variety of applications depending on the need (Ayata et al., 2020). IoT-enabled gadgets are also known as smart devices or network devices (Ashima et al., 2021). Sensors, electronics, software, embedded systems, actuators, and other devices can all communicate on the IoT platform. The data-intensive IoT healthcare network is built on cloud computing which aids in the smartening of health monitoring systems (Garbhapu & Gopalan, 2017) (Table 4.1). The system makes use of data-driven, network-driven, and

TABLE 4.1   IoT Applications (Garbhapu and Gopalan, 2017)

Applications of IoT	Description
Business Models Connectivity	Several technologies like LTE (Pal et al., 2020), Wi-Fi, Bluetooth, WiMax, LORAWAN
Smart Homes	Technology like AI or IoT-enabled with smart homes
Smart Cities	IoT-enabled smart homes make the city smart with modern security system and smart energy tools
Healthcare Industry	No need to visit doctor physically. Patient can discuss wirelessly on time and data stored on the cloud server automatically
Security & Privacy	With the induction of technology, systems provide more safety to individuals

cloud-driven IoT, all of which operate under separate standards, strategies, and protocols. Gateways are frequently employed, which can be utilized as a hub between the body and personal or local area networks. This chapter introduces the Smart e-Health (Li et al., 2017) Access concept, which has the potential to improve usage of IoT infrastructures for healthcare applications (Bhardwaj et al., 2022, 2019). This chapter also describes the Smart e-Health Gateway prototype and demonstrates the design and implementation of proof of this concept (Bansal and Raj, 2016).

IoT-enabled gadgets have made information gathering and remote monitoring of patients (Hassan et al., 2020) a routine affair with the potential to keep patients safe and healthy while also allowing physicians to provide superior treatment (Boutry et al., 2019). IoT has spawned smart health, with the goal of increasing operational efficiency and producing a cost-effective system while retaining quality, providing health records and data privacy (Singh et al., 2020), resulting in providing excellent healthcare to users. As a result, the system architectures based on the basic model are being proposed by researchers wherein IoT devices are used to obtain information about the patient's body parameters. Figure 4.1 shows one such typical architecture.

As per the figure, it has three stages of health monitoring system through IoT in terms of layers as follows:

  i. Sensing layer

 ii. Transport layer

iii. Application layer.

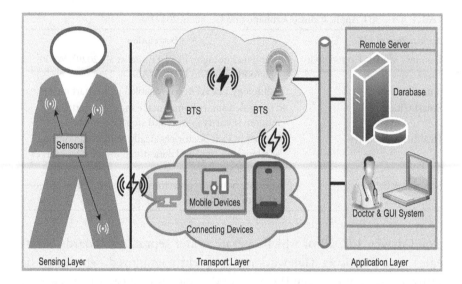

FIGURE 4.1   IoT-enabled health monitoring system architecture (Garbhapu and Gopalan, 2017).

The available networks systems, like the vertical base stations seems to be towers called blood transfusion service (BTS) provide the mobile and internet connectivity and so one tower is connected with nearest BTS and similarly global network is established for the simplicity of communication system (Gopal and Raj, 2013). The BTS transmit the signals to connect all devices in their range with the network like laptops, mobile devices or tablets, etc. The connecting procedure is all done in the transport layer and these are basically applicable to make the communication in between the sensing layer called human beings to be observed or are in the process to be monitored. All sensing devices are connected with the human body like wireless electrodes, sensing belt wrist watch used for the measurement of respiration/heart pulse, oxygen level, etc. These come under the wearable devices category (Goyal et al., 2018, 2019). The sensors are basically connected near the chest and left-arm side. These devices continuously transmit the recorded data on the storage device connected like laptop or hard drive with it or live data are transmitted for the observation or monitoring. This data is further transmitted for the remote area or server so that globally patients can be monitored remotely and advised by doctors for their health accordingly (Jain et al., 2016, 2018). This remote procedure is done with the help of application layer.

4.1.2 IoMT-Based Heart Monitoring

This technology takes data from heart patients (Meteier et al., 2021) and sends it to a healthcare center, where a deep neural network learns the characteristics of heart illness from previous analyses and improves accuracy by manipulating complicated data (Jain and Raj, 2018a, 2018b, 2019a, 2019b). The accuracy (Singh et al., 2020) reported as 99.03%, indicating that this method may reliably anticipate cardiac illness and reduce mortality by issuing an early alert for the monitored individuals and clinicians presents an IoT-based Biomedical Measurement System (BMS) for cardiac illness that collects data from the human body using an android app, a pulsometer, and a pedometer as a sensor. Table 4.2 shows the various health parameters required as per the indicators.

Internet of Medical Things (IoMT)-based BMS mostly use wearable devices like smart watches, smart bracelets, glasses, and so on (Bayoumy et al., 2021) to assess vital signs (heart rate, pulse rate, body temperature, blood pressure, oxygen concentration, lungs contraction volume, blood sugar level, respiration rate, and so on) in the physical layer (Figure 4.2).

TABLE 4.2   Monitoring Parameters for Health (Chen et al., 2020a,b)

Indicators	Sampling Frequency (Period)
ECG	128 Hz
Blood Pressure	2 s
SpO_2	2 s
Pulse Rate	2 s

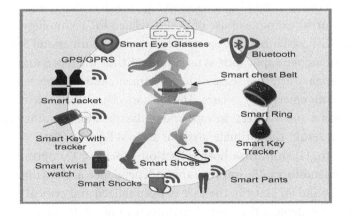

FIGURE 4.2   Smart wearable measurement devices (Bayoumy et al., 2021).

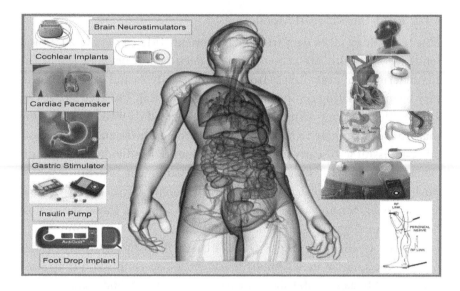

FIGURE 4.3   Smart implantable measurement device.

IoT makes it possible to measure patients' body parameters in real time as complexity shown in Figure 4.3. Sensors capture patients' body characteristics and send the data to the cloud (Kaur & Pal, 2019), which the doctor can access at any time by establishing a wireless link between the doctor and the patients (Jiao et al., 2020; Kandasamy et al., 2020). IoT devices may be used to monitor and operate emergency notification systems from a distance (Brunete et al., 2021). As contacts with doctors have become simpler and more effective, it has also boosted patient appointments and satisfaction (Kaur et al., 2021a, 2021b). All data collected from patients are stored in a cloud computing environment. Health research data collection is a noteworthy example of use of health-related IoT technology.

An ECG-based heart disease detection system (Kumar and Saini, 2021) in which a mobile application is used for real-time diagnosis and monitoring of coronary artery disease or heart ailment, and the app sends out an alert once an emergency occurs. The authors claim that their monitoring system has a 100% detection rate and a classification accuracy of above 85%. As a result, the ultimate goals of an IoMT-based (Patel et al., 2019) BMS are to: (1) minimize hospitalization expenses, (2) optimize public health expenditures, (3) improve the independence and quality of life of the elderly, and (4) assist in the care of hospitalized and critical patients.

Figure 4.4 depicts the overall architecture of an IoMT-based system (Rubí et al., 2019). Unlike the other designs described in the literature,

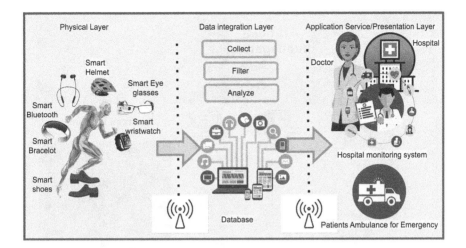

FIGURE 4.4   IoMT system architecture.

TABLE 4.3   IoT Technology-Based Smart Medical Devices with Monitored Data
(Lim et al., 2020)

Vital Sign	Measurement Activity	Safety
Weight measuring	Walking time	Fall detection device
Blood pressure measuring device	Step counting device	Personal safety and tracking device
ECG	Calorie spent	Not required
Blood glucose measuring device	Time spent in rest/sleeping	Not required

which are tailored to the applications for which they were created, this is a generic architecture that reports the common components of all IoT-based BMS presented in Table 4.3. The layers of this system are: (1) physical, (2) data integration, and (3) application service/presentation.

4.1.3 Artificial Intelligence in Healthcare

Artificial Intelligence (AI) techniques (Alluhaidan et al., 2023) enable machines to mimic human behavior and natural processes. AI (Nagarajan et al., 2021) allows machines to learn from their past experiences. By digesting enormous volumes of data and identifying patterns in them, the machines alter their responses in reaction to new inputs, allowing them to do human-like jobs. As a result, AI, machine learning, and deep learning are all subsets of one another.

Figure 4.5 shows the various components of AI. AI algorithms (Nam et al., 2019) vary from humans in terms of algorithms are literal: once a

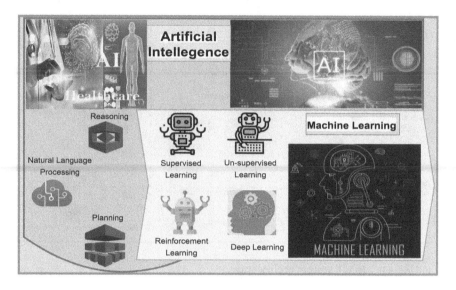

FIGURE 4.5   Organization of Artificial Intelligence.

goal is established, the algorithm learns solely from the input data and can only comprehend that data. AI is becoming more sophisticated at doing what people do, but more effectively, faster, and for less money (Larradet et al., 2020; Liaqat et al., 2021). AI-based systems have enormous promise in healthcare (Yin et al., 2020). They are increasingly becoming a component of our healthcare eco-system, just as they are in our daily lives. The processes such as image analysis, robotic surgery, virtual assistants, and clinical decision support are the most significant fields (Yin et al., 2020). Some of the applications of AI in healthcare are as below.

4.1.3.1 Decision-Making
Predictive analytics and priority administrative activities can help clinical decision-making and actions to improve treatment by aligning massive health (He et al., 2020) data with suitable and timely judgments.

4.1.3.2 Maintaining Electronic Medical Records
It is a recognized fact that maintaining Electronic Health Records, or EHR, results in strategic improvements in healthcare (Kelly et al., 2020), but it is not easy due to issues such as cognitive overload, user burnout, and unending documentation. However, using AI, one can truly automate these mundane procedures and improve the user interfaces.

4.1.3.3 Clinical Documentation

Clinical documentation consumes a significant amount of time, but with the use of voice recognition and dictation, as well as natural language processing (Yeh et al., 2021), a significant amount of time and effort may be saved. Because information retrieval is a key element of AI, this is a huge benefit for doctors. AI provides a more user-friendly interface for saving data. Its usage results in a significant shift in the way patients are handled. Doctors no longer have to worry about drug overdoses, incorrect combinations, or allergies because all this data can be recorded in the cloud (Kaur & Pal, 2019) and can be analyzed and acted upon at the appropriate moment.

Patients with a history of infections can also benefit from the technology because it is now simpler to see trends and provide alerts. AI can handle regular requests in addition to information storage and retrieval and pattern recognition (Lim et al., 2020; Luz et al., 2016). Here are a few examples:

a. It would send messages to the concerned patient if a patient had an overdue lab test.

b. A patient's medicine is going to expire. The request for a pharmaceutical refill will be delivered quickly.

c. It can determine which of the numerous patients requires immediate attention and assign a priority to them.

4.1.3.4 Disease Diagnosis

AI approach has been utilized to treat a range of ailments (Li et al., 2017). Each of these strategies is stated as having a "training aim" to ensure that "classifications agree as much as feasible with the outcomes…". To show some specifics for illness diagnosis/classification, Artificial Neural Networks (ANN) and Bayesian Networks are two separate methodologies utilized in the categorization of certain disorders. ANN was shown to be superior and capable of more correctly classifying diabetes and CVD (Rincon et al., 2020). The inability to access instances with comparable clinical origins remains a substantial hurdle for clinicians which can be tackled successfully using AI.

4.2 LITERATURE SURVEY

Swapna et al. (2018) used deep learning algorithms to diagnose cardiac arrhythmias based on ECG signals with the least amount of data preprocessing possible. Various approaches such as convolutional neural networks (CNNs) and recurrent structures such as long short-term memory (LSTM) were used. With CNN-LSTM, authors were able to identify between normal and abnormal (cardiac arrhythmia) ECGs with a five-fold cross-validation accuracy of 0.834.

Li et al. (2017) suggested a pervasive monitoring system that may convey real-time physical indicators from patients to remote medical applications. The data collecting and transmission portions of the system make up the majority of the system (Pal et al., 2020; Palanivel Rajan, 2015). The data acquisition part's essential element is the monitoring scheme (monitoring parameters and frequency for each parameter), which authors devised based on conversations with medical professionals. Multiple bodily indications (blood pressure, ECG, SpO$_2$, heart rate, pulse rate, blood fat, and blood glucose) are designed to be gathered at various rates over time. Finally, a working prototype is created to show how the system works (Raj et al., 2010; Raza et al., 2021).

According to Garbhapu and Gopalan (2017), healthcare facilities are still unavailable to a substantial percentage of the population, particularly those having low income and living in rural or isolated places. A low-cost IoT-based biomedical kit has been developed that can monitor vital signs with a 98 percent accuracy for temperature readings and 95 percent accuracy for blood pressure measurements (Saiphani Kumar et al., 2018). The sensor nodes are comprised of a microprocessor MSP430G2553 and a wireless transceiver nRF24L01. The data collected at the hub can be sent to the doctor using the Raspberry Pi 3's built-in IEEE 802.11 (Wi-Fi protocol).

Thakur and Patel (2021) proposed a system with a Wi-Fi module to continuously upload patient data to the cloud. The CNN Deep Adaptive learning will detect the type of arrhythmia based on the ECG. Data gathered in this manner can also be used for research purposes.

Li et al. (2017) described IoT devices to access patient's health status and send data to faraway data centers immediately. This direct interconnection of a large number of devices is utilized to store, process, and retrieve medical records on the cloud, allowing more effective and efficient treatment (Sharma et al., 2021, 2019). In this research, the authors attempted to work with ECG signals and build the necessary procedures to achieve high accuracy. The specifications and characteristics of IoT systems are reviewed in the article, as well as the effective use of ECG for utilizing and offering a mechanism for arrhythmia classification (Singh et al., 2016a, 2016b, 2017, 2018a, 2018b, 2018c, 2018d, 2019). The goal of IoT-based healthcare support services for arrhythmia is to provide a system that improves flexibility, cost-effectiveness, optimization capability, availability, and scalability in order to reduce errors.

Iqbal et al. (2018) reported that deep learning approaches have sparked renewed interest in electrocardiography analysis. Advances in 3D cardiac imaging enhanced by AI launched the concept of virtual hearts. Changing lifestyles have made population-based diagnosis of atrial fibrillation possible in previously inconceivable ways.

Patel et al. (2019), who are medical AI researchers, worked on real-time patient monitoring. According to them, IoT devices can produce a digital biomarker that is objective and reflect real-world and copious data. The IoT is strongly linked to medical AI. IoT-based attempts to identify and treat people with chronic diseases have previously been made. Real-time monitoring of physical activity such as spinal posture is now being researched for use in the field of medicine.

He et al. (2020) worked on machine learning in healthcare. Their finding was that while such technologies will almost certainly never be able to fully replace clinical practitioners, they have the potential to alter the healthcare industry. They described a deep CNN-based automated heart sound categorization method that incorporates time-frequency heat map representations.

Gjoreski et al. (2020) described a technique for detecting chronic heart failure using heart sounds. The technique combines traditional machine learning with end-to-end deep learning models (Singh and Raj, 2018a, 2018b, 2019a, 2019b, 2020).

Chen et al. (2020) were of the view that the IoT techniques appear promising because they relied on centralized data collecting approaches; however, they may have limited use in the actual world as they may lead users and data owners to be concerned about their privacy. Edge devices are critical medical tools for detecting and preventing cardiovascular problems in real time. Clearly, the convergence of health informatics and mobile edge cloud computing, as well as the development of ECG devices based on IoT, is unavoidable.

Hassan et al. (2020) state that remote ECG monitoring plays an important role in early diagnosis and prevention of CVDs. EdgeCNN, a novel hybrid intelligent healthcare architecture based on CNNs and cloud computing, was presented. This system can learn medical data from edge devices in a flexible manner. They proposed an efficient ECG edge computing diagnostic model and learning algorithm (Tomar et al., 2013; Wadhera et al., 2019). The model can infer ECG in real time closer to the data source, resulting in a favorable balance of diagnostic accuracy and resource loss. They also suggested using a deep convolution generative adversarial network (DCGAN) to improve ECG. DCGAN is a reliable network architecture built on CNN extension that offers a high level of unsupervised learning credibility. For ECG diagnosis, data augmentation can give enough amount and type of data. The experimental findings reveal that after the data augmentation of ECG data-related categories, the deep learning model's overall accuracy as well as the number of ECG categories that the model can diagnose increase, thus considerably improving the system's practical usefulness.

Antonio et al. looked back on the history of EP's involvement in occupational health. They outlined the advantages of developing wearable and smart devices for cardiovascular monitoring and their potential applications, as well as the trends in the use of mobile ECG devices in various environments and demographics.

Khairuddin et al. (2017) not only examined prior work on traditional ECG devices to highlight their shortcomings, but they also provided some new perspectives into how the IoT has the potential to develop medical applications in ECG devices.

Liu et al. (2019) merged mobile cloud computing and the field of health informatics to create a system for ECG extraction and analysis utilizing mobile computing, which they intend to implement in a commercial setting (Wadhwa et al., 2019; Wadhwa and Raj, 2018).

Pereira et al. employed CNN to detect handwritten graphics in order to assist diagnosis of Parkinson's disease in its early stages. Their algorithm learns characteristics from the signals of a smart pen, which employs sensors to capture handwriting movements during personal assessments (Wang et al., 2018; Xu et al., 2020). The efficacy of LSTM in evaluating and recognizing multivariate time series patterns of medical measures in the critical care unit was investigated.

Hannun et al. (2019) used ECG data from 53,549 individuals to create a 34-layer CNN model that could categorize the 12 heart rhythm abnormalities. The final classification accuracy is higher than human specialists' diagnostic accuracy.

To diagnose ECG, Chauhan et al. employed LSTM in a recurrent neural network. Without any additional data preparation, ECG signals may be immediately entered into the network using this way.

Jin et al. (2020) employed a neural network to extract a complicated portion of ECG signals' QRS waves, which they subsequently used for user authentication. This system's user authentication accuracy is as high as 99%.

Zihlmann et al. (2017) built two models, CNN and LSTM, and trained and tested them using the PhysioNet/CinC 2017 dataset. The LSTM model received an F1-score of the outcomes comparison of 82.1% accuracy, which is better than the CNN model.

Wang et al. (2018) developed DMSFNet, a five-class model that classifies atrial fibrillation using the 12-lead CPSC 2018 and PhysioNet/CinC 2017 datasets.

Zhang et al. (2020a) created a STA-CRNN model with an attention mechanism for eight classifications, with an F1-score of 0.835. These ECG diagnostic models' training and reasoning are conducted on a resource-rich server or cloud. Because cardiac disease is characterized by its abrupt onset, deep learning in mobile devices is required for real-time monitoring. Many researchers have used mobile applications to execute tasks such as identifying junk in photos using CNN. However, investigations demonstrate that these apps continue to consume a lot of resources. The prediction results are returned in 5.6 s; however, it uses 83% of the CPU and 67 MB of RAM.

Ravi et al. (2017) presented the creation of a mobile device fitness application that classifies human activities using deep learning. They found that DNN models on resource-constrained devices frequently contain fewer hidden layers, resulting in poor performance. To support intelligent IoT applications, Nguyen et al. presented a conceptual hardware and software infrastructure.

Zhang et al. (2020a) used DCGAN to improve Electroencephalogram (EEG) data and compared it to other approaches such as geometric transformation, autoencoder, and variational autoencoder. The results reveal that DCGAN performs better in terms of enhancement (Yadav et al., 2018, 2020).

DCGAN was also utilized by Zanini and Colombini (2020) to improve Electromyography (EMG) in the case of Parkinson's disease. By learning the patient's distinct tremor frequency and amplitude, this model grows the patient's tremor dataset and applies it to different workout program sets.

To balance the quantity of samples across different categories and improve the diversity of samples, Cao et al. (2020) developed a unique data augmentation technique based on duplication, concatenation, and re-sampling of ECG events (Yang et al., 2019).

Salamon and Bello (2017)employed a number of audio data improvement strategies to investigate the influence of different enhancement approaches on the suggested CNN architecture's performance (Zhang et al., 2020b, 2020c; Zhou et al., 2020).

Perez and Wang (2017) investigated and compared various approaches to the problem of data augmentation in image classification, including one that attempted to use a GAN to generate images of various styles, and discussed the method's success and shortcomings on various datasets.

4.3 CONCLUSION

Global internet connectivity is improving as a result of advancements in communication technologies. When the internet is connected to global things, it is referred to as the IoT, and it allows things to become smarter. In heartbeat classifications, segmentation techniques, feature descriptions, and learning algorithms, the physiological signal (ECG) has been employed to detect various anomalies. With the help of IoT and AI, doctors' counseling can be offered to a larger number of CVD patients while also receiving feedback. Doctors can utilize IoMT to track patient information, medical crises, blood information, and health information in real time. In terms of supporting healthcare practitioners, computational diagnostic tools for ECG signal analysis have a lot of potential.

Funding: Not applicable.

Data Availability Statement: Not applicable.

Acknowledgments: The authors express their gratitude to the Department of Electronics and Communication Engineering at the National Institute of Technical Teachers Training and Research in Chandigarh for their interest in this work and for providing useful comments to help finalize the paper. The authors also acknowledge the support of the AICTE QIP (Poly) Schemes department of the Government of India. Additionally, the authors would like to thank NITTTR Chandigarh for providing lab facilities and a research environment that allowed them to carry out this work.

Conflicts of Interest: There is no conflict of interest declared by the authors.

REFERENCES

Ali, H., Naing, H. H., & Yaqub, R. (2021). An IoT assisted real-time high CMRR wireless ambulatory ECG monitoring system with arrhythmia detection. *Electronics*, 10(16), 1871.

Alluhaidan, A. S. et al. (2023). An automatic threshold selection using ALO for healthcare duplicate record detection with reciprocal neuro-fuzzy inference system. *Computers, Materials & Continua*, 74(3), 5821–5836.

Anuradha, Singh, J., Raj, B., & Khosla, M. (2018). Design and performance analysis of nano-scale memristor-based nonvolatile SRAM. *Journal of Sensor Letter*, American Scientific Publishers, 16, 798–805.

Ashima, Vaithiyanathan, D., & Raj, B. (2021). Performance analysis of charge plasma induced graded channel Si nanotube. *Journal of Engineering Research (JER)*, EMSME Special Issue, 146–154.

Ayata, D., Yaslan, Y., & Kamasak, M. E. (2020). Emotion recognition from multimodal physiological signals for emotion aware healthcare systems. *Journal of Medical and Biological Engineering*, 40(2), 149–157.

Bandodkar, A. J., Molinnus, D., Mirza, O., Guinovart, T., Windmiller, J. R., Valdés-Ramírez, G., Andrade, F. J., Schöning, M. J., & Wang, J. (2014). Epidermal tattoo potentiometric sodium sensors with wireless signal transduction for continuous non-invasive sweat monitoring. *Biosensors and Bioelectronics*, 54, 603–609.

Bansal, P., & Raj, B. (2016). Memristor modeling and analysis for linear dopant drift kinetics. *Journal of Nanoengineering and Nanomanufacturing*, American Scientific Publishers, 6, 1–7.

Bayoumy, K., Gaber, M., Elshafeey, A., Mhaimeed, O., Dineen, E. H., Marvel, F. A., … Elshazly, M. B. (2021). Smart wearable devices in cardiovascular care: Where we are and how to move forward. *Nature Reviews Cardiology*, 18, 1–19.

Bhardwaj, A., Kumar, P., Raj, B., & Anand, S. (2022). Design and performance optimization of doping-less vertical nanowire TFET using gate stack technique. *Journal of Electronic Materials (JEMS)*, Springer, 41(7), 4005–4013.

Bhardwaj, A. K., Gupta, S., Raj, B., & Singh, A. (2019). Impact of double gate geometry on the performance of carbon nanotube field effect transistor structures for low power digital design. *Computational and Theoretical Nanoscience*, ASP, 16, 1813–1820.

Boutry, C. M., Beker, L., Kaizawa, Y., Vassos, C., Tran, H., Hinckley, A. C., Pfattner, R., Niu, S., Li, J., & Claverie, J. (2019). Biodegradable and flexible arterial-pulse sensor for the wireless monitoring of blood flow. *Nature Biomedical Engineering*, 3, 47–57.

Brunete, A., Gambao, E., Hernando, M., & Cedazo, R. (2021). Smart assistive architecture for the integration of IoT devices, robotic systems, and multimodal interfaces in healthcare environments. *Sensors*, 21(6), 2212.

Cao, P., Li, X., Mao, K., Lu, F., & Pan, Q. (2020). A novel data augmentation method to enhance deep neural networks for detection of atrial fibrillation. *Biomedical Signal Processing and Control*, 56, 101675

Chen, L. Y., Tee, B. C. K., Chortos, A. L., Schwartz, G., Tse, V., Lipomi, D. J., Wong, H. S. P., McConnell, M. V., & Bao, Z. (2014). Continuous wireless pressure monitoring and mapping with ultra-small passive sensors for health monitoring and critical care. *Nature Communications*, 5, 1–10.

Chen, T. M., Huang, C. H., Shih, E. S., Hu, Y. F., & Hwang, M. J. (2020a). Detection and classification of cardiac arrhythmias by a challenge-best deep learning neural network model. *Iscience*, 23(3), 100886.

Chen, X., Zhu, H., Geng, D., Liu, W., Yang, R., & Li, S. (2020b). Merging RFID and blockchain technologies to accelerate big data medical research based on physiological signals. *Journal of Healthcare Engineering*, 17 pages, Article ID 2452683, 2020. https://doi.org/10.1155/2020/2452683

Garbhapu, V. V., & Gopalan, S. (2017). IoT based low cost single sensor node remote health monitoring system. *Procedia Computer Science*, 113, 408–415.

Gjoreski, M., Gradišek, A., Budna, B., Gams, M., & Poglajen, G. (2020). Machine learning and end-to-end deep learning for the detection of chronic heart failure from heart sounds. *IEEE Access*, 8, 20313–20324.

Gopal, M., & Raj, B. (2013). Low power 8T SRAM cell design for high stability video applications, *ITSI Transaction on Electrical and Electronics Engineering*, 1(5), 91–97.

Goyal, C., Ubhi, J. S., & Raj, B. (2018). A reliable leakage reduction technique for approximate full adder with reduced ground bounce noise. *Journal of Mathematical Problems in Engineering*, Hindawi, 2018, 16 pages.

Goyal, C., Ubhi, J. S., & Raj, B. (2019). Low leakage zero ground noise nanoscale full adder using source biasing technique. *Journal of Nanoelectronics and Optoelectronics*, American Scientific Publishers, 14, 360–370.

Hannun, A.Y., Rajpurkar, P., Haghpanahi, M., Tison, G.H., Bourn, C., Turakhia, M.P., & Ng, A.Y. (2019). Cardiologist-level arrhythmia detection and classification in ambulatory electrocardiograms using a deep neural network. *Nature Medicine* 25, 65.

Hassan, S. R., Ahmad, I., Ahmad, S., Alfaify, A., & Shafiq, M. (2020). Remote pain monitoring using fog computing for e-Healthcare: An efficient architecture. *Sensors*, 20(22), 6574.

He, Y., Fu, B., Yu, J., Li, R., & Jiang, R. (2020). Efficient learning of healthcare data from IoT devices by edge convolution neural networks. *Applied Sciences*, 10(24), 8934.

Huang, C. Y., Chan, M. C., Chen, C. Y., & Lin, B.S. (2014). Novel wearable and wireless ring-type pulse oximeter with multi-detectors. *Sensors*, 14, 17586–17599.

Iqbal, U., Wah, T. Y., ur Rehman, M. H., Mujtaba, G., Imran, M., & Shoaib, M. (2018). Deep deterministic learning for pattern recognition of different cardiac diseases through the internet of medical things. *Journal of Medical Systems*, 42(12), 1–25.

Jain, A., Sharma, S., & Raj, B. (2016). "Design and analysis of high sensitivity photosensor using cylindrical surrounding gate MOSFET for low power sensor applications. *Engineering Science and Technology, an International Journal*, Elsevier's, 19(4), 1864–1870.

Jain, A., Sharma, S., & Raj, B. (2018). Analysis of Triple Metal Surrounding Gate (TM-SG) III-V nanowire MOSFET for photosensing application. *Opto-Electronics Journal*, Elsevier, 26(2), 141–148.

Jain, N., & Raj, B. (2018a). Analysis and performance exploration of high-k SOI FinFETs over the conventional low-k SOI FinFET toward analog/RF design. *Journal of Semiconductors (JoS)*, IOP Science, 39(12), 124002-1-7.

Jain, N., & Raj, B. (2018b). Parasitic capacitance and resistance model development and optimization of raised source/drain SOI FinFET structure for analog circuit applications. *Journal of Nanoelectronics and Optoelectronics*, ASP, USA, 13, 531–539.

Jain, N., & Raj, B. (2019a). Dual-k Spacer region variation at the drain side of asymmetric SOI FinFET structure: Performance analysis towards the analog/RF design applications. *Journal of Nanoelectronics and Optoelectronics*, American Scientific Publishers, 14, 349–359.

Jain, N., & Raj, B. (2019b). Thermal stability analysis and performance exploration of Asymmetrical Dual-k underlap Spacer (ADKUS) SOI FinFET for security and privacy applications. *Indian Journal of Pure & Applied Physics (IJPAP)*, 57, 352–360.

Jiao, Z., Xiao, Y., Jin, Y., & Chen, X. (2020). Tianxia120: A multimodal medical data collection bioinformatic system for proactive health management in internet of medical things. *Journal of Healthcare Engineering*, 2020, 8828738, 11 pages. https://doi.org/10.1155/2020/8828738.

Jin, D., Adams, H., Cocco, A. M., Martin, W. G., & Palmer, S. (2020). Smartphones and wearable technology: benefits and concerns in cardiology. *Medical Journal of Australia*, 212(2), 54–56.

Kandasamy, N., Ahmad, F., Ajitha, D., Raj, B., & Telagam, N. (2020). Quantum dot cellular automata based scan flip flop and boundary scan register. *IETE Journal of Research*.

Kaur, M., Gupta, N., Kumar, S., Raj, B., & Singh, A. K. (2021a). Comparative RF and crosstalk analysis of carbon based nano interconnects. *IET Circuits, Devices & Systems*, 15(6), 493–503.

Kaur, P., Buttar, A. S., & Raj, B. (2021b). A comprehensive analysis of nanoscale transistor based biosensor: A review. *Indian Journal of Pure and Applied Physics*, 59, 304–318.

Kaur, T., & Pal, P. (2019). Cloud computing network security for various parameters, and its application. *International Journal of Advanced Science and Technology*, 28(20), pp. 897–904.

Kelly, J. T., Campbell, K. L., Gong, E., & Scuffham, P. (2020). The Internet of Things: Impact and implications for health care delivery. *Journal of Medical Internet Research*, 22(11), e20135.

Khairuddin, A.M., Azir, K.N.F.K., & Kan, P.E. (2017). Limitations and future of electrocardiography devices: A review and the perspective from the Internet of Things. In *Proceedings of the 2017 International Conference on Research and Innovation in Information Systems (ICRIIS)*, Langkawi, Malaysia, 16–17 July 2017.

Kumar, A., and Saini, G. (2021). Comparative study of biomedical physiological based ECG signal heart monitoring for human body, In *International Conference on Emerging Technologies: AI, IoT, and CPS for Science & Technology Applications* (5870, 0–2), NITTTR Chandigarh, India.

Larradet, F., Niewiadomski, R., Barresi, G., Caldwell, D. G., & Mattos, L. S. (2020). Toward emotion recognition from physiological signals in the wild: Approaching the methodological issues in real-life data collection. *Frontiers in Psychology*, 11, 1111.

Li, C., Hu, X., & Zhang, L. (2017). The IoT-based heart disease monitoring system for pervasive healthcare service. *Procedia Computer Science*, 112, 2328–2334.

Liaqat, S., Dashtipour, K., Zahid, A., Arshad, K., Ullah, S., Assaleh, K., & Ramzan, N. (2021). A review and comparison of the state-of-the-art techniques for atrial fibrillation detection and skin hydration. *Frontiers in Communications and Networks*, 2, 679502.

Lim, H. R., Kim, H. S., Qazi, R., Kwon, Y. T., Jeong, J. W., & Yeo, W. H. (2020). Advanced soft materials, sensor integrations, and applications of wearable flexible hybrid electronics in healthcare, energy, and environment. *Advanced Materials*, 32, 1901924.

Liu, Q., Liu, A., Zhang, X., Chen, X., Qian, R., & Chen, X. (2019). Removal of EMG artifacts from multichannel EEG signals using combined singular spectrum analysis and canonical correlation analysis. *Journal of Healthcare Engineering*, 2019, 4159676, 13 pages. https://doi.org/10.1155/2019/4159676.

Luz, E. J. D. S., Schwartz, W. R., Cámara-Chávez, G., & Menotti, D. (2016). ECG-based heartbeat classification for arrhythmia detection: A survey. *Computer Methods and Programs in Biomedicine*, 127, 144–164.

Meteier, Q., Capallera, M., Ruffieux, S., Angelini, L., Abou Khaled, O., Mugellini, E., ... Sonderegger, A. (2021). Classification of drivers' workload using physiological signals in conditional automation. *Frontiers in Psychology*, 12, 268.

Nagarajan, V. D., Lee, S. L., Robertus, J. L., Nienaber, C. A., Trayanova, N. A., & Ernst, S. (2021). Artificial intelligence in the diagnosis and management of arrhythmias. *European Heart Journal*, 42(38), 3904–3916.

Nam, K. H., Kim, D. H., Choi, B. K., & Han, I. H. (2019). Internet of things, digital biomarker, and artificial intelligence in spine: Current and future perspectives. *Neurospine*, 16(4), 705.

Pal, P., Kaur, T., Sethi, D., Kumar, A., Kumar, S., Lamba, A., & Rastogi, U. (2020). Vertical Handoff in Heterogeneous Mechanism for Wireless LTE Network-An Optimal Approach. In *2020 International Conference on Emerging Trends in Communication, Control and Computing (ICONC3)* (pp. 1–5). IEEE, Lakshmangarh, India. DOI: 10.1109/ICONC345789.2020.9117281.

Pal, P., & Pali, L. (2018). Congestion free analysis for emergency vehicles response in tri-city (Panchkula-Chandigarh Mohali) using LTE-A. *Modelling, Measurement and Control A*, 91(2), 66–72. DOI: 10.18280/mmc_a.910206

Palanivel Rajan, S. (2015). Review and investigations on future research directions of mobile based telecare system for cardiac surveillance. *Journal of Applied Research and Technology*, 13(4), 454–460.

Patel, W., Patel, C., & Valderrama, C. (2019). IoMT based efficient vital signs monitoring system for elderly healthcare using neural network. *International Journal of Research*, 8(I), 239–245.

Perez, L., & Wang, J. (2017). The effectiveness of data augmentation in image classification using deep learning. *arXiv*, arXiv:1712.04621.

Pushparaj, K., & Saini, G. (2021). Comparative Study of Biomedical Physiological based ECG Signal heart monitoring for Human body. In *2021 International Conference on Emerging Technologies: AI, IoT and CPS for Science and Technology Applications, ICET 2021.* urn:nbn:de:0074-3058-1

Raj, B., Mitra, J., Bihani, D. K., Rangharajan, V., Saxena, A. K., & Dasgupta, S. (2010). Analysis of noise margin, power and process variation for 32 nm FinFET based 6T SRAM cell. *Journal of Computer (JCP)*, Academy Publisher, FINLAND, 5(6).

Ravi, D., Wong, C., Deligianni, F., Berthelot, M., Andreu-Perez, J., Lo, B., & Yang, G.Z. (2017). Deep Learning for Health Informatics. *IEEE Journal of Biomedical and Health Informatics*, 21, 4–21.

Raza, A., Tran, K. P., Koehl, L., & Li, S. (2021). Designing ECG Monitoring Healthcare System with Federated Transfer Learning and Explainable AI. arXiv preprint arXiv:2105.12497.

Rincon, J. A., Guerra-Ojeda, S., Carrascosa, C., & Julian, V. (2020). An IoT and Fog computing-based monitoring system for cardiovascular patients with automatic ECG classification using deep neural networks. *Sensors*, 20(24), 7353.

Rubí, S., Jesus, N., & Gondim, P. R. L. (2019). IoMT platform for pervasive healthcare data aggregation, processing, and sharing based on OneM2M and OpenEHR. *Sensors*, 19(19), 4283.

Saiphani Kumar, G., Singh, A., & Raj, B. (2018). Design and analysis of gate all around CNTFET based SRAM cell design. *Journal of Computational Electronics*, Springer, 17(1), 138–145.

Salamon, J., & Bello, J. P. (2017). Deep convolutional neural networks and data augmentation for environmental sound classification. *IEEE Signal Processing Letters*, 24(3), 279–283.

Sharma, D., Mehra, R., & Raj, B. (2021). Comparative analysis of photovoltaic technologies for high efficiency solar cell design. *Superlattices and Microstructures*, Elsevier, 153, 106861.

Sharma, S. K.., Raj, B., & Khosla, M. (2019). Enhanced photosensivity of highly spectrum selective cylindrical gate $In_{1-x}Ga_xAs$ nanowire MOSFET photodetector. *Modern Physics Letter-B*, 33(12), 1950144.

Shukla, S., Hassan, M. F., Khan, M. K., Jung, L. T., & Awang, A. (2019). An analytical model to minimize the latency in healthcare internet-of-things in fog computing environment. *PLoS One*, 14(11), e0224934.

Singh, A., Khosla, M., & Raj, B. (2016a). Circuit compatible model for electrostatic doped Schottky barrier CNTFET. *Journal of Electronic Materials*, Springer, 45(12), 4825–4835.

Singh, A., Khosla, M., & Raj, B. (2019). Design and analysis of dynamically configurable electrostatic doped carbon nanotube tunnel FET. *Microelectronics Journal*, Elsevier, 85, 17–24.

Singh, A., Khosla, M., Raj, B. (2017). Analysis of electrostatic doped Schottky barrier carbon nanotube FET for low power applications. *Journal of Materials Science: Materials in Electronics*, Springer, 28, 1762–1768.

Singh, D., Pushparaj, M. K., Mishra, A. Lamba, & S. Swagatika. (2020) "Security issues in different layer of IoT and their possible mitigation. *International Journal of Scientific & Technology Research*, 9(04), 2762–2771.

Singh, G., Sarin, R. K., & Raj, B. (2016b). A novel robust Exclusive-OR function implementation in QCA nanotechnology with energy dissipation analysis. *Journal of Computational Electronics*, Springer, 15(2), 455–465.

Singh, G., Sarin, R. K., & Raj, B. (2018a). Fault-tolerant design and analysis of quantum-dot cellular automata based circuits. *IEEE/IET Circuits, Devices & Systems*, 12, 638–664.

Singh, J., & Raj, B. (2018a). Comparative analysis of memristor models for memories design. *JoS*, IoP, 39(7), 074006-1-12.

Singh, J., & Raj, B. (2018b). Modeling of mean barrier height levying various image forces of metal insulator metal structure to enhance the performance of conductive filament based memristor model. *IEEE Nanotechnology*, 17(2), 268–267.

Singh, J., & Raj, B. (2019a). An accurate and generic window function for non-linear memristor model. *Journal of Computational Electronics*, Springer, 18(2), 640–647.

Singh, J., & Raj, B. (2019b). Design and investigation of 7T2M NVSARM with enhanced stability and temperature impact on store/restore energy. *IEEE Transactions on Very Large Scale Integration Systems*, 27(6), 1322–1328.

Singh, J., & Raj, B. (2019c). Tunnel current model of asymmetric MIM structure levying various image forces to analyze the characteristics of filamentary memristor. *Applied Physics A*, Springer, 125(3), 203.1 to 203.11.

Singh, J., Sharma, S., Raj, B., & Khosla, M. (2018b). Analysis of barrier layer thickness on performance of $In_{1-x}Ga_xAs$ based Gate Stack Cylindrical Gate Nanowire MOSFET. *JNO*, ASP, 13, 1473–1477.

Singh, R., Mehta, R., & Rajpal, N. (2018c). Efficient wavelet families for ECG classification using neural classifiers. *Procedia Computer Science*, 132, 11–21.

Singh, S., & Raj, B. (2020). A 2-D analytical surface potential and drain current modeling of double-gate vertical t-shaped tunnel FET. *Journal of Computational Electronics*, Springer, 19, 1154–1163.

Singh, S., Vishvakarma, S. K., & Raj, B. (2018d). Analytical modeling of split-gate junction-less transistor for a biosensor application. *Sensing and Bio-Sensing*, Elsevier, 18, 31–36.

Swapna, G., Soman, K. P., & Vinayakumar, R. (2018). Automated detection of cardiac arrhythmia using deep learning techniques. *Procedia Computer Science*, 132, 1192–1201.

Thakur, S. T., & Patel, D. P. (2021). Patient Health Monitoring and Inferencing Arrhythmia Using ECG_Data. 17 May 2021, PREPRINT (Version 1) available at Research Square [https://doi.org/10.21203/rs.3.rs-509103/v1]

Tomar, A. S., Magraiya, V. K., & Raj, B. (2013). Scaling of access and data transistor for high performance DRAM cell design. *Quantum Matter*, 2, 412–416.

Wadhera, T., Kakkar, D., Wadhwa, G., & Raj, B. (2019). Recent advances and progress in development of the field effect transistor biosensor: A review. *Journal of Electronic Materials*, Springer, 48(12), 7635–7646.

Wadhwa, G., Kamboj, P., Raj, B. (2019). Design optimisation of junction-less TFET biosensor for high sensitivity. *Advances in Natural Sciences: Nanoscience and Nanotechnology*, 10(7), 045001.

Wadhwa, G., & Raj, B. (2018). Parametric variation analysis of charge-plasma-based dielectric modulated JLTFET for biosensor application. *IEEE Sensor Journal*, 18(15), 6070–6077.

Wang, C., Pun, T., & Chanel, G. (2018). A comparative survey of methods for remote heart rate detection from frontal face videos. *Frontiers in Bioengineering and Biotechnology*, 6, 33.

Xu, H., Li, P., Yang, Z., Liu, X., Wang, Z., Yan, W., ... Zhang, Z. (2020). Construction and application of a medical-grade wireless monitoring system for physiological signals at general wards. *Journal of Medical Systems*, 44(10), 1–15.

Yadav, D., Chouhan, S. S., Vishvakarma, S. K., & Raj, B. (2018). Application specific microcontroller design for IoT based WSN. *Sensor Letter*, ASP, 16, 374–385.

Yadav, D., Raj, B., & Raj, B. (2020). Design and simulation of low power micro-controller for IoT applications. *Journal of Sensor Letters*, ASP, 18, 401–409.

Yang, J. C., Mun, J., Kwon, S.Y., Park, S., Bao, Z., & Park, S. (2019). Electronic skin: Recent progress and future prospects for skin-attachable devices for health monitoring, robotics, and prosthetics. *Advanced Materials*, 31, 1904765.

Yeh, L. R., Chen, W. C., Chan, H. Y., Lu, N. H., Wang, C. Y., Twan, W. H., ... Chen, T. B. (2021). Integrating ECG monitoring and classification via IoT and deep neural networks. *Biosensors*, 11(6), 188.

Yin, M., Tang, R., Liu, M., Han, K., Lv, X., Huang, M., ... Gai, Y. (2020). Influence of optimization design based on artificial intelligence and internet of things on the electrocardiogram monitoring system. *Journal of Healthcare Engineering*, 2020, 8840910, 8 pages. https://doi.org/10.1155/2020/8840910.

Zanini, R., & Colombini, E. (2020). Parkinson's disease EMG data augmentation and simulation with DCGANs and style transfer. *Sensors*, 20, 2605.

Zhang, J., Liu, A., Gao, M., Chen, X., Zhang, X., & Chen, X. (2020a). ECG-based multi-class arrhythmia detection using spatio-temporal attention-based convolutional recurrent neural network. *Artificial Intelligence in Medicine*, 106, 101856.

Zhang, X., Liu, J., Shen, J., Li, S., Hou, K., Hu, B., ... Zhang, T. (2020b). Emotion recognition from multimodal physiological signals using a regularized deep fusion of kernel machine. *IEEE Transactions on Cybernetics*, 51(9), 4386–4399.

Zhang, Z., Li, Z., & Li, Z. (2020c). An improved real-time R-wave detection efficient algorithm in exercise ECG signal analysis. *Journal of Healthcare Engineering*, 2020, 8868685, 7 pages. https://doi.org/10.1155/2020/8868685.

Zhou, T., Cha, J. S., Gonzalez, G., Wachs, J. P., Sundaram, C. P., & Yu, D. (2020). Multimodal physiological signals for workload prediction in robot-assisted surgery. *ACM Transactions on Human-Robot Interaction (THRI)*, 9(2), 26 pages. https://doi.org/10.1145/3368589.

Zihlmann, M.; Perekrestenko, D.; Tschannen, M. (2017). Convolutional recurrent neural networks for electrocardiogram classification. In *Computing in Cardiology*; IEEE: Piscataway, NJ, pp. 124–132.

CHAPTER 5

Fast Image Desmogging for Road Safety Using Optimized Dark Channel Prior

Akshay Juneja

Thapar Institute of Engineering and Technology

Vijay Kumar

Dr. B.R. Ambedkar National Institute of Technology

Sunil Kumar Singla

Thapar Institute of Engineering and Technology

CONTENTS

DOI: 10.1201/9781003230113-5

5.1 INTRODUCTION

In the presence of weather degrading variants such as fog, haze, smoke, smog, rain and dust, the images collected are degraded and endure poor visibility issues. The majority of researchers design the architecture to produce clear scene radiance for the input images degraded due to haze, fog and rain. The costs of car accidents to human lives and property are significant. In the European Union, in excess of 40,000 individuals lost their lives and around a million are harmed every year due to road accidents. Over the time, there is fast improvement of automatic directing strategies such as intelligent transportation systems and unmanned ground vehicles. The computation strategies have taken over the market and smog-removing algorithms are much needed tasks to accomplish to save human lives. However, dissimilarities in the environmental factors and illumination conditions make the task challenging [1]. It is problematic to design a restoration model for smoggy images because smog is combination of two degrading variants, namely fog and smoke. In real-world, restoration of smoggy images is equally important as foggy or hazy images. The dehazing algorithms present in literature cannot produce smog-free image of desired quality, so a modified model is necessary. The two important factors which are estimated to obtain the clear scene radiance from a smoggy input image are airlight and transmission map.

The algorithms present in literature are mainly categorized as depth map estimation, filtering-based techniques, meta-heuristics-based algorithms, enhancement-based and fusion-based methods to obtain clear scene radiance for smoggy input. He et al. [2] proposed dark channel prior (DCP) technique in which the color channel with maximum number of low intensity pixels was selected. The dark channel was evaluated and refined to restore the image. In Kim et al. [3], pixels of all color channels having peak intensity were used to estimate airlight followed by bilateral filters for edge preservation. Fattal [4] designed a local color-line model in which transmission map was maximized using Gauss–Markov random field.

In Wang et al. [5], regression technique was utilized to evaluate transmission map and the clear scene radiance was obtained using scattering model. The model designed by Su et al. [6] exhibited gradient reversal artifact and halo effect. It utilized bilateral filter for edge preservation.

To provide smoothness at edges, a desmogging model was designed by Zhao et al. [7]. It presented multi-scale tone manipulation method to review local contrast, but the results generated were not of desired level for images with large smog gradients. Reported paper [8] designed a supervised learning technique for synthetic images which used linear transformation to estimate map. However, the results were better than DCP but this model was not efficient for real-world images. The algorithm presented in Kumari and Sahoo [9] extracted edges using difference between the original and filtered images. The median filter and gamma correction factor helped to design look-up table. Reported paper [10] proposed a desmogging model to estimate transmission based on mean vector L2-norm, followed by guided image to refine transmission map. Reported paper [11] proposed change-of-detail prior approach which made local smoggy regions stable but unable to preserve the edges. Reported paper [12] designed a model to preserve the edges using weighted guided filter based on Koschmieder's law.

Reported paper [13] presented a desmogging model based on bi-histogram modification which not only measured the smog density but also provided measure against smog formation due to which sometimes significant information got lost. Reported paper [14] presented gain intervention-based refinement filter used in combination with DCP to reduce halo effect in desmogged images. The superpixel algorithm presented by Reported paper [15] for desmogging eliminates the possibility of halo artifacts and prioritizes color restoration in sky region. Reported paper [16] presented a method to work on dark and bright channel prior simultaneously to estimate the transmission map and airlight for black and white pixels, respectively. In Reported paper [17], the desmogged images had less halo effect and color distortion because of gamma correction and segmentation operation. Also, edges were preserved using median filter. Reported paper [18] designed a regression-based model to obtain desmogged images. The transmission vector was obtained by solving support vector regression. Reported paper [19] implemented a multi-scale wavelet model to achieve the goal. The low frequency part of the image was analyzed using DCP while the high-frequency part was used to preserve the texture information.

In Reported paper [20], a gain-coefficient-based trilateral filter was presented to overcome the drawback of using DCP while desmogging the objects with no shadows or their illumination properties were similar to airlight. Also, in 2018, an integrated algorithm presenting the combination of dark and bright channel prior was proposed in Ref. [21]. This method eliminated the issue of halo and gradient reversal artifacts. Singh and Raj [22] implemented anisotropic diffusion image filter to obtain clear scene radiance. This filter utilized the ratio of gradient and local activity to achieve the goal. Singh et al. [23] focused on edge and color restoration, and to improve the texture of images by designing gradient-sensitive loss to obtain depth map and window-based integrated means filter to estimate transmission map from input smoggy image. Reported paper . [24] proposed gradient profile prior (GPP)-based desmogging model which utilized iterative learning-based (L0) filter to refine the transmission map. Its modified version was presented in Ref. [25] that implemented gradient channel prior (GCP) instead of GPP.

5.1.1 Atmospheric Scattering Model

There are multiple foggy datasets that exist in the literature [26]. However, real-time smoggy datasets are not available. Thus, deep learning-based desmogging models are trained for synthetic smoggy images only. The desmogging model as depicted in various computer vision problems [27–30] is represented as Eq. (5.1). This model is used to estimate transmission map and atmospheric light.

$$S_i(y) = S_o(y)\tau(y) + \alpha(1 - \tau(y)) \tag{5.1}$$

where $S_i(y)$ is the smoggy image and $S_o(y)$ is the smog-free image.

The global atmospheric light α signifies the intensity of light in R, G and B channels. The part of light which is not scattered during the transmission is represented by $\tau(y)$.

This transmitted light $\tau(y)$ is expressed in Eq. (5.2):

$$\tau(y) = e^{-\beta d(y)} \tag{5.2}$$

where β is defined as the scattering coefficient of the atmosphere and d is the depth of the object.

Figure 5.1 represents atmospheric scattering model under a smoggy environment.

The highlights of this chapter are as follows:

- Improving DCP-based algorithm by calculating contrast energy (CE).

- Optimization of image entropy (IE) of prior-based generated result.

- Performance metrics are calculated for sample images and comparison is made with existing techniques.

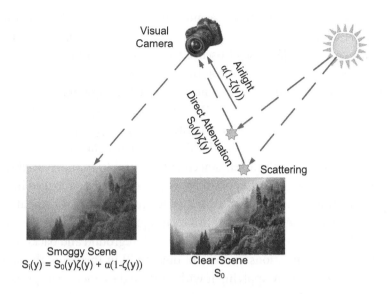

FIGURE 5.1   Atmospheric scattering model under smoggy environment.

The chapter is categorized as follows: A literature survey on existing dehazing and desmogging techniques is discussed in Section 5.2. The proposed desmogging model and the mathematics involved are discussed in Section 5.3. Section 5.4 presents the comparative analysis of performance metrics of proposed technique with existing algorithms. Section 5.5 discusses the concluding remarks.

5.2 RELATED WORK

Reported paper [31] presented a method to simultaneously desmog and denoise a distorted smoggy image. The desmogging algorithm utilized polarized scattering effect to estimate airlight and transmission map. These polarized images were used from 0° to 90°. This algorithm was followed by blind contrast assessment to reduce noising in the image [32]. Reported paper [33] utilized the polarization attributes of round polarization light and set up a polarization imaging framework with round polarization light as dynamic lighting. Once the light strength map was obtained, the Stokes vector of light was calculated, and the line polarization light and the round polarization light were individually obtained in the polarized image to recover the differential polarized smog-free image. Reported paper [34] emphasized on airlight scattering model to estimate constant-time airlight and transmission map for obtaining clear scene radiance images.

Reported paper [35] proposed a multi-scale fusion technique in which smog-free image was obtained using DCP map, clarity map and saliency map. Reported paper [36] used Koschmieder's law to minimize edge distortion and color distortion in the smog-free image using Retinex constraint. In Reported paper [37], initially the atmospheric veil was obtained for smoggy image using boundary conditions. The improved atmospheric veil was estimated by local contrast using bilateral filter. In Reported paper [38], the desmogging technique firstly utilized DCP to obtain airlight and transmission map followed by logarithmic enhancement method to improve brightness in the clear scene radiance. Reported paper [39] restored desmogged images using GCP. This technique worked better for texture images compared to other techniques. The drawback of this technique was that it does not show good results for images with similar objects in foreground and background.

However, the limitations of conventional DCP in images with uneven smog were overcome by applying it with saturated extraction as proposed by Reference [40]. Reported paper [41] designed an external gradient prior to obtain clear scene radiance from smoggy images, but it was only applicable to images with thin smog. In Reported paper [42], the estimated transmission map was improved using optimal patch-wise and pixel-wise fusion model to obtain smog-free image. Reported paper [43] proposed a unified variation model in which scene transmission and inverted scene radiance were calculated separately for each channel (Red, Green and Blue) to design a desmogging framework. Reported paper [44] discussed Siamese network architecture which utilized unmatched images to learn new features to train the model. A color channel transfer was proposed by Reported paper [45] to obtain loss-free color channel in desmogged image. In Reported paper [46], two total generalized variation regularizations were utilized to improve image density and transmission map. Reported paper [47] proposed a desmogging algorithm based on supervised learning using generative adversarial network. In this algorithm, a pair of discriminator and generator produced smog-free image. Reported paper [48] modified the conventional Multi-Scale Convolution Neural Network (MSCNN) with holistic edges in which transmission map was estimated using coarse scale and refined using fine scale.

Reported paper [49] utilized wavelet transformation to extract high and low frequency components and analyzed them separately to recover smog-free image. Reported paper [50] proposed a pyramid channel-based feature attention network consisting of multi-scale extraction module, feature attention module formed from a pyramid channel, and an image reconstruction module. Reported paper [51] designed a self-constructing image fusion technique to obtain clear scene radiance from a smoggy input without obtaining airlight and transmission map. The edge was restored perfectly using this technique. Reported paper [52] prioritized color preservation by eliminating additional airlight component to obtain smog-free images. This method utilized nearest-neighbor regularization to obtain smog-free pixels.

In Reported paper [53], the smoggy image was categorized in normal and bright regions such that transmission estimation for bright and normal regions was performed using atmospheric veil correction and DCP, respectively. Also, smoothing quantization and image matting was performed to obtain alpha map. Both the parameters act as input in fusion transmission model. Reported paper [54] presented a dense pyramid residual network in which edges of smoggy input images were restored using structure similarity index metric (SSIM). A feed forward network was presented by Reported paper [55] to achieve the goal using semi-supervised approach, i.e., supervised losses were calculated for synthetic smoggy images and unsupervised losses were calculated for real smoggy images. Reported paper [56] designed a deep learning model consisting of feature extraction, non-linear mapping, deconvolution and activation function. This model blocked artifacts and eliminated halo effect.

Reported paper [57] designed a fusion-based scheme in which various derived maps such as exposure map, saliency map and gamma correction map were fused with a U-shaped convolution neural network (CNN) to obtain smog-free images. Reported paper [58] produced a desmogged image using the combination of two fusion techniques, namely multi-region fusion and exposure fusion technique to estimate transmission map. A convex model based on sparse DCP was designed in the study by Reported paper [59] to obtain smog-free images. This method utilized various techniques such as L1 regularization, data-fitting and two total variation regularization models to achieve the goal. Reported paper [60] used support vector machine classifier to verify if the obtained image was desmogged to the desired level or not after the implementation of contrast-limited adaptive histogram equalization, DCP and Retinex algorithm. In Reported paper [61], channel-wise and spatial-wise modules were designed and the interdependencies of their features were studied.

In Reported paper [62], an illumination channel prior was designed and implemented to estimate atmospheric light and transmission map followed by its refining using gradient magnitude-based image filter. An information gain-based filter called bilateral filter or spatially invariant Gaussian kernel-based image filter was used in Reported paper [28]. The pixels are evaluated in patches such that the value of central pixel is replaced using weighted average. A non-dominated sorting genetic algorithm was used in Reported paper [29] for tuning the resultant image computed using integrated variational regularized model and integrated transmission map estimation. The color was restored and artifacts are suppressed to restore visibility using this method.

Reported paper [27] proposed an oblique GPP using computed smog gradient to estimate depth map. An energy minimization function was implemented to refine the transmission map. The smog gradient prediction model proposed in Ref. [30] utilized CNN consisting of four layers of convolution, rectified linear unit and maximum pooling to extract features from input smoggy images and compute them. The probability density function is evaluated using softmax. Reported paper [63] proposed a cycle CNN-based desmogging model using the concept of visible light polarization. The encoder–decoder structure used in this model is coupled using residual blocks.

5.3 EXPERIMENTAL WORK

The smoggy images have dense regions which are opaque in nature and the remaining regions are covered in light black fumes. One of the most useful prior-based techniques for this purpose is DCP. In the proposed approach, the processing of input image using DCP is presented to highlight the smoggy regions by increasing its visibility. Then various features of the processed image such as CE and entropy are optimized to enhance the regions covered in smoke. Finally, the smog-free image is recovered after applying mathematical operation between the two techniques.

5.3.1 Conventional Dark Channel Prior

It is one of the most common techniques applied to improve the visibility of images distorted due to weather degraded variants [2]. The normalized form of Eq. (5.1) is written as:

$$\frac{S_i^c(y)}{\alpha^c} = \frac{S_{o1}^c(y)}{\alpha^c}\tau(y)+\left(1-\tau(y)\right) \tag{5.3}$$

where S_{o1} is assumed as the output of DCP technique and 'c' represents the color channel, which means each channel is processed separately using DCP.

Assuming the transmission map in a local patch $\Omega(x)$ and applying minimum filter on both sides of Eq. (5.3),

$$\min_{y \in \Omega(y)} \left(\min_c \frac{S_i^c(y)}{\alpha^c} \right) = \overline{\tau}(y) \min_{y \in \Omega(y)} \left(\min_c \frac{S_{o1}^c(y)}{\alpha^c} \right) + \left(1 - \overline{\tau}(y)\right). \quad (5.4)$$

The dark channel present in clear image S_o is almost zero after DCP. The atmospheric airlight α^c is always positive. Therefore,

$$\min_{y \in \Omega(y)} \left(\min_c \frac{S_{o1}^c(y)}{\alpha^c} \right) = 0. \quad (5.5)$$

Using Eqs. (5.4) and (5.5), transmission map is calculated as

$$\overline{\tau}(y) = 1 - \min_{y \in \Omega(y)} \left(\min_c \frac{S_i^c(y)}{\alpha^c} \right). \quad (5.6)$$

To maintain the originality of smog, a small factor 'ρ' is introduced in the image for distant object. Thus, the estimated transmission map is given by Eq. (5.7). The range of ρ is 0–1. The value of ρ is fixed at 0.75 for all the results reported in this chapter.

$$\overline{\tau}(y) = 1 - \rho \min_{y \in \Omega(y)} \left(\min_c \frac{S_i^c(y)}{\alpha^c} \right) \quad (5.7)$$

This map is refined using soft matting. A sparse linear system is used to obtain the refined result.

$$\left(L + \lambda U\right)\tau(y) = \lambda \overline{\tau}(y) \quad (5.8)$$

where L is the matting Laplacian matrix,
λ is the weight and U is the identity matrix of the same size as L.

The next component to be estimated is airlight. Since the clear image has less airlight than the distorted image, and also sunlight reaching the object is a part of atmospheric light, it can be represented as:

$$S_{o1}(y) = R(y)(\alpha + \text{SL}), \quad (5.9)$$

where $R < 1$ is the reflectance of the objects and SL is the sunlight.

From Eqs. (5.1) and (5.10) it is concluded that

$$S_i(y) = R(y)(\alpha + \text{SL})\tau(y) + \alpha(1 - \tau(y)) < \alpha. \tag{5.10}$$

The clear image is obtained using Eq. (5.11) such that gamma operation increases the exposure of output image to light. In the proposed scheme, a minimum amount of smog in $\tau(y)$ is preserved and is assumed as τ_0 with value 0.0001.

$$S_{o1}(y) = \frac{S_i(y) - \alpha}{\max(\tau(y), \tau_0)} + \alpha \tag{5.11}$$

5.3.2 Feature Enhancement

DCP is mainly used for fog and haze removal. It does not give desired output for smoggy images. Various features such as CE and entropy are to be estimated to achieve better result. For this purpose, a feature enhancement system is cascaded to the DCP output. The CE refers to the contrast of the input image [64]. This feature is extracted individually from each color channel in c_1 (grayscale, yellow-blue and red-green). The distorted image is rectified using convolution of DCP output image and Gaussian second-order derivative filters [65] having horizontal and vertical kernels represented as k_h and k_v, respectively. This introduces noise η^c in the system. The computation of CE is performed as:

$$\text{CE}(S_{o1}^{c_1}) = \frac{\gamma \times \sqrt{(S_{o1}^{c_1} * k_h)^2 + (S_{o1}^{c_1} * k_v)^2}}{\sqrt{(S_{o1}^{c_1} * k_h)^2 + (S_{o1}^{c_1} * k_v)^2 + \gamma k}} - \eta^{c_1}, \tag{5.12}$$

where γ is the maximum value of the term $\sqrt{(S_{o1}^{c_1} * k_h)^2 + (S_{o1}^{c_1} * k_v)^2}$ and k is the contrast gain.

The second feature which is needed to be enhanced is IE. The image is computed in grayscale for the desired result. It is represented as:

$$\text{IE}(S_{o1}^{\text{gray}}) = -\sum_{\forall i} p_i \log(p_i), \tag{5.13}$$

where p_i is histogram probability of pixel intensity i.

For the dehazed output S_{o2}, Eq. (5.2) is used to calculate the dehazed patch $S_{o2}^{c_1}(\tau_i)$. The optimized transmission map is given as:

$$\text{Opt}(t_i) = \text{CE}\left[\left(S_{o2}^{c_1}(\tau_i)\right)\right] \times \text{IE}\left[\left(S_{o2}^{\text{gray}}(\tau_i)\right)\right]. \tag{5.14}$$

Since atmospheric light was estimated to the best in first stage, there is no need to perform the operation again. The clear image is obtained using Eq. (5.15) such that gamma operation increases the exposure of output image to light. In the proposed scheme, a minimum amount of smog in $\tau(y)$ is preserved and is assumed as τ_0 with value 0.0001.

$$S_{o2}(y) = \frac{S_{o1}(y) - \alpha}{\left[\max(\tau(y),\tau_0)\right]^{\text{gamma}}} + \alpha \tag{5.15}$$

5.3.3 Desmogged Output

The final output image is obtained by performing mathematical operation between the output of two stages to compensate the effect of over-estimation of transmission map. It is given as:

$$S_o(y) = a \times S_{o1}(y) - b \times S_{o2}(y), \tag{5.16}$$

where a and b are constants. Here, assumed values of a and b are 1.5 and 0.5, respectively.

Figure 5.2 represents the block diagram and architecture of proposed technique to recover $S_{o2}(y)$ from $S_i(y)$.

5.4 RESULTS AND DISCUSSION

This section discusses the qualitative and quantitative analysis of the optimized DCP and the generated results are compared with the existing algorithms.

5.4.1 Qualitative Analysis

The online databases having smoggy images are rare. Some sample images are selected from Ref. [66] for implementing the proposed technique.

The sample images are processed using the proposed approach and results are compared with existing algorithms such as multilayer perceptron [67], optimal transmission map and adaptive airlight (OTM-AAL) [68], and improved color attenuation prior (ICAP) [69]. The results

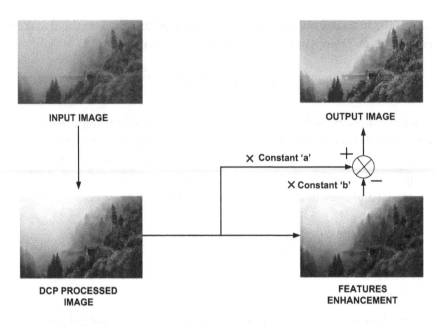

INPUT IMAGE

OUTPUT IMAGE

X Constant 'a'   +

X Constant 'b'   −

DCP PROCESSED
IMAGE

FEATURES
ENHANCEMENT

FIGURE 5.2   Proposed desmogging algorithm.

generated are shown in Table 5.1. These techniques prioritize the refining of transmission map and estimation of airlight is secondary task. In multilayer perceptron technique, the dynamic range of restored image is improved using minimum channel and contrast stretching technique. The transmission map estimated in OTM-AAL is refined by extracting various features such as local standard deviation, IE, contrast and normalized dispersion optimal. The ICAP refines the transmission map using guided image filter.

Image titled '01.tif' has dense smoggy regions which are difficult to process as they become opaque in nature. But the surrounding regions with thin black fumes are computed to improve visibility. Image '02.tif' is captured from a certain height such that a layer of smog covers the city, and in image '03.tif' an empty street with a couple of object is shown. Similarly, the images '04.tif', '05.tif' and '06.tif' are computed using the mentioned techniques.

The existing techniques are helpful for fog or haze removal, but they are not giving desired result for smoggy images. The brightness in the output images is reduced and background noise is present.

In the proposed optimized DCP, the transmission map is optimized by enhancing CE and IE for the desmogged patch. Although it increases the brightness, colors get distorted.

TABLE 5.1   Comparison with Existing Dehazing Techniques

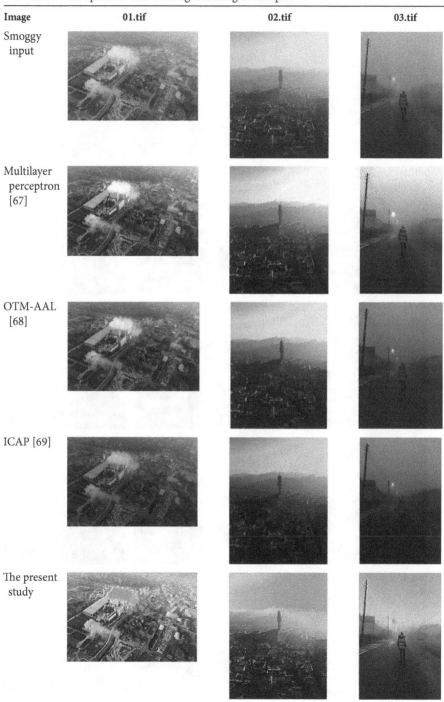

(Continued)

TABLE 5.1 (Continued)   Comparison with Existing Dehazing Techniques

Image	04.tif	05.tif	06.tif
Smoggy input			
Multilayer perceptron [67]			
OTM-AAL [68]			
ICAP [69]			
The present study			

5.4.2 Quantitative Analysis

The sample images are desmogged using the novel prior-based enhancement technique as shown in Table 5.1. To analyze the functioning of the proposed approach, various performance metrics can be calculated [70]. In this chapter, only two of those metrics are discussed. These performance parameters are SSIM and peak signal to noise ratio (PSNR). SSIM returns the comparison of contrast, luminance and structural comparisons of output and input image.

A smaller value of SSIM is preferred for distorted and computed image. PSNR gives the ratio of signal to the noise returning the index of the image distortion. A larger value of PSNR is preferred for less distortion. Figure 5.3

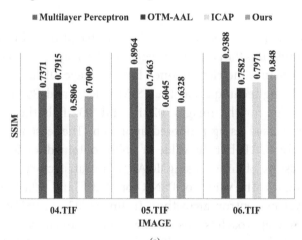

(a)

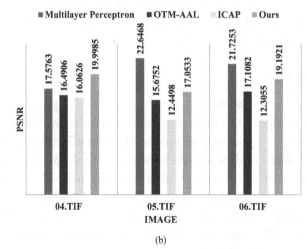

(b)

FIGURE 5.3   Performance comparison based on (a) SSIM and (b) PSNR.

TABLE 5.2   Performance Comparison of Various Visibility Restoration Techniques

Dehazing Technique	Performance Metrics	01.tif	02.tif	03.tif
Multilayer perceptron [67]	SSIM	0.8531	0.8238	0.8311
	PSNR	17.0066	20.2682	19.5960
OTM-AAL [68]	SSIM	0.7539	0.7504	0.7516
	PSNR	13.9179	17.7166	15.8325
ICAP [69]	SSIM	0.7026	0.6380	0.5823
	PSNR	11.6471	14.8766	14.9967
The present study	SSIM	0.6278	0.6685	0.6348
	PSNR	17.7651	17.6448	18.1822

presents the comparison of various techniques based on SSIM and PSNR. Table 5.2 summarizes the parameter metrics of the images shown in Table 5.1.

The performance metrics obtained for the image '01.tif' are best compared to existing techniques as the SSIM is least and PSNR is highest. Similarity index for the images '02.tif' and '03.tif' is the second lowest when processed using proposed approach. The least value of SSIM is obtained for ICAP, but the value of PSNR obtained for ICAP is least. Thus, the results obtained using ICAP is unsatisfactory compared to other techniques. The values of PSNR for '02.tif' and '03.tif' are highest for multilayer perceptron algorithm. In image '02.tif', PSNR calculated using proposed approach is close to the value obtained when OTM-AAL is used. PSNR obtained in image '03.tif' using optimized DCP is the second highest, making this technique overall better than the existing discussed techniques. Similarly, the performance metrics for other images are compared in Figure 5.3a and b.

5.5 SUMMARY

In this chapter, an optimized DCP technique is proposed. Initially the smoggy images are computed using conventional DCP technique. Although DCP is a powerful technique, it is not effective for the images where it is difficult to differentiate between sky and non-sky regions. The color of objects in such images is similar to the color of airlight. Due to this reason, the estimated transmission map only highlights the smoggy regions and separates the sky and non-sky region. Thus, the estimation of airlight gives the desired result. But the computed image has various drawbacks such as low brightness, poor contrast and background noise. Various features such as CE and IE are extracted and implemented on the desmogged images computed using DCP. The convolution at each stage increases the computation time.

The enhanced image has overestimated transmission map, so, the output of first stage, i.e., DCP and second stage, i.e., feature enhancement is performed to compensate its effect. The SSIM and PSNR are calculated for the sample images. The results obtained using optimized DCP are compared with the existing desmogging techniques such as multilayer perceptron, optimal transmission map and adaptive atmospheric light, and ICAP. The overall results of proposed approach are better as compared to existing mentioned algorithms based on calculation of performance metrics. Also, the brightness is improved and visibility is restored for thin smoggy areas in clear scene radiance. But the computed image has color distortion and there is no such provision for dense smoggy areas because the smog gradients have condensed and region has become opaque.

ACKNOWLEDGMENT

This research is supported by the Council of Scientific and Industrial Research (CSIR), India. The sanction number of the scheme is 22(0801)/19/EMR-II.

REFERENCES

1. J. Bala, and K. Lakhwani, "Performance Evaluation of Various Desmogging Techniques for Single Smoggy Images", *Modern Physics Letters B*, Vol. 33, No. 5, 2019.
2. K. He, J. Sun, and X. Tang, "Single Image Haze Removal Using Dark Channel Prior", *IEEE Transactions on Pattern Analysis and Machine Intelligence*, Vol. 33, No. 12, pp. 2341–2353, 2011.
3. J. H. Kim, W. D. Jang, J. Y. Sim, and C. S. Kim, "Optimized Contrast Enhancement for Real-Time Image and Video Dehazing", *Journal of Visual Communication and* Image Representation, Vol. 24, No. 3, p. 410, 2013.
4. R. Fattal, "Dehazing Using Color-Lines", *ACM Transactions on Graphics (TOG)*, Vol. 34, No. 1, p. 13, 2014.
5. L. Wang, L. Xiao, and Z. Wei, "Image Dehazing Using Two-Dimensional Canonical Correlation Analysis", *IET Computer Vision*, Vol. 9, No. 6, p. 903, 2015.
6. W. Sun, H. Wang, C. Sun, B. Guo, W. Jia, and M. Sun, "Fast Single Image Haze Removal Via Local Atmospheric Light Veil Estimation", *Computers & Electrical Engineering*, Vol. 46, p. 371, 2015.
7. H. Zhao, C. Xiao, J. Yu, and X. Xu, "Single Image Fog Removal Based on Local Extrema", *IEEE/CAA Journal of Automatica Sinica*, Vol. 2, No. 2, pp. 158, 2015.
8. G. Ge, Z. Wei, and J. Zhao, "Fast Single-Image Dehazing Using Linear Transformation", *Optik*, Vol. 126, No. 21, p. 3245, 2015.

9. A. Kumari and S. K. Sahoo, "Fast Single Image and Video Deweathering Using Look-Up-Table Approach", *AEU - International Journal of Electronics and Communications*, Vol. 69, No. 12, p. 1773, 2015.

10. M. Ding and L. Wei, "Single-Image Haze Removal Using the Mean Vector L2-Norm of RGB Image Sample Window", *Optik*, Vol. 126, No. 23, p. 3522, 2015.

11. H. Singh, P. Kumar, and B. Raj, "Performance Analysis of Majority Gate SET Based 1-bit Full Adder", *International Journal of Computer and Communication Engineering (IJCCE)*, IACSIT Press Singapore, ISSN: 2010-3743, Vol. 2, No. 4, 2013.

12. A. K. Bhardwaj, S. Gupta, and B. Raj, "Investigation of Parameters for Schottky Barrier (SB) Height for Schottky Barrier Based Carbon Nanotube Field Effect Transistor Device", *Journal of Nanoelectronics and Optoelectronics*, ASP, Vol. 15, pp. 783–791, 2020.

13. P. Bansal, and B. Raj, "Memristor: A Versatile Nonlinear Model for Dopant Drift and Boundary Issues", *JCTN*, American Scientific Publishers, Vol. 14, No. 5, pp. 2319–2325, 2017.

14. N. Jain, and B. Raj, "An Analog and Digital Design Perspective Comprehensive Approach on Fin-FET (Fin-Field Effect Transistor) Technology - A Review", *Reviews in Advanced Sciences and Engineering (RASE)*, ASP, Vol. 5, pp. 1–14, 2016.

15. S. Sharma, B. Raj, and M. Khosla, "Subthreshold Performance of $In_{1-x}Ga_xAs$ Based Dual Metal with Gate Stack Cylindrical/Surrounding Gate Nanowire MOSFET for Low Power Analog Applications", *Journal of Nanoelectronics and Optoelectronics*, American Scientific Publishers, USA, Vol. 12, pp. 171–176, 2017.

16. B. Raj, A. K. Saxena, and S. Dasgupta, "Analytical Modeling for the Estimation of Leakage Current and Subthreshold Swing Factor of Nanoscale Double Gate FinFET Device" *Microelectronics International, UK*, Vol. 26, pp. 53–63, 2009.

17. S. S. Soniya, G. Wadhwa, and B. Raj, "An Analytical Modeling for Dual Source Vertical Tunnel Field Effect Transistor", *International Journal of Recent Technology and Engineering (IJRTE)*, Vol. 8, No. 2, pp. 1–8, 2019.

18. S. Singh, and B. Raj, "Design and Analysis of Heterojunction Vertical T-shaped Tunnel Field Effect Transistor", *Journal of Electronics Material*, Springer, Vol. 48, No. 10, pp. 6253–6260, 2019.

19. C. Goyal, J. S. Ubhi, and B. Raj, "A Low Leakage CNTFET Based Inexact Full Adder for Low Power Image Processing Applications", *International Journal of Circuit Theory and Applications*, Wiley, Vol. 47, No. 9, pp. 1446–1458, 2019.

20. B. Raj, A. K. Saxena, and S. Dasgupta, "A Compact Drain Current and Threshold Voltage Quantum Mechanical Analytical Modeling for FinFETs", *Journal of Nanoelectronics and Optoelectronics (JNO), USA*, Vol. 3, No. 2, pp. 163–170, 2008.

21. G. Wadhwa, and B. Raj, "An Analytical Modeling of Charge Plasma Based Tunnel Field Effect Transistor with Impacts of Gate Underlap Region", *Superlattices and Microstructures*, Elsevier, Vol. 142, pp. 106512, 2020.

22. S. Singh, and B. Raj, "Modeling and Simulation Analysis of SiGe Heterojunction Double Gate Vertical t-Shaped Tunnel FET", *Superlattices and Microstructures*, Elsevier Vol. 142, pp. 106496, 2020
23. A. Singh, D. K. Saini, D. Agarwal, S. Aggarwal, M. Khosla, and B. Raj, "Modeling and Simulation of Carbon Nanotube Field Effect Transistor and its Circuit Application", *Journal of Semiconductors (JoS)*, IOP Science, Vol. 37, pp. 074001–074006, 2016.
24. N. Jain, and B. Raj, "Device and Circuit Co-Design Perspective Comprehensive Approach on FinFET Technology - A Review", *Journal of Electron Devices*, Vol. 23, No. 1, pp. 1890–1901, 2016.
25. S. Kumar and B. Raj, "Analysis of I_{ON} and Ambipolar Current for Dual-Material Gate-Drain Overlapped DG-TFET", *Journal of Nanoelectronics and Optoelectronics*, American Scientific Publishers, USA, Vol. 11, pp. 323–333, 2016.
26. J. Singh, and B. Raj, "Enhanced Nonlinear Memristor Model Encapsulating Stochastic Dopant Drift", *JNO*, ASP, 14, 958–963, 2019.
27. N. Anjum, T. Bali, and B. Raj, "Design and Simulation of Handwritten Multiscript Character Recognition", *International Journal of Advanced Research in Computer and Communication Engineering*, Vol. 2, No. 7, pp. 2544–2549, 2013.
28. S. Sharma, B. Raj, and M. Khosla, "A Gaussian Approach for Analytical Subthreshold Current Model of Cylindrical Nanowire FET with Quantum Mechanical Effects", *Microelectronics Journal*, Elsevier, Vol. 53, pp. 65–72, 2016.
29. K. Singh, and B. Raj, "Performance and Analysis of Temperature Dependent Multi-Walled Carbon Nanotubes as Global Interconnects at Different Technology Nodes," *Journal of Computational Electronics*, Springer, Vol. 14, No. 2, pp. 469–476, 2015.
30. S. Kumar and B. Raj, "Compact Channel Potential Analytical Modeling of DG-TFET Based on Evanescent–Mode Approach", *Journal of Computational Electronics*, Springer, Vol. 14, No. 2, pp. 820–827, 2015.
31. K. Singh, and B. Raj, "Temperature Dependent Modeling and Performance Evaluation of Multi-Walled CNT and Single-Walled CNT as Global Interconnects", *Journal of Electronic Materials*, Springer, Vol. 44, No. 12, pp. 4825–4835, 2015.
32. V. K. Sharma, M. Pattanaik, and B. Raj, "INDEP Approach for Leakage Reduction in Nanoscale CMOS Circuits", *International Journal of Electronics*, Taylor & Francis, Vol. 102, No. 2, pp. 200–215, 2014.
33. K. Singh, and B. Raj, "Influence of Temperature on MWCNT Bundle, SWCNT Bundle and Copper Interconnects for Nanoscaled Technology Nodes", *Journal of Materials Science: Materials in Electronics*, Springer, Vol. 26, No. 8, pp. 6134–6142, 2015.
34. N. Anjum, T. Bali, and B. Raj, "Design and Simulation of Handwritten Gurumukhi and Devanagri Numerical Recognition", *International Journal of Computer Applications*, Published by Foundation of Computer Science, New York, USA, Vol. 73, No. 12, pp. 16–21, 2013.

35. S. Khandelwal, V. Gupta, B. Raj, and R. D. Gupta, "Process Variability Aware Low Leakage Reliable Nano Scale DG-FinFET SRAM Cell Design Technique", *Journal of Nanoelectronics and Optoelectronics*, Vol. 10, No. 6, pp. 810–817, 2015.

36. V. K. Sharma, M. Pattanaik, and B. Raj, "ONOFIC Approach: Low Power High Speed Nanoscale VLSI Circuits Design", *International Journal of Electronics*, Taylor & Francis, Vol. 101, No. 1, pp. 61–73, 2014.

37. S. Khandelwal, B. Raj, and R. D. Gupta, "FinFET Based 6T SRAM Cell Design: Analysis of Performance Metric, Process Variation and Temperature Effect", *Journal of Computational and Theoretical Nanoscience*, ASP, USA, Vol. 12, pp. 2500–2506, 2015.

38. S. Singh, Y. Shekhar, R. Jagdeep, S. Anurag, and B. Raj, "Impact of HfO$_2$ in Graded Channel Dual Insulator Double Gate MOSFET", *Journal of Computational and Theoretical Nanoscience*, American Scientific Publishers, Vol. 12, No. 6, pp. 950–953, 2015.

39. V. K. Sharma, M. Pattanaik, and B. Raj, "PVT Variations Aware Low Leakage INDEP Approach for Nanoscale CMOS Circuits", *Microelectronics Reliability*, Elsevier, Vol. 54, pp. 90–99, 2014.

40. B. Raj, A. K. Saxena and S. Dasgupta, "Quantum Mechanical Analytical Modeling of Nanoscale DG FinFET: Evaluation of Potential, Threshold Voltage and Source/Drain Resistance", *Elsevier's Journal of Material Science in Semiconductor Processing*, Elsevier, Vol. 16, No. 4, pp. 1131–1137, 2013.

41. M. Gopal, S. S. D. Prasad, and B. Raj, "8T SRAM Cell Design for Dynamic and Leakage Power Reduction", *International Journal of Computer Applications*, Published by Foundation of Computer Science, New York, USA, Vol. 71, No. 9, pp. 43–48, 2013.

42. M. Pattanaik, B. Raj, S. Sharma, and A. Kumar, "Diode Based Trimode Multi-Threshold CMOS Technique for Ground Bounce Noise Reduction in Static CMOS Adders", *Advanced Materials Research*, Trans Tech Publications, Switzerland, Vol. 548, pp. 885–889, 2012.

43. B. Raj, A. K. Saxena, and S. Dasgupta, "Nanoscale FinFET Based SRAM Cell Design: Analysis of Performance Metric, Process variation, Underlapped FinFET and Temperature effect", *IEEE Circuits and System Magazine*, Vol. 11, No. 2, pp. 38–50, 2011.

44. V. K. Sharma, M. Pattanaik, and B. Raj, "Leakage Current ONOFIC Approach for Deep Submicron VLSI Circuit Design", *International Journal of Electrical, Computer, Electronics and Communication Engineering*, World Academy of Sciences, Engineering and Technology, Vol. 7, No. 4, pp. 239–244, 2013.

45. T. Chawla, M. Khosla, and B. Raj, "Design and simulation of Triple metal Double-Gate Germanium on Insulator Vertical Tunnel Field Effect Transistor", *Microelectronics Journal*, Elsevier, Vol. 114, pp. 105125, 2021.

46. P. Kaur, S. S. Gill, and B. Raj, "Comparative Analysis of OFETs Materials and Devices for Sensor Applications", *Journal of Silicon*, Springer, Vol. 14, pp. 4463–4471, 2022

47. S. K. Sharma, P. Kumar, B. Raj, and B. Raj, "In$_{1-x}$Ga$_x$As Double Metal Gate-Stacking Cylindrical Nanowire MOSFET for Highly Sensitive Photo detector", *Journal of Silicon*, Springer, Vol. 14, pp. 3535–3541, 2022

48. B. Raj, A. K. Saxena, and S. Dasgupta, "Analytical Modeling of Quasi Planar Nanoscale Double Gate FinFET with Source/Drain Resistance and Field Dependent Carrier Mobility: A Quantum Mechanical Study", *Journal of Computer (JCP)*, Academy Publisher, FINLAND, Vol. 4, No. 9, pp. 1–7, 2009.

49. S. Bhushan, S. Khandelwal, and B. Raj, "Analyzing Different Mode FinFET Based Memory Cell at Different Power Supply for Leakage Reduction", Seventh International Conference on Bio-Inspired Computing: Theories and Application, (BIC-TA 2012), *Advances in Intelligent Systems and Computing*, Vol. 202, pp. 89–100, 2013.

50. J. Singh, and B. Raj, "Temperature Dependent Analytical Modeling and Simulations of Nanoscale Memristor", *Engineering Science and Technology, an International Journal*, Elsevier's, Vol. 21, pp. 862–868, 2018.

51. S. Singh, S. Bala, B. Raj, and B. Raj, "Improved Sensitivity of Dielectric Modulated Junctionless Transistor for Nanoscale Biosensor Design", *Sensor Letter*, ASP, Vol. 18, pp. 328–333, 2020.

52. V. Kumar, S. K. Vishvakarma, and B. Raj, "Design and Performance Analysis of ASIC for IoT Applications", *Sensor Letter*, ASP, Vol. 18, pp. 31–38, 2020.

53. A. Jaiswal, R. K. Sarin, B. Raj, and S. Sukhija, "A Novel Circular Slotted Microstrip-fed Patch Antenna with Three Triangle Shape Defected Ground Structure for Multiband Applications", *Advanced Electromagnetic (AEM)*, Vol. 7, No. 3, pp. 56–63, 2018.

54. G. Wadhwa, and B Raj, "Label Free Detection of Biomolecules Using Charge-Plasma-Based Gate Underlap Dielectric Modulated Junctionless TFET", *Journal of Electronic Materials (JEMS)*, Springer, Vol. 47, No. 8, pp. 4683–4693, 2018.

55. G. Singh, R. K. Sarin, and B. Raj, "Design and Performance Analysis of a New Efficient Coplanar Quantum-Dot Cellular Automata Adder", *Indian Journal of Pure & Applied Physics (IJPAP)*, Vol. 55, pp. 97–103, 2017.

56. A. Singh, M. Khosla, and B. Raj, "Design and Analysis of Electrostatic Doped Schottky Barrier CNTFET Based Low Power SRAM", *International Journal of Electronics and Communications, (AEÜ)*, Elsevier, Vol. 80, pp. 67–72, 2017.

57. P. Kaur, V. Pandey, and B. Raj, "Comparative Study of Efficient Design, Control and Monitoring of Solar Power using IoT", *Sensor Letter*, ASP, Vol. 18, pp. 419–426, 2020.

58. G. Wadhwa, P. Kamboj, J. Singh, B. Raj, "Design and Investigation of Junctionless DGTFET for Biological Molecule Recognition", *Transactions on Electrical and Electronic Materials*, Springer, Vol. 22, pp. 282–289, 2020.

59. T. Chawla, M. Khosla, and B. Raj, "Optimization of Double-Gate Dual Material GeOI-Vertical TFET for VLSI Circuit Design", *IEEE VLSI Circuits and Systems Letter*, Vol. 6, No. 2, pp. 13–25, 2020.

60. S. K. Verma, S. Singh, G. Wadhwa and B. Raj, "Detection of Biomolecules Using Charge-Plasma Based Gate Underlap Dielectric Modulated Dopingless TFET", *Transactions on Electrical and Electronic Materials (TEEM)*, Springer, Vol. 21, pp. 528–535, 2020.
61. N. Jain, and B. Raj, "Impact of Underlap Spacer Region Variation on Electrostatic and Analog/RF Performance of Symmetrical High-k SOI FinFET at 20 nm Channel Length", *Journal of Semiconductors (JoS)*, IOP Science, Vol. 38, No. 12, pp. 122002, 2017.
62. S. Singh, and B. Raj, "Analytical Modeling and Simulation Analysis of T-Shaped III-V Heterojunction Vertical T-FET", *Superlattices and Microstructures*, Elsevier, Vol. 147, pp. 106717, 2020.
63. G. Singh, R. K. Sarin, and B. Raj, "Design and Analysis of Area Efficient QCA Based Reversible Logic Gates", *Journal of Microprocessors and Microsystems*, Elsevier, Vol. 52, pp. 59–68, 2017.
64. A. Singh, M. Khosla, and B. Raj, "Compact Model for Ballistic Single Wall CNTFET under Quantum Capacitance Limit", *Journal of Semiconductors (JoS)*, IOP Science, Vol. 37, pp. 104001–104008, 2016.
65. S. Singh, M. Khosla, G. Wadhwa, and B. Raj, "Design and Analysis of Double-Gate Junctionless Vertical TFET for Gas Sensing Applications", *Applied Physics A*, Springer, Vol. 127, No. 16, pp. 1–6, 2021.
66. I. Singh, B. Raj, M. Khosla, and B. K. Kaushik, "Potential MRAM Technologies for Low Power SoCs", *SPIN World Scientific Publisher, SCIE*; Vol. 10, No. 04, p. 2050027, 2020.
67. S. Singh, and B. Raj, "Parametric Variation Analysis on Hetero-Junction Vertical t-Shape TFET for Suppressing Ambipolar Conduction", *Indian Journal of Pure and Applied Physics*, Vol. 58, pp. 478–485, 2020.
68. S. S. Soniya, G. Wadhwa, and B. Raj, "Design and Analysis of Dual Source Vertical Tunnel Field Effect Transistor for High Performance", *Transactions on Electrical and Electronics Materials*, Springer, Vol. 21, pp. 74–82, 2019.
69. M. Kaur, N. Gupta, S. Kumar, B. Raj, and A. K. Singh, "RF Performance Analysis of Intercalated Graphene Nanoribbon Based Global Level Interconnects", *Journal of Computational Electronics*, Springer, Vol. 19, pp. 1002–1013, 2020.
70. G. Wadhwa, and B. Raj, "Design and Performance Analysis of Junctionless TFET Biosensor for High Sensitivity", *IEEE Nanotechnology*, Vol. 18, pp. 567–574, 2019.

CHAPTER 6

Face Mask Detection Using Artificial Intelligence

Preetiyanka
J.C. Boss University (YMCA)

Balwant Raj
Panjab University SSG Regional Centre

Meenakshi Devi
University of Oxford Brookes

Balwinder Raj
National Institute of Technical Teachers Training and Research
Dr. B.R. Ambedkar National Institute of Technology

CONTENTS

DOI: 10.1201/9781003230113-6

6.1 INTRODUCTION

COVID-19 research demonstrates that a threefold increase in the likelihood of preventing an outbreak in a community happens for every 10% increase in mask wear, while other techniques, such as social distancing, are not nearly as effective [1–5]. As a result, mandating the usage of a face mask is critical. The majority of states in the US have passed legislation requiring the wearing of masks in public. Implementing the mandate only through human force is not only time consuming owing to the required level of focus, but it is also dangerous due to the heightened danger to the enforcer. A face mask detection algorithm makes it feasible to tell whether or not someone is wearing a mask. There are many benefits to using an automatic face mask detector. There are many diverse uses for the face mask detector [6–10]. In sensitive regions where masking is illegal, face mask detection can be used to identify a masked subject in surveillance footage. There is a lot of interest in face mask detection because of the wide range of applications it has. Masks can be detected using the Haar cascade classifier (HCC). Using the simple Haar cascade technique and three additional weak classifiers, these researchers came up with a new solution. For efficient and high-performance human detection, a range of occluding and illuminating techniques, as well as rotations, are employed. Face and eye identification using HCCs has been established with high accuracy [11–14]. Face masks are becoming increasingly common in public as the number of COVID-19 infections increases around the world. Most people don't use a face mask to safeguard their health from air pollution, but rather to keep their emotions disguised from those around them who might be tempted to examine their current actions, as recently discovered in a survey. When it comes to preventing the transmission of the corona virus, face masks are becoming increasingly mandatory [15–18]. An international pandemic was declared in 2020 after some COVID fatalities spread rapidly, resulting in a huge number of deaths. More than 6 million new cases have been recorded in 180 countries in the last 10 days alone. It is more likely that you will contract this virus from someone near to you if you are in a crowded area or a closed room. Wearing a face mask is becoming increasingly vital to halt spreading the disease. Wearing a face mask when out in public has increased as a result of the global outbreak of COVID-19. Residents of COVID-19 refuse to wear masks in order to avoid exposure to air pollution. To achieve a more subdued image, many choose to mask their feelings through their facial expressions. According to one person's theory, wearing a face mask might help decrease the transmission of the COVID-19 virus. COVID-19 has emerged as a serious threat to human health in the 21st century. The WHO has declared COVID-19 a worldwide pandemic because to its rapid spread. COVID-19 expanded to more than 5 million users in 188 countries in less than 6 months. The virus spreads through intimate contact in heavily crowded places. There has never been a better opportunity for worldwide collaboration in science than since the corona virus pandemic. Combating COVID-19 will need the use of machine learning (ML) and deep learning techniques. ML techniques may be used to build pandemic early warning systems and a classification system for people who are more sensitive to the disease than the rest of the population. In many nations, the wearing of face masks in public is a popular practice. Rules and regulations are frequently enacted to keep pace with an increasing number of events and fatalities in a wide variety of sectors of endeavour. Consequently, it is difficult to identify those who wear masks. "No entrance with no mask" has been implemented in numerous nations due to the outbreak of a coronavirus infection. The identification of COVID-19 face masks is critical for security reasons. The usage of masks by medical workers reduces the danger of infection from an infected individual, even if they don't exhibit any symptoms of their own illness [19–23]. In addition to airports and hospitals, schools and workplaces also utilize face mask detection. It is more difficult to identify a person's face if they are wearing a mask because it is more difficult to extract masked facial traits than ordinary facial characteristics. For now, you'll have to use your imagination to fill in the blanks.

Using this method, mask-wearing categorization predictions can be made in milliseconds. Similar research on face mask recognition has been performed to recognize masked faces from all the other faces for security or perhaps anti-terrorist purposes. However, the design rationale for medical face mask detection is the same for all types of false negatives. Using the proposed technology, it will be possible to detect whether or not people are following safety regulations automatically. A thorough examination of many deep learning algorithms is done in order to track the evolution of disease using medical imaging. A new study based on temperature sensors, face mask recognition, and social distance suggests the use of Internet of Things (IoT)-based COVID-19. Computer vision algorithms on the Raspberry Pi handle mask identification and social separation, while Arduino Uno handles infrared temperature monitoring. In this chapter, we describe a novel mask identification approach that uses face detection and picture super-resolution. Accurate identification of people wearing masks is the algorithm's forte. As long as there is sufficient light, these models can be utilized. The new technique is both more efficient and more accurate than the previous one. Automatic quantification of mask identification and social distance in real time is achieved using a computer vision-based deep learning technique. A wide range of jobs may be simulated with Pi models. The spread of COVID-19 is considerably minimized if this technique is followed. COVID-19 may be identified using an IoT-based deep learning system. Using the approach described, an X-ray of the chest is used to detect a pandemic. The accuracy of the COVID-19 identification using computational intelligence and neuroscience has been demonstrated, and this has been extremely useful to medical professionals [24–30]. Open-source computer vision techniques are proposed in this chapter to identify veiled individuals. This strategy has proven to be successful in industrial settings. In this section, we'll discuss how IoT and sensors can be used to track out and battle the infection. Electronic health services for COVID-19 management and IoT networks in a post-pandemic context are studied in this research. In addition, the methodologies for detecting COVID-19 are described in detail. This review also discusses the challenges that may arise in the future when using these technologies. IoT-powered wearable sensors, In vitro diagnostics (IVDs), and deep

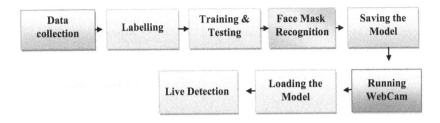

FIGURE 6.1   Model architecture for face mask detection.

learning involving X-rays are just some of the technologies featured in the report. The fine condition of the regions with convolutional neural networks (R-CNN) and particular area recommendation criteria can be used to detect a mask-wearing face. Extraordinary skills are put to use through unconventional means. It is extremely accurate with R-context CNN. Each feature is extracted using the K-Nearest Neighbour approach, which has a high accuracy in precision and recall. A real-time system has been evaluated using the generic detection idea. This systemic can be improved by adding more parameters, despite the fact that it requires a long time to run. The researchers also reported a computationally simplified but still powerful deep learning-based face mask detector. Feature extraction has been improved through regression modules. Recently, a number of deep learning-based techniques for mask identification have emerged. Convolutional models based on automated recognition are used to quickly and accurately detect and extract facial features when operating in low-light conditions. IoT-based models can be augmented by systems based on super-resolution image processing. Convolution, automatic facial recognition, and computer vision all work together to fill in any gaps that may exist in current facial recognition systems. In the suggested approach, COVID-19's negative impacts are mitigated by utilizing R-CNNs [1, 31–36]. The model architecture for face mask detection is given in Figure 6.1.

6.2 TECHNIQUES FOR FACE MASK DETECTION

A deep neural network (DNN) is one that uses CNNs, which take their inspiration from biological processes (CNNs). Back-propagation is the approach employed by CNNs to learn the spatial patterns of input independently and fluidly, and it is made of different components, including a convolution layer, a pooling layer, and eventually a fully connected layer. Each image position has a unique set of CNN kernels, making it an extremely parameter-efficient algorithm. Because of these characteristics,

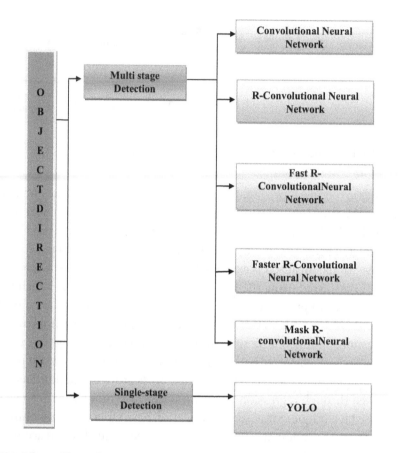

FIGURE 6.2   Object detection.

the CNN is an excellent choice for computer vision problems. Because of significant advances in Graphics processing unit (GPU) computer power, deep learning technologies have taken off in recent years. It appears that object recognition is a major focus of computer vision research. Figure 6.2 depicts the current object detection methods in accordance with the recommended recommendations and improvement tactics [37–43].

6.2.1 Multi-Stage Detectors

After creating an enormous number of region recommendations for each image using heuristic algorithms like CNN, the two-stage method classifies and slows down these eligible provinces. Deep learning was used to detect the first object. Figure 6.3 depicts the retinal face detection model architecture. Detection of the masked face goes through a number of steps, as illustrated in Figure 6.3.

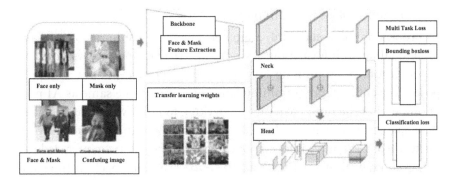

FIGURE 6.3 Architecture of retina facemask.

6.3 ARTIFICIAL INTELLIGENCE (AI)

John McCarthy created the term "artificial intelligence" in 1956. This is "the science and engineering of creating intelligent devices", he said. AI is a branch of computer science that focuses on the development of intelligent agents that are capable of recognizing and responding to their environment in order to maximize their chances of success. Alan Turing, a mathematician, presented the question of whether or not computers may reason and learn on their own in the same manner that people do [44–51]. To see if "machines can think", Alan Turing put his theories and assumptions to the test. After a long series of investigations, robots can attain thinking and learning similar to humans (later known as the Turing Test, a method to test if robots can answer questions in the same way as humans). As a result, one definition of AI is "the ability to simultaneously hold two different thoughts in mind while still remaining functional". However, for AI to be useful, it needs to be able to draw conclusions quickly, learn from past mistakes, and use logic to make decisions. Also, it must be able to prioritize and deal with ambiguity and complexity. AI is a hot issue right now, and we are going to focus on it in this section. Here are some of the most crucial components of AI that will help us better comprehend AI and how it can help us defend ourselves from the impending technological trend. Some AI algorithms will also be discussed in this chapter. Machines using AI may execute tasks that would otherwise need human intellect. Symbolic inference, or reasoning in the machine, is the scientific goal of AI, which aims to construct computer programs that display intelligent behaviour. An AI definition is not time-independent. A straightforward approach to measure a system's efficiency is to check how long it takes to execute a set of predetermined operations [52–57].

6.3.1 Features of AI Programming

In Brook's opinion, standard computer languages are incapable of handling qualitative information. As a result, AI machines are designed to use a custom programming language they've created just for this purpose. Conventional programming languages are not the same as AI programmes. For the most part, they are written to modify qualitative rather than quantitative data. Rather of relying on algorithmic context, they make use of declarative information. They have the ability to infer, deduce, and even guess at data. They have the option of going back in time and rethinking their decisions [58–63].

6.3.2 Components of AI

AI has four main components:
   a. "Expert systems or knowledge-based systems"
   b. "Using heuristics to solve problems"
   c. "Natural Language Processing"
   d. "Vision"

Even though they were managed by experts, expert systems (ES) offer outcomes in instances where they are applicable. Heuristic problem resolution may need some educated judgement in order to arrive at a close approximation to the best answer [64–70]. Because of the use of natural language processing (NLP), human–robot communication is now possible. The human visual system comprises a built-in capacity to detect shapes, features, and other components of the visual environment.

6.4 EXPERT SYSTEM

ES that mix human and machine knowledge may make a wide range of intelligent recommendations, explanations, and arguments. An ES relies on a vast library of well-defined specific knowledge on a given field. The process of producing these programmes is called as "Knowledge Engineering" in this company [71–76]. Algorithms having expert-level expertise in handling issues in particular job domains by using knowledge are known as knowledge-based systems or ES. Instead of depending only on textbooks, this system's data are produced from real-world experience. A crucial aspect of these "expert" systems is that they are able to make suggestions to users who are not as well versed in their respective professions as the experts themselves. The amount of time it takes for this knowledge to be transferred varies depending on the work at hand. An ES is far easier to develop than one that relies solely on common sense. A task domain is represented by them. An action that is goal-oriented and problem-solving is referred to as a task, and the domain is the area where the activity is taking place. In the early days of symbolic mathematics, one of the earliest ES consisted of a loosely coupled collection of list processing (LISP) functions. In order to train people in various areas of expertise, such as design and troubleshooting, several different ES have been developed. ES are still in the developmental stages [77,82].

6.4.1 Benefits of Expert Systems

The following are the benefits of expert system:

a. "Expert systems have demonstrated to do a better job than individuals. They are less prone to blunders and more trustworthy in their advise".
b. "Artificial Knowledge is typically cheaper compared to human expertise".
c. "Training non-experts and even boosting the comprehension of specialists was a big triumph for them".
d. "They may manage the mechanical kind of repetitive tasks of specialists, so that professionals may correctly concentrate on their distinctive skills in the subject".
e. "Many managers' decision-making processes can accommodate them".
f. "This group has the power to condone actions that are cruel to other people".
g. "They boost the productivity of industry" [2, 83–88].

6.5 CONVOLUTIONAL NEURAL NETWORK

Low processing costs and the ability to extract spatial information make CNNs essential for pattern identification applications. CNN performs convolution sections on the input photos in order to exclude the most evident components from the input images. The study strategy uses Deep Learning, OpenCV, TensorFlow, and Keras to aid in the detection of masks on faces. This method helps to ensure everyone's safety [89–94]. This method of authentic mask identification uses the MobileNetV2 and CNN framework as a classifier and can be implemented in embedded devices because it is small, lightweight, and only has a few parameters. Face recognition, face patterns, and facial characteristics for detection algorithms can all benefit from the data because it was gathered from a variety of sources. Prathmes, you might think about creating a detection system for digital healthcare face masks. OpenCV can be used to access the live video stream and to perform image pre-processing on the captured images. In order to detect faces, Haar cascade will be used, which is a highly effective method. As shown in Figure 6.4, the system's design functions automatically to prevent COVID-19 from expanding. As a result of this research, facial features can be recognized and the person's mask usage can be determined. Facial mask detection and transmission rate reduction are both made possible by the system. Receptionists and doctors have limited access to digital tools under the system [3].

Until vaccines can be developed, wearing a mask and avoiding close contact with others are essential methods for limiting the spread of disease, according to the World Health Organization. As a result, it is imperative that people be made to wear masks in public. Detecting and alerting those who are not wearing a face mask can be a challenge in densely populated areas. As a result, image processing techniques are being used to identify people wearing facemasks and those who aren't. Raspberry Pi embedded development kit collects images from the camera in real time and processes them. Wearing or not wearing a mask is detected using real-time camera images compared to the trained dataset. ML is used to create the training dataset, which is the deciding factor in the outcome. Using a trained dataset, an algorithm will be able to distinguish between people who are wearing face masks and those who are not [4].

i. Face detection

Preliminary face detection ensures that a face and its landmarks are present in the image before face recognition can proceed. In computer vision, a face detection system is a method for determining the human face in any given image [95–98]. Face localization is the process of locating the facial features in a digital image, and ignoring any other objects in the image. Face detection can be accomplished in a variety of ways, including template matching for face detection and localization, feature invariant approaches for feature detection, and appearance-based methods like Eigen face, neural networks, and information theory. These methods all rely on calculating the relationship between an input image and a model face pattern. The technique's collective application, on the other hand, remains a big question mark. Colour segmentation based on skin colour detection and facial parts detection is used in the proposed work to identify faces in images.

ii. Feature Extraction

Detection of faces is an ever-evolving field that is constantly improving itself by utilizing various facial characteristics. Face-extracting algorithms have been developed over the course of this technology's evolution, and they fall into three broad categories: features, appearance, and template-based templates. Identifying the face region, estimating the costs, and compiling the attributes each have their own advantages and disadvantages. In order for any of the alternatives to work, they all require a relatively simple model that does not currently exist.

It is possible to locate and extract face components (eyes, nose, mouth, etc.) from photos of real people using feature-based facial image retrieval. Face tracking, face recognition, and face recognition identification are just a few of the many face processing methods that rely on this initial step. Major feature extraction techniques are presented in Figure 6.4.

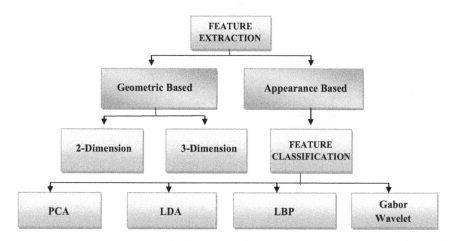

FIGURE 6.4   Major feature extraction techniques.

6.5.1 Image Classification and Recognition

This step is used to classify an image based on the features extracted from the input image and determine whether or not the saved database recognizes the input image. Neural networks are used as a classifier "to extract features from the input image and" use them as a basis for classification.

a. Image Recognition

Face images should be recognized under a variety of lighting and expression conditions, so the recognition method should be capable of doing so. Pattern recognition researchers face a significant challenge when trying to identify human faces. Particularly, the structure of the human face is nearly identical, with only minor variations among individuals [99–102].

In reality, they are restricted to a single category of human face. In addition, changes in lighting conditions, facial expressions, and body positions make face recognition more difficult. In order to match the images before recognition, image classification is performed. Normalization of the face and compensation for lighting Image Extracting Feature Sets from a Face Matching of Facial Feature Locations Images Submitted to the Enrolment Database Identification of a face using a standard classifier and a feature vector. Various steps have been identified to complete this process in accordance with the concept given in Figure 6.5.

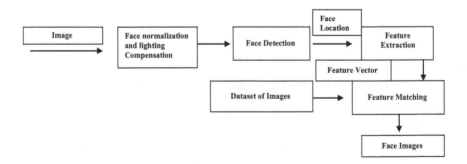

FIGURE 6.5 Image classification and identification steps.

b. Face Recognition

In reality, they are restricted to a single category of human face. In addition, changes in lighting conditions, facial expressions, and body positions make face recognition more difficult. In order to match the images before recognition, image classification is performed. Normalization of the face and compensation for lighting Image Extracting Feature Sets from a Face Matching of Facial Feature Locations Images Submitted to the Enrolment Database Identification of a face using a standard classifier and a feature vector. Various steps have been identified to complete this process in accordance with the concept shown in Figure 6.6.

Feature-oriented methods use face images to find the right features for face recognition. Curvature, descriptive statistics, and analogous face components are all considered for face recognition. In the holistic approach to face recognition, the entire face is selected as an input. There are a number of methods in this category such as Eigen faces, Fisher faces, and support vector machine-based methods. Combination of these two approaches is another option [103–106]. Facial images and local features are combined in this

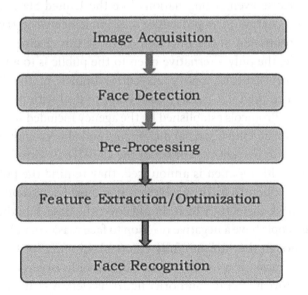

FIGURE 6.6   Steps of face recognition system applications.

class of procedures for face recognition. When it comes to recognizing faces, an image recognition system that has been trained to think like a human is more intelligent. Human intelligence is taken into account and incorporated into the proposed work by using a neural network that incorporates human characteristics. Two types of facial recognition exist: verification (or authentication) and identification (or re-identification) (or recognition). One-to-one comparison is used to match a topic image with an authentic template image when performing template matching or authentication. Face identification and authentication use one-to-many matching to compare an input face photo against all of the template faces in order to identify the output photo. Because of Canada's first automated face recognition system, the efficiency of face recognition systems has greatly improved. It is now possible to perform real-time face recognition for photographs taken in limited lighting [5].

Suddenly, the world grinds to a halt. Lockdowns in numerous nations have been implemented as a precaution against this deadly illness. People were ordered to stay indoors and not leave their homes. If you're reading this, you've already been exposed to the deadly COVID-19 virus, which is spreading at an ever-increasing rate because even strong nations like the United States and Japan couldn't contain it. A procedure was implemented to try and slow the transmission of the infection. Because the vaccine is no longer available, the only alternative open to the public is to adhere to the government's health policy. Executive branch of the Philippines established the Inter-Agency Task Force to deal with new infectious illnesses. Protocols established by the agency included wearing a face mask and face shield, social distancing, and always sanitizing hands "in order to prevent the spread of the COVID-19 virus". Every time a new health regimen is announced, they remind the public to follow and adhere to it. The problem is that most people don't apply the facial mask correctly, which should cover the nose, mouth, and chin. Some people have a negative reaction to face masks in public settings, even though they are carefully enforced. In order for them to wear the face mask, it must be ordered by an authority figure, and they will remove it after the authority figure has left. A virus can enter the nose, eyes, or mouth of a person who wears a face mask incorrectly. The goal of this research is to assess whether or not a person is sufficiently defending themselves from the COVID-19 virus by utilizing a face mask. In order to ensure that face masks are being used correctly, extensive testing will be carried out [6].

Analytical model development, often known as data analysis, is automated by ML. A subset of AI, which is built on preprocessed data that systems may learn from and identify patterns based on previous data, this technology makes prior decisions with minimal human participation. To explore if computers can learn without being taught for specific activities, researchers turned to pattern recognition and the hypothesis that computers may quickly learn without having to be programmed to accomplish some specific jobs. The iterative nature of ML is critical because it allows models to adjust to new data on their own. Some variables that have made Bayesian Analysis and data mining more popular than ever have sparked a surge in interest in ML. The most powerful and cost-effective forms of computational processing, data, and data storage are all available. Finance, retail, healthcare, oil and gas, and transportation are among the many industries that make heavy use of ML. Eventually, the accuracy of the output data will improve due to the system's ability to predict and evaluate data in succeeding steps.

6.6 DEEP LEARNING

In other words, it's a form of education that mimics the structure and functioning of the human brain. It is also known as a subset of ML, which is one of the most prominent technologies at the moment. When compared to the human brain because of the presence of neural networks in the working process, this is known as artificial neural networks (ANNs). Most of the time, it doesn't require any human involvement, and it can even function with datasets that aren't labelled or structured at all. The entire training procedure for ML algorithms is carried out using a hierarchical standard of ANNs. The primary neuron nodes of ANNs are linked together in a spider web-like pattern, mimicking the structure of the human brain. Deep learning makes use of three different types of neural networks [7].

It's difficult to pin down exactly what constitutes learning or intelligence because they encompass such a wide range of activities. "To gain knowledge or understanding of, or skill in, via study, instruction, or experience", and "modification of a behavioural propensity through experience" are among the definitions provided by the dictionary. Animal and human learning is the focus of the work of zoologists and psychologists.

In this chapter, we concentrate on how computers learn. Animal learning and ML share a number of similarities [107–110]. To be sure, psychologists' efforts to use computer models to refine beliefs about animal and human learning have had a significant influence on many ML techniques. ML concepts and approaches may potentially shed light on aspects of biological learning, according to some experts. A computer is considered to be learning when it makes changes to its code, data, or structure to better its expected future performance. This is a general definition of what it means to learn. A database entry, for example, is under the scope of other disciplines and is not always better understood for being labelled learning. After hearing a speech sample a few times, the machine's capacity to consistently distinguish it rises; thus, we may assume that the system has trained. The evolution of computer systems executing AI-related operations is typically referred to as "machine learning" (AI). This type of work involves a variety of skills, including as pattern identification, diagnostics, planning, robot control, and prediction, for example. It's possible that the "changes" be improvements to currently functioning systems or the creation of entirely new ones from scratch. This agent is able to perceive and model its surroundings, and then decide on the best course of action based on what it knows about the consequences of its actions. Learning may occur if any of the components depicted in the figure are modified. Depending on which subsystem is being altered, different learning processes may be used. In this chapter, we'll take a look at a number of various approaches to education.

6.6.1 Supervised Machine Learning

The input–output connection of a system may be studied using supervised learning, a ML methodology that employs paired input–output training instances. A sample of training data can be used to label an input dataset; hence, it can be referred to as "labelled training datasets" or "supervised training datasets". Learning from Labelled Data or Inductive Machine Learning is some names for this method, the objective of supervised learning is to create an artificial system that can learn the link between inputs and outputs and anticipate the system's result given fresh data. Using a learned mapping, data may be categorized if the output values represent the input class labels. Although output values do not change, input regression rises. Inputs and outputs are commonly explained by learning-model parameters. An estimate approach is needed for training samples learning system do have not clearly disclosed these qualities. Supervised learning training data requires supervised or labelled information, but unsupervised training data does not (i.e., simply the inputs) because of the difference between supervised and unsupervised learning (i.e., merely the inputs). Learning strategies are developed using data from both supervised and unstructured sources. As the training progresses, an algorithm will ask a user or an instructor for a label at different times [8].

6.6.2 Unsupervised Machine Learning

When it comes to unsupervised learning, it's the same. For so-called unsupervised learning, the machine doesn't mark the content in a specific direction throughout the learning process but relies on the machine itself to finish analysis of information data. It is more practical to let the computer pick up simple concepts and content on its own before giving it more freedom to acquire more complex concepts and content, such as tree roots for example. Overall, ML content has become more diverse as a result of staged progress. Deep belief networks and auto encoders are examples of current unsupervised learning methods. Such conditions are favourable for resolving clustering issues and are useful in the growth of numerous industries.

6.6.3 Reinforcement Machine Learning

Reinforcement learning may be utilized in ML applications in addition to supervised and unsupervised learning. The systematic acquisition of knowledge is known as "reinforcement learning". The data gathered in the previous period will be used in the specific application procedure. A closed data processing loop is created by organizing and processing the feedback information from a specific component. Reinforcement learning, on the whole, is a form of learning that uses statistics and dynamic learning to expand data collecting. Robot control is the primary application of these techniques.

The Q-learning algorithm and the temporal difference learning algorithm are two of its most representative learning methods [9].

A major distinction between supervised learning and "unsupervised learning" is that the latter focuses on the discovery of structure in large datasets that have not been labelled. Learning that is reinforced despite their appearance, ML paradigms do not easily fit into either supervised or unsupervised categories. Reinforcement learning can be seen of as an unsupervised approach because it doesn't rely on examples of good conduct, but it attempts to maximize a reward signal rather than search for a hidden pattern. In order to maximize a reward signal, reinforcement learning can benefit from revealing structure in an agent's experience, but this alone is not enough. There are several different ways to teach a computer to learn, and we consider reinforcement learning to be one of them. An interesting trade-off exists in reinforcement learning: between exploration and exploitation. In order to gain a high quantity of reward, reinforcement learning agents must choose tasks that they have previously done and demonstrated to be effective. However, in order to discover these activities, it must first try out new things. Exploration is required in order for the agent to enhance future action options as well as to apply what it now knows to receive a reward. Without a failure, neither exploration nor exploitation can be undertaken in a vacuum. The agent must test a wide range of choices and select the ones that appear to be most effective. A lot of trial-and-error is required to get a decent sense of how each action will affect the outcome. The exploration–exploitation conundrum has been studied by mathematicians for decades. Instead, let's note that the purest forms of supervised and unsupervised learning don't even attempt to strike a balance between exploration and exploitation in the learning process [10].

6.7 ARTIFICIAL NEURAL NETWORKS

AI is a branch of computer science that deals with algorithms that can learn over time. ML algorithms may classify emails as spam or not spam by looking at the user's behaviour. "AI converts data into knowledge" is another typical definition. While AI refers to the ability of a machine to learn, ML is an algorithmic technique to achieving that intelligence. Supervised and unsupervised algorithms for ML are the two main classifications. Unsupervised algorithms do not need tagged datasets, whereas supervised algorithms must. Classification and regression are two of the most common supervised learning problems. When doing a classification job, the input is assigned a category, but when performing a regression work, the input is mapped to a real-valued outputting dataset. Deep learning is another algorithmic method to AI. Machine learning, in turn, may be described as a subset of AI because this method is used to implement ML. The depth of a neural network is what is meant by the term "deep". It was feasible to train incredibly DNNs because of advances in algorithms, computer power, and imaging technologies. Because deep learning algorithms do not require manual feature engineering, they are superior than ML methods. Unlike ML algorithms, deep learning algorithms are able

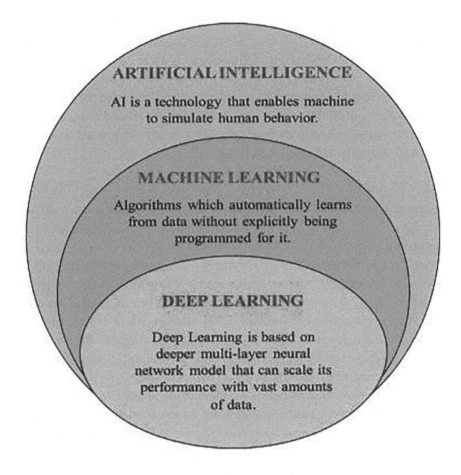

FIGURE 6.7   Relationship between artificial intelligence, ML, and deep learning.

to grow with the amount of data, but ML algorithms tend to saturate. A subset of AI known as machine learning and a subset of deep learning are both subsets of AI [11] (Figure 6.7).

Outside of the ANN system, the input layer will be used to receive data. To the next layer, every neuron in this input layer is connected (hidden layer). "The input layer comprises of a number" of neurons and the hidden layer receives data from these neurons. As a result, neurons in the output layer will receive the information from "the neurons in this hidden layer. The purpose of the hidden layer" is to make the network more powerful, making it easier for people to execute their duties. Without hidden layers, ANN's capabilities are severely constrained. One or more layers may be hidden beneath the surface. Each layer has a fixed number of neurons. When it came to the optimal number of neurons and hidden layers in ANNs, there was no recognized formula. For a long time, users of ANNs couldn't tell how many layers and neurons were concealed in the system (ANN). ANN architecture's ideal number of hidden layers and neurons will be discussed in this research, according to the author. To conduct this research, researchers looked at examples of the letter patterns A–E and the pattern identification of geometric shapes (such as triangles, squares, and circles) [12].

6.8 EVOLUTION OF CONVOLUTIONAL NEURAL NETWORKS

Like more traditional neural networks like ANNs, CNNs also learn as they go along. Each neuron will do an action because of a scalar product and a non-linear function (such as non-linear function). In order to arrive at a final grade, the network's nodes all apply the same perceptual scoring formula (the weight). For the last layer, ANN-specific loss functions are required. When it comes to pattern identification in images, there is only one major distinction between the CNN and the ANN: CNNs are predominantly employed in this area. For image-focused jobs, this allows us to embed image-specific properties into our architecture, minimizing the number of parameters needed to set up the model [13].

ML has the potential to reduce human labour by allowing machines to learn from their own mistakes and previous experiences in one of three ways: learning under supervision, learning without supervision, or learning with some degree of monitoring. Feature extraction is a precondition for conventional ML approaches, which necessitates the assistance of a domain expert. Aside from that, picking the right features for a certain challenge is a difficult task. As a result, deep learning approaches avoid the difficulty of feature selection by automatically identifying the most important features from raw data for a given situation. A deep learning model is made up of a number of processing layers, each of which is capable of learning different aspects of the data it is fed. As the network progresses through its tiers, it is able to pick up new features. With regard to image and audio identification, subject classification or sentiment analysis, translation and interpretation of non-verbal communication, as well as NLP, deep learning has shown great promise for a variety of applications. Deep learning designs include CNNs, convolutional belief networks, and a variety of other types of networks. For generalization, convent is better than networks with all levels linked because of its deep feed-forward architecture. describes CNN as the concept of hierarchical feature detectors derived from biological principles. With a vast range of abstract qualities, our machine can easily learn and recognize them all. The following are some of the advantages CNN has over more traditional models. As a result of reducing the number of factors that need to be memorized, the idea of weight sharing improves generalization. Because there are fewer parameters in CNN, overfitting is not an issue. Both feature extraction and classification are accomplished through the use of a learning strategy. ANNs are far more difficult to employ than CNNs to develop large networks. Car detection, diabetic retinopathy, as well as other facial expressions can all benefit from CNNs. CNN has long been a topic of interest, and this study's goal is to expand our knowledge and comprehension of it. These findings aim to provide a comprehensive overview of the fundamental principles behind CNNs, together with information on the general model and the three most frequent designs and ML techniques. ADAM, a revolutionary method of learning proposed by, has also been explained in detail. In addition, it calculates the learning rate for each parameter. The sections are organized as follows. It serves as an introduction and a statement of intent for the research being conducted. All of CNN's fundamental themes are explained in detail here. It introduces a number of different CNN designs. It shows how the algorithm for learning works [14].

6.8.1 CNN Architecture

Images are the primary kind of input for CNNs, and this is why they are so popular. Focusing the architecture on a certain type of data sets the stage for the greatest possible solution. A CNN's layers are distinguished by their three-dimensional character from the network's overall neurons. The activation volume, the number of ANN layers, and the depth of an ANN are the only three factors. The neurons in each layer are only connected to a tiny section of each layer before it is completed, which varies from ordinary ANNs [15].

All CNN architectures feature convolution and pooling (or sub sampling) layers that are organized into modules, regardless of their structure or size. One or more fully linked layers follow these modules, much like a regular feed-forward neural network would [111–113]. It is a common practice to stack modules on top of one another while building a deep model. An image is sent immediately to the network, "where it is subjected to several rounds of convolution and pooling. Afterward, the outcomes of these operations are fed into one or more layers that are fully interconnected". Layers above the output layer feed information into this layer's neuronal processor, which then uses that information to perform computations and produce an output. Despite the fact that this is the most often used base architecture, a number of design modifications have been proposed in recent years in an effort to improve the accuracy of image categorization while also reducing computation costs.

In the field of deep learning, these neural networks serve a critical role in image and video processing projects, as well as in other applications. Building blocks of these NN are kernel filters; these kernels extract features from the input data utilizing the convolution operation as the primary method of extraction for these NNs. For the most part, CNN is useful since it automatically applies NN filters without explicitly stating that they are doing so, and because it assists in extracting the most useful features from the input data [16].

6.8.2 Deep Learning Using Convolutional Neural Network for Computer Vision

CNNs presented in Figure 6.8 are a type of deep learning model that is used to analyse visual input. Some refer to it as a "convolutionary neural network" instead. An additional name for these ANNs is shift-invariant ANNs or space-invariant ANNs because of its shared-weights design and translation invariance properties. Algorithms may be used to construct recommendation systems, classify pictures, perform medical image analysis, and evaluate the intelligibility of language in order to recognize photographs and videos. In the next section, CNN's architecture and components, as well as how pictures are processed, are addressed. CNN's

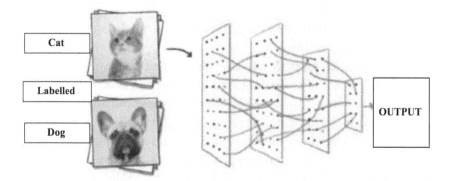

FIGURE 6.8   Convolutional neural networks.

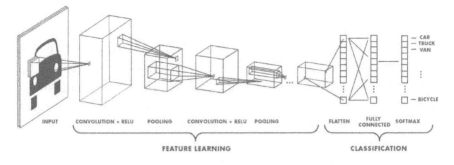

FIGURE 6.9   Architecture of a CNN.

viewers benefit from CNN's ability to analyse images and data in order to achieve their goals (Figure 6.9).

6.8.3 Basic CNN Components

i. "Convolutional Layer"

It's a "convolutional neural network", or CNN, which is built for two-dimensional image input, but it can also be utilized for one-dimensional and three-dimensional data as well. A channel is used to carry out the convolution process (a small matrix whose size may be chosen). In order to accurately duplicate an image's properties over the whole picture network, the original pixel values are needed. When all the increases are totalled together at the end of the process, the result is a single number. The channel advances rightward by n units while performing a comparison action (this number may vary). An information grid that was previously generated is reduced in size by travelling over each location in its entirety.

ii. "Pooling Layer"

Simplifying a map's dimensionality while yet keeping the most important information is possible using spatial pooling (also known as subsampling or down-sampling). There are many ways in which spatial pooling can occur: The expressions maximum, average, and total are all examples of quantifiers. The largest component from the redressed highlight map within a defined spatial neighbour-hood is selected when Max Pooling happens. For example, instead of picking just the most significant component, we could select the average (Average Pooling) or the total of all components included in the window. The effectiveness of Max Pooling has grown over time [8]. Using the example described below, Max Pooling selects the largest component from the corrected feature map. In the standard pooling method, selecting the largest component is the same as selecting the largest component. The term "sum pooling" describes the process of collecting all of the elements in an element map into one location. Before convolution, it is important to add a pooling (subsampling) layer in CNN, following the feature maps. In order to reduce the size of the convolution feature, the pooling layer is responsible for doing just that. As a result of the reduction in dimensionality, less processing power is required on the computers. To retain the model's practical training, it helps to extract leading features that are invariant to position and rotation. To save time and avoid overtraining, groups train together. To achieve the best results, a pool must use both the maximum and the average amount of resources.

iii. "Fully Connected Layer"

It is only possible to create a feed-forward neural network by using a totally linked layer. At the bottom of the network, there are layers that are completely connected. The output layer of the final pooling or convolutional layer is provided as input to a fully connected layer, which is flattened before it is received as input. Convolutional and pooling layers are unwound into a single vector, and then the output is flattened out (3D matrix). Neurons in the two layers above and below the "fully connected" layer are directly linked to each other, not connected to anything else. Normal AN models use the same arrangement of neuronal cells [17].

6.8.4 Applications of Deep Learning

This section describes the foundation of this review by discussing several of fields that have been applied with deep learning algorithm.

6.8.4.1 Automatic Speech Recognition (ASR)

For the first time in 2012, Google voice search took a new direction by using DNN to represent the sounds of a language. DNN supplanted the 30-year-old Gaussian Mixture Model in the industry. As a result of this, DNN has shown that it is better at determining which sound a user is generating at any given time, and with this they have significantly boosted speech recognition accuracy.

In terms of performance, both ASR and ML have hit a new peak with the introduction of deep learning. Shallow layer learning uses exemplars to represent high-dimensional but frequently empty speech qualities, whereas deep layer learning employs numerous layers of non-linear transformations to extract features.

6.8.4.2 Image Recognition

Photos of breast histology with deep Max-Pooling CNNs may be used to identify mitosis. Mitosis is a tough process to recognize. When it comes to mitosis, the cell nucleus undergoes a series of changes. Use of the DNN algorithm as a pixel classifier requires no human input, making it ideal for this type of application. The visual features of DNNs may be observed in this example. An open dataset shows that DNN beats all other competing approaches, even when processing images are as large as 4 MPixels, which can be done in only minutes on an average laptop. As a result of the ImageNet LSVRC-2010 competition, more than 1.2 million high-resolution photos have been used to sort into more than 1,000 separate categories. Error rates for the top 1 and top 5 places were lowered by 37.5% and 17.0%, respectively, when compared to prior information. Waiting for better GPUs and more datasets can improve all research.

6.8.4.3 Natural Image Processing

Deep learning algorithms have recently been successfully applied to a number of languages and information retrieval applications. Useful for every task at any level of abstraction, deep learning approaches leverage deep architectures to find the hidden patterns and features in training data. Deep Structured Semantic Models were proposed in 2013 by the authors of Ref. [12]. When it comes to ranking documents, they employ a DNN, as shown above. The query and documents are first mapped to a shared semantic space using a non-linear projection. Using the cosine similarity between their vectors in the semantic space, each document's relevance to the question is determined. Click-through data are used to train neural network models in a way that maximizes the conditional likelihood of the clicked document given the query. On a real-world web document ranking job, the new models are tested with real-world data. Before this study, other latent semantic models had been considered state-of-the-art in terms of performance but were found to be drastically underperforming by comparison with the suggested model [18].

6.9 AI ALGORITHMS AND MODELS

AI relies heavily on algorithms and models, which are derived from scientific results in the fields of math, statists, and biology. In this study, I'll cover some of the most popular AI models: Neural Network, Deep Learning. Support vector machine (SVM) and ANN are two examples of artificial neural networks (Figure 6.10).

    i. Support vector machine is used to build classification models by identifying an ideal hyperplane for each training example as demonstrated in Figure 6.10. For example, diagnosing power transformer faults, diagnosing diseases, and optimizing treatment are all possible uses of this technique.

    ii. Understanding thoughts and actions in terms of physical connections between neurons is represented by an ANN. As illustrated in Figure 6.10, ANN has been used to solve a wide range of problems by allowing the machine to construct mathematical models that mimic natural behaviours. With this algorithm, machines will be able to solve any problem much like a human [19].

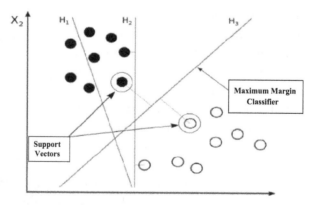

FIGURE 6.10   Describes how SVM algorithm is represented in AI.

6.10 SUMMARY

Face mask identification in images taken with the COVID-19 precaution may now be done using a CNN utilizing the approach that has been proposed. A thorough evaluation of the proposed methodologies has been performed using the datasets. A wide range of classifiers were examined. In order to detect human masks, prototypes of the project are now being created. Our effort is designed to stop the spread of COVID-19, which poses a danger to the public. People's data were saved on our server as a result of our use of the deep learning concept. It was clear to us from the results that the results generated by a symbolic method were superior to those generated by a traditional method.

Action is required to limit the spread of the COVID-19 pandemic. Identification of a person's face by their mask. At the beginning of this chapter, we briefly stated the purpose of our study. A visual depiction of the model's learning and performance difficulties was then shown. The system has a respectable level of accuracy thanks to the use of simple ML tools and approaches. There are a plethora of potential uses. Due to the conditions surrounding COVID-19, wearing a mask may soon be required. Several public service organizations mandate their employees to wear masks. The public health care system will benefit greatly from the approach's implementation. In the near future, people may be able to know if they're wearing the mask appropriately. The model may be updated to assess whether or not the mask is virus-prone, i.e., surgical, N95, or otherwise.

Neural networks have been shown using CNNs and motion learning methods. The dataset we utilized for model development, validation, and testing includes both masked and exposed photos of people's faces. Kaggle and GitHub are among the many places where these photographs were sourced. Photos and real-time video feeds were used to generate the model. We narrowed our search for a starting point by using measures such as precision, accuracy, and recall, and we chose CNN's design as having the most aesthetic appeal. For example, this face mask detector may be used to identify those who are following the rules and those who aren't in places with significant traffic such as shopping malls, airports, and other high-risk zones. A brief description of the project's motivations was given at the beginning. Afterwards, the model's capacity to learn and perform was shown. Simple machine learning (ML) methods and approaches were used to get a respectable level of accuracy in the strategy. The possibilities for its application are virtually limitless. As a result of the COVID-19 event, it's reasonable to assume that wearing a mask will become mandatory in the near future. In order to use several public services, you must wear a face mask or other protective gear. If the technique is applied, the public health system will tremendously benefit. It has the potential to be improved such that it can detect whether or not a mask is being worn appropriately. It is also possible to modify the model such that the patient's mask is virus-resistant (i.e., whether they are using a N95 surgical mask).

REFERENCES

1. A. Kushwaha, "Face Mask Detection Using Deep Learning and Computer Vision", *International Journal* of *Engineering* Research & *Technology*, Vol. 10, No. 12, pp. 461–464, 2021.
2. G. Singh, A. Vedrtnam, and D. Sagar, "An Overview of Artificial Intelligence," 2013.
3. F. A., Mohammed Ali, and S. H. Al-Tamimi, "Face Mask Detection Methods and Techniques: A Review", *International Journal of Nonlinear Analysis and Applications*, Vol. 13, pp. 3811–3823, , 2022.
4. R. Senthilkumar, "Face Mask Detection Using AI and IOT a Project Report Submitted by Bachelor of Engineering in Electronics and Communication Engineering Institute of Road and Transport Technology, Erode Anna University: Chennai 600 025," Research gate, 2021.
5. D. Deepika, "Pose Invariant in Face Recognition", 2021.
6. A. Gupta, G. Anjali, S. Saxena, and R. Kaliyaperumal, "Face Mask Detector Using Machine Learning Applications", 2022.
7. R. Bhogavalli, "Face Mask Detection Using Machine Learning", 2021.
8. Q. Liu, and Y. Wu, "Supervised Learning", 2015.
9. W. Jin, "Research on Machine Learning and Its Algorithms and Development", 2020. doi: 10.1088/1742–6596/1544/1/012003.
10. R. S. S. and A. G. Barto, *"Reinforcement Learning: An Introduction"*, MIT Press, Cambridge, MA, 2015.
11. A. Bhardwaj, P. Kumar, B. Raj, and S. Anand, "Design and Performance Optimization of Doping-Less Vertical Nanowire TFET Using Gate Stack Technique," *Journal of Electronic Materials (JEMS)*, Springer, Vol. 41, No. 7, pp. 4005–4013, 2022.
12. J. Singh, and B. Raj, "Tunnel Current Model of Asymmetric MIM Structure Levying Various Image Forces to Analyze the Characteristics of Filamentary Memristor", *Applied Physics A*, Springer, Vol. 125, No. 3, pp. 203.1 to 203.11, 2019.
13. C. Goyal, J. S. Ubhi, and B. Raj, "Low Leakage Zero Ground Noise Nanoscale Full Adder Using Source Biasing Technique", *Journal of Nanoelectronics and Optoelectronics*, American Scientific Publishers, Vol. 14, pp. 360–370, 2019.

14. G. Singh, R. K. Sarin, and B. Raj, "A Novel Robust Exclusive-OR Function Implementation in QCA Nanotechnology with Energy Dissipation Analysis", *Journal of Computational Electronics*, Springer, Vol. 15, No. 2, pp. 455–465, 2016.
15. T. Wadhera, D. Kakkar, G. Wadhwa, and B. Raj, " Recent Advances and Progress in Development of the Field Effect Transistor Biosensor: A Review" *Journal of Electronic Materials*, Springer, Vol. 48, No. 12, pp. 7635–7646, 2019.
16. G. Wadhwa, P. Kamboj, and B. Raj, "Design Optimisation of Junctionless TFET Biosensor for High Sensitivity", *Advances in Natural Sciences: Nanoscience and Nanotechnology*, Vol. 10, No. 7, p. 045001, 2019.
17. P. Bansal, and B. Raj, "Memristor Modeling and Analysis for Linear Dopant Drift Kinetics", *Journal of Nanoengineering and Nanomanufacturing*, American Scientific Publishers, Vol. 6, pp. 1–7, 2016.
18. A. Singh, M. Khosla, and B. Raj, "Circuit Compatible Model for Electrostatic Doped Schottky Barrier CNTFET," *Journal of Electronic Materials*, Springer, Vol. 45, No. 12, pp. 4825–4835, 2016.
19. Ashima, D. Vaithiyanathan, and B. Raj, "Performance Analysis of Charge Plasma induced Graded Channel Si Nanotube", *Journal of Engineering Research (JER)*, EMSME Special Issue, pp. 146–154, 2021.
20. A. S. Tomar, V. K. Magraiya, and B. Raj, "Scaling of Access and Data Transistor for High Performance DRAM Cell Design", *Quantum Matter*, Vol. 2, pp. 412–416, 2013.
21. N. Jain, and B. Raj, "Parasitic Capacitance and Resistance Model Development and Optimization of Raised Source/Drain SOI FinFET Structure for Analog Circuit Applications", *Journal of Nanoelectronics and Optoelectronins*, ASP, USA, Vol. 13, pp. 531–539, 2018.
22. S. Singh, S. K. Vishvakarma, and B. Raj, "Analytical Modeling of Split-Gate Junction-Less Transistor for a Biosensor Application", *Sensing and Bio-Sensing*, Elsevier, Vol. 18, pp. 31–36, 2018.
23. M. Gopal, and B. Raj, "Low Power 8T SRAM Cell Design for High Stability Video Applications", *ITSI Transaction on Electrical and Electronics Engineering*, Vol. 1, No. 5, pp. 91–97, 2013.
24. B. Raj, J. Mitra, D. K. Bihani, V. Rangharajan, A. K. Saxena, and S. Dasgupta, "Analysis of Noise Margin, Power and Process Variation for 32 nm FinFET Based 6T SRAM Cell", *Journal of Computer (JCP)*, Academy Publisher, FINLAND, Vol. 5, No. 6, pp. 1–8, 2010.
25. D. Sharma, R. Mehra, and B. Raj, "Comparative Analysis of Photovoltaic Technologies for High Efficiency Solar Cell Design", *Superlattices and Microstructures*, Elsevier, Vol. 153, pp. 106861, 2021.
26. P. Kaur, A. S. Buttar, and B. Raj, "A Comprehensive Analysis of Nanoscale Transistor Based Biosensor: A Review", *Indian Journal of Pure and Applied Physics*, Vol. 59, pp. 304–318, 2021.
27. D. Yadav, B. Raj, and B. Raj, "Design and Simulation of Low Power Microcontroller for IoT Applications", *Journal of Sensor Letters*, ASP, Vol. 18, pp. 401–409, 2020.

28. S. Singh, and B. Raj, "A 2-D Analytical Surface Potential and Drain Current Modeling of Double-Gate Vertical t-Shaped Tunnel FET", *Journal of Computational Electronics*, Springer, Vol. 19, pp. 1154–1163, 2020.

29. J. Singh, and B. Raj, "An Accurate and Generic Window function for Non-linear Memristor Model" *Journal of Computational Electronics*, Springer, Vol. 18, No. 2, pp. 640–647, 2019.

30. M. Kaur, N. Gupta, S. Kumar, B. Raj, and A. K. Singh, "Comparative RF and Crosstalk Analysis of Carbon Based Nano Interconnects", *IET Circuits, Devices & Systems*, Vol. 15, No. 6, pp. 493–503, 2021.

31. N. Kandasamy, F. Ahmad, D. Ajitha, B. Raj, and N. Telagam, "Quantum Dot Cellular Automata Based Scan Flip Flop and Boundary Scan Register", *IETE Journal of Research*, Vol. 69, 2020.

32. S. K. Sharma, B. Raj, and M. Khosla, "Enhanced Photosensitivity of Highly Spectrum Selective Cylindrical Gate $In_{1-x}Ga_xAs$ Nanowire MOSFET Photodetector", *Modern Physics Letter-B*, Vol. 33, No. 12, p. 1950144, 2019.

33. J. Singh, and B. Raj, "Design and Investigation of 7T2M NVSARM with Enhanced Stability and Temperature Impact on Store/Restore Energy", *IEEE Transactions on Very Large Scale Integration Systems*, Vol. 27, No. 6, pp. 1322–1328, 2019.

34. A. K. Bhardwaj, S. Gupta, B. Raj, and A. Singh, "Impact of Double Gate Geometry on the Performance of Carbon Nanotube Field Effect Transistor Structures for Low Power Digital Design", *Computational and Theoretical Nanoscience*, ASP, Vol. 16, pp. 1813–1820, 2019.

35. N. Jain, and B. Raj, "Thermal Stability Analysis and Performance Exploration of Asymmetrical Dual-k Underlap Spacer (ADKUS) SOI FinFET for Security and Privacy Applications", *Indian Journal of Pure & Applied Physics (IJPAP)*, Vol. 57, pp. 352–360, 2019.

36. A. Singh, M. Khosla, and B. Raj, "Design and Analysis of Dynamically Configurable Electrostatic Doped Carbon Nanotube Tunnel FET", *Microelectronics Journal*, Elsevier, Vol. 85, pp. 17–24, 2019.

37. N. Jain, and B. Raj, "Dual-k Spacer Region Variation at the Drain Side of Asymmetric SOI FinFET Structure: Performance Analysis towards the Analog/RF Design Applications", *Journal of Nanoelectronics and Optoelectronics*, American Scientific Publishers, Vol. 14, pp. 349–359, 2019.

38. J. Singh, S. Sharma, B. Raj, and M. Khosla, "Analysis of Barrier Layer Thickness on Performance of $In_{1-x}Ga_xAs$ Based Gate Stack Cylindrical Gate Nanowire MOSFET", *JNO*, ASP, Vol. 13, pp. 1473–1477, 2018.

39. N. Jain, and B. Raj, "Analysis and Performance Exploration of High-k SOI FinFETs over the Conventional Low-k SOI FinFET toward Analog/RF Design", *Journal of Semiconductors (JoS)*, IOP Science, Vol. 39, No. 12, pp. 124002-1-7, 2018.

40. C. Goyal, J. S. Ubhi, and B. Raj, "A Reliable Leakage Reduction Technique for Approximate Full Adder with Reduced Ground Bounce Noise", *Journal of Mathematical Problems in Engineering*, Hindawi, Vol. 2018, Article ID 3501041, 16 pages, 2018.

41. Anuradha, J. Singh, B. Raj, and M. Khosla, "Design and Performance Analysis of Nano-Scale Memristor-Based Nonvolatile SRAM", *Journal of Sensor Letter*, American Scientific Publishers, Vol. 16, pp. 798–805, 2018.
42. G. Wadhwa, and B. Raj, "Parametric Variation Analysis of Charge-Plasma-Based Dielectric Modulated JLTFET for Biosensor Application", *IEEE Sensor Journal*, Vol. 18, No. 15, pp. 6070–6077, 2018.
43. J. Singh, and B. Raj, "Comparative Analysis of Memristor Models for Memories Design", *JoS, IoP*, Vol. 39, No. 7, pp. 074006-1-12, 2018.
44. D. Yadav, S. S. Chouhan, S. K. Vishvakarma, and B. Raj, "Application Specific Microcontroller Design for IoT Based WSN", *Sensor Letter*, ASP, Vol. 16, pp. 374–385, 2018.
45. G. Singh, R. K. Sarin, and B. Raj, "Fault-Tolerant Design and Analysis of Quantum-Dot Cellular Automata Based Circuits", *IEEE/IET Circuits, Devices & Systems*, Vol. 12, pp. 638–664, 2018.
46. J. Singh, and B. Raj, "Modeling of Mean Barrier Height Levying Various Image Forces of Metal Insulator Metal Structure to Enhance the Performance of Conductive Filament Based Memristor Model", *IEEE Nanotechnology*, Vol. 17, No. 2, pp. 268–275, 2018.
47. A. Jain, S. Sharma, and B. Raj, "Analysis of Triple Metal Surrounding Gate (TM-SG) III-V Nanowire MOSFET for Photosensing Application", *Opto-Electronics Journal*, Elsevier, Vol. 26, No. 2, pp. 141–148, 2018.
48. A. Jain, S. Sharma, and B. Raj, "Design and Analysis of High Sensitivity Photosensor Using Cylindrical Surrounding Gate MOSFET for Low Power Sensor Applications", *Engineering Science and Technology, an International Journal*, Elsevier's, Vol. 19, No. 4, pp. 1864–1870, 2016.
49. A. Singh, M. Khosla, and B. Raj, "Analysis of Electrostatic Doped Schottky Barrier Carbon Nanotube FET for Low Power Applications," *Journal of Materials Science: Materials in Electronics*, Springer, Vol. 28, pp. 1762–1768, 2017.
50. G. Saiphani Kumar, A. Singh, B. Raj, "Design and Analysis of Gate All around CNTFET Based SRAM Cell Design", *Journal of Computational Electronics*, Springer, Vol. 17, No.1, pp. 138–145, 2018.
51. G. P. Singh, B. S. Sohi, and B. Raj, "Material Properties Analysis of Graphene Base Transistor (GBT) for VLSI Analog Circuits", *Indian Journal of Pure & Applied Physics (IJPAP)*, Vol. 55, pp. 896–902, 2017.
52. S. Kumar and B. Raj, "Estimation of Stability and Performance Metric for Inward Access Transistor Based 6T SRAM Cell Design Using n-type/p-type DMDG-GDOV TFET", *IEEE VLSI Circuits and Systems Letter*, Vol. 3, No. 2, pp. 25–39, 2017.
53. S. Sharma, A. Kumar, M. Pattanaik, and B. Raj, "Forward Body Biased Multimode Multi-Threshold CMOS Technique for Ground Bounce Noise Reduction in Static CMOS Adders", *International Journal of Information and Electronics Engineering*, Vol. 3, No. 3, pp. 567–572, 2013.
54. H. Singh, P. Kumar, and B. Raj, "Performance Analysis of Majority Gate SET Based 1-bit Full Adder", *International Journal of Computer and Communication Engineering (IJCCE)*, IACSIT Press Singapore, ISSN: 2010-3743, Vol. 2, No. 4, 2013.

55. A. K. Bhardwaj, S. Gupta, and B. Raj, "Investigation of Parameters for Schottky Barrier (SB) Height for Schottky Barrier Based Carbon Nanotube Field Effect Transistor Device", *Journal of Nanoelectronics and Optoelectronics*, ASP, Vol. 15, pp. 783–791, 2020.

56. P. Bansal, and B. Raj, "Memristor: A Versatile Nonlinear Model for Dopant Drift and Boundary Issues", *JCTN*, American Scientific Publishers, Vol. 14, No. 5, pp. 2319–2325, 2017.

57. N. Jain, and B. Raj, "An Analog and Digital Design Perspective Comprehensive Approach on Fin-FET (Fin-Field Effect Transistor) Technology - A Review", *Reviews in Advanced Sciences and Engineering (RASE)*, ASP, Vol. 5, pp. 1–14, 2016.

58. S. Sharma, B. Raj, and M. Khosla, "Subthreshold Performance of $In_{1-x}Ga_xAs$ Based Dual Metal with Gate Stack Cylindrical/Surrounding Gate Nanowire MOSFET for Low Power Analog Applications", *Journal of Nanoelectronics and Optoelectronics*, American Scientific Publishers, USA, Vol. 12, pp. 171–176, 2017.

59. B. Raj, A. K. Saxena, and S. Dasgupta, "Analytical Modeling for the Estimation of Leakage Current and Subthreshold Swing Factor of Nanoscale Double Gate FinFET Device" *Microelectronics International, UK*, Vol. 26, pp. 53–63, 2009.

60. S. S. Soniya, G. Wadhwa, and B. Raj, "An Analytical Modeling for Dual Source Vertical Tunnel Field Effect Transistor", *International Journal of Recent Technology and Engineering (IJRTE)*, Vol. 8, No. 2, 2019.

61. S. Singh, and B. Raj, "Design and Analysis of Hetrojunction Vertical T-Shaped Tunnel Field Effect Transistor", *Journal of Electronics Material*, Springer, Vol. 48, No. 10, pp. 6253–6260, 2019.

62. C. Goyal, J. S. Ubhi, and B. Raj, "A Low Leakage CNTFET Based Inexact Full Adder for Low Power Image Processing Applications", *International Journal of Circuit Theory and Applications*, Wiley, Vol. 47, No. 9, pp. 1446–1458, 2019.

63. B. Raj, A. K. Saxena, and S. Dasgupta, "A Compact Drain Current and Threshold Voltage Quantum Mechanical Analytical Modeling for FinFETs", *Journal of Nanoelectronics and Optoelectronics (JNO)*, USA, Vol. 3, No. 2, pp. 163–170, 2008.

64. G. Wadhwa, and B. Raj, "An Analytical Modeling of Charge Plasma Based Tunnel Field Effect Transistor with Impacts of Gate Underlap Region", *Superlattices and Microstructures*, Elsevier, Vol. 142, p. 106512, 2020.

65. S. Singh, and B. Raj, "Modeling and Simulation Analysis of SiGe Heterojunction Double Gate Vertical t-Shaped Tunnel FET", *Superlattices and Microstructures*, Elsevier, Vol. 142, p. 106496, 2020.

66. A. Singh, D. K. Saini, D. Agarwal, S. Aggarwal, M. Khosla, and B. Raj, "Modeling and Simulation of Carbon Nanotube Field Effect Transistor and Its Circuit Application", *Journal of Semiconductors (JoS)*, IOP Science, Vol. 37, pp. 074001–074006, 2016.

67. N. Jain, and B. Raj, "Device and Circuit Co-Design Perspective Comprehensive Approach on FinFET Technology - A Review", *Journal of Electron Devices*, Vol. 23, No. 1, pp. 1890–1901, 2016.

68. S. Kumar and B. Raj, "Analysis of I_{ON} and Ambipolar Current for Dual-Material Gate-Drain Overlapped DG-TFET", *Journal of Nanoelectronics and Optoelectronics*, American Scientific Publishers, USA, Vol. 11, pp. 323–333, 2016.

69. N. Anjum, T. Bali, and B. Raj, "Design and Simulation of Handwritten Multiscript Character Recognition", *International Journal of Advanced Research in Computer and Communication Engineering*, Vol. 2, No. 7, pp. 2544–2549, 2013.

70. S. Sharma, B. Raj, and M. Khosla, "A Gaussian Approach for Analytical Subthreshold Current Model of Cylindrical Nanowire FET with Quantum Mechanical Effects", *Microelectronics Journal*, Elsevier, Vol. 53, pp. 65–72, 2016.

71. K. Singh, and B. Raj, "Performance and Analysis of Temperature Dependent Multi-Walled Carbon Nanotubes as Global Interconnects at Different Technology Nodes", *Journal of Computational Electronics*, Springer, Vol. 14, No. 2, pp. 469–476, 2015.

72. S. Kumar and B. Raj, "Compact Channel Potential Analytical Modeling of DG-TFET Based on Evanescent–Mode Approach", *Journal of Computational Electronics*, Springer, Vol. 14, No. 2, pp. 820–827, 2015.

73. K. Singh, and B. Raj, "Temperature Dependent Modeling and Performance Evaluation of Multi-Walled CNT and Single-Walled CNT as Global Interconnects", *Journal of Electronic Materials*, Springer, Vol. 44, No. 12, pp. 4825–4835, 2015.

74. V. K. Sharma, M. Pattanaik, and B. Raj, "INDEP Approach for Leakage Reduction in Nanoscale CMOS Circuits", *International Journal of Electronics*, Taylor & Francis, Vol. 102, No. 2, pp. 200–215, 2014.

75. K. Singh, and B. Raj, "Influence of Temperature on MWCNT Bundle, SWCNT Bundle and Copper Interconnects for Nanoscaled Technology Nodes", *Journal of Materials Science: Materials in Electronics*, Springer, Vol. 26, No. 8, pp. 6134–6142, 2015.

76. N. Anjum, T. Bali, and B. Raj, "Design and Simulation of Handwritten Gurumukhi and Devanagri Numerical Recognition", *International Journal of Computer Applications*, Published by Foundation of Computer Science, New York, USA, Vol. 73, No. 12, pp. 16–21, 2013.

77. S. Khandelwal, V. Gupta, B. Raj, and R. D. Gupta, "Process Variability Aware Low Leakage Reliable Nano Scale DG-FinFET SRAM Cell Design Technique", *Journal of Nanoelectronics and Optoelectronics*, Vol. 10, No. 6, pp. 810–817, 2015.

78. V. K. Sharma, M. Pattanaik, and B. Raj, "ONOFIC Approach: Low Power High Speed Nanoscale VLSI Circuits Design", *International Journal of Electronics*, Taylor & Francis, Vol. 101, No. 1, pp. 61–73, 2014.

79. S. Khandelwal, B. Raj, and R. D. Gupta, "FinFET Based 6T SRAM Cell Design: Analysis of Performance Metric, Process Variation and Temperature Effect", *Journal of Computational and Theoretical Nanoscience*, ASP, USA, Vol. 12, pp. 2500–2506, 2015.

80. S. Singh, Y. Shekhar, R. Jagdeep, S. Anurag, and B. Raj, "Impact of HfO_2 in Graded Channel Dual Insulator Double Gate MOSFET", *Journal of Computational and Theoretical Nanoscience*, American Scientific Publishers, Vol. 12, No. 6, pp. 950–953, 2015.

81. V. K. Sharma, M. Pattanaik, and B. Raj, "PVT Variations Aware Low Leakage INDEP Approach for Nanoscale CMOS Circuits", *Microelectronics Reliability*, Elsevier, Vol. 54, pp. 90–99, 2014.

82. B. Raj, A. K. Saxena and S. Dasgupta, "Quantum Mechanical Analytical Modeling of Nanoscale DG FinFET: Evaluation of Potential, Threshold Voltage and Source/Drain Resistance", *Elsevier's Journal of Material Science in Semiconductor Processing*, Elsevier, Vol. 16, No. 4, pp. 1131–1137, 2013.

83. M. Gopal, S. S. D. Prasad, and B. Raj, "8T SRAM Cell Design for Dynamic and Leakage Power Reduction", *International Journal of Computer Applications*, Published by Foundation of Computer Science, New York, USA, Vol. 71, No. 9, pp. 43–48, 2013.

84. M. Pattanaik, B. Raj, S. Sharma, and A. Kumar, "Diode Based Trimode Multi-Threshold CMOS Technique for Ground Bounce Noise Reduction in Static CMOS Adders", *Advanced Materials Research*, Trans Tech Publications, Switzerland, Vol. 548, pp. 885–889, 2012.

85. B. Raj, A. K. Saxena, and S. Dasgupta, "Nanoscale FinFET Based SRAM Cell Design: Analysis of Performance Metric, Process Variation, Underlapped FinFET and Temperature Effect", *IEEE Circuits and System Magazine*, Vol. 11, No. 2, pp. 38–50, 2011.

86. V. K. Sharma, M. Pattanaik, and B. Raj, "Leakage Current ONOFIC Approach for Deep Submicron VLSI Circuit Design", *International Journal of Electrical, Computer, Electronics and Communication Engineering*, World Academy of Sciences, Engineering and Technology, Vol. 7, No. 4, pp. 239–244, 2013.

87. T. Chawla, M. Khosla, and B. Raj, "Design and Simulation of Triple Metal Double-Gate Germanium on Insulator Vertical Tunnel Field Effect Transistor", *Microelectronics Journal*, Elsevier, Vol. 114, p. 105125, 2021.

88. P. Kaur, S. S. Gill, and B. Raj, "Comparative Analysis of OFETs Materials and Devices for Sensor Applications", *Journal of Silicon*, Springer, Vol. 14, pp. 4463–4471, 2022.

89. S. K. Sharma, P. Kumar, B. Raj, and B. Raj, "$In_{1-x}Ga_xAs$ Double Metal Gate-Stacking Cylindrical Nanowire MOSFET for Highly Sensitive Photo Detector", *Journal of Silicon*, Springer, Vol. 14, pp. 3535–3541, 2022.

90. B. Raj, A. K. Saxena, and S. Dasgupta, "Analytical Modeling of Quasi Planar Nanoscale Double Gate FinFET with Source/Drain Resistance and Field Dependent Carrier Mobility: A Quantum Mechanical Study", *Journal of Computer (JCP)*, Academy Publisher, FINLAND, Vol. 4, No. 9, 2009.

91. S. Bhushan, S. Khandelwal, and B. Raj, "Analyzing Different Mode FinFET Based Memory Cell at Different Power Supply for Leakage Reduction", Seventh International Conference on Bio-Inspired Computing: Theories and Application, (BIC-TA 2012), *Advances in Intelligent Systems and Computing*, Vol. 202, pp. 89–100, 2013.

92. J. Singh, and B. Raj, "Temperature Dependent Analytical Modeling and Simulations of Nanoscale Memristor", *Engineering Science and Technology, an International Journal*, Elsevier's, Vol. 21, pp. 862–868, pp. 742–748, 2018.

93. S. Singh, S. Bala, B. Raj, and B. Raj, "Improved Sensitivity of Dielectric Modulated Junctionless Transistor for Nanoscale Biosensor Design", *Sensor Letter*, ASP, Vol. 18, pp. 328–333, 2020.

94. V. Kumar, S. K. Vishvakarma, and B. Raj, "Design and Performance Analysis of ASIC for IoT Applications", *Sensor Letter*, ASP, Vol. 18, pp. 31–38, 2020.

95. A. Jaiswal, R. K. Sarin, B. Raj, and S. Sukhija, "A Novel Circular Slotted Microstrip-fed Patch Antenna with Three Triangle Shape Defected Ground Structure for Multiband Applications", *Advanced Electromagnetic (AEM)*, Vol. 7, No. 3, pp. 56–63, 2018.

96. G. Wadhwa, and B Raj, "Label Free Detection of Biomolecules Using Charge-Plasma-Based Gate Underlap Dielectric Modulated Junctionless TFET", *Journal of Electronic Materials (JEMS)*, Springer, Vol. 47, No. 8, pp. 4683–4693, 2018.

97. G. Singh, R. K. Sarin, and B. Raj, "Design and Performance Analysis of a New Efficient Coplanar Quantum-Dot Cellular Automata Adder", *Indian Journal of Pure & Applied Physics (IJPAP)*, Vol. 55, pp. 97–103, 2017.

98. A. Singh, M. Khosla, and B. Raj, "Design and Analysis of Electrostatic Doped Schottky Barrier CNTFET Based Low Power SRAM", *International Journal of Electronics and Communications, (AEÜ)*, Elsevier, Vol. 80, pp. 67–72, 2017.

99. P. Kaur, V. Pandey, and B. Raj, "Comparative Study of Efficient Design, Control and Monitoring of Solar Power Using IoT", *Sensor Letter*, ASP, Vol. 18, pp. 419–426, 2020.

100. G. Wadhwa, P. Kamboj, J. Singh, B. Raj, "Design and Investigation of Junctionless DGTFET for Biological Molecule Recognition", *Transactions on Electrical and Electronic Materials*, Springer, Vol. 22, pp. 282–289, 2020.

101. T. Chawla, M. Khosla, and B. Raj, "Optimization of Double-Gate Dual Material GeOI-Vertical TFET for VLSI Circuit Design", *IEEE VLSI Circuits and Systems Letter*, Vol. 6, No. 2, pp. 13–25, 2020.

102. S. K. Verma, S. Singh, G. Wadhwa and B. Raj, "Detection of Biomolecules Using Charge-Plasma Based Gate Underlap Dielectric Modulated Dopingless TFET", *Transactions on Electrical and Electronic Materials (TEEM)*, Springer, Vol. 21, pp. 528–535, 2020.

103. N. Jain, and B. Raj, "Impact of Underlap Spacer Region Variation on Electrostatic and Analog/RF Performance of Symmetrical High-k SOI FinFET at 20 nm Channel Length", *Journal of Semiconductors (JoS)*, IOP Science, Vol. 38, No. 12, p. 122002, 2017.

104. S. Singh, and B. Raj, "Analytical Modeling and Simulation Analysis of T-Shaped III-V Heterojunction Vertical T-FET", *Superlattices and Microstructures*, Elsevier, Vol. 147, p. 106717, 2020.
105. G. Singh, R. K. Sarin, and B. Raj, "Design and Analysis of Area Efficient QCA Based Reversible Logic Gates", *Journal of Microprocessors and Microsystems*, Elsevier, Vol. 52, pp. 59–68, 2017.
106. A. Singh, M. Khosla, and B. Raj, "Compact Model for Ballistic Single Wall CNTFET under Quantum Capacitance Limit", *Journal of Semiconductors (JoS)*, IOP Science, Vol. 37, pp. 104001–104008, 2016.
107. S. Singh, M. Khosla, G. Wadhwa, and B. Raj, "Design and Analysis of Double-Gate Junctionless Vertical TFET for Gas Sensing Applications", *Applied Physics A*, Springer, Vol. 127, No. 16, 2021.
108. I. Singh, B. Raj, M. Khosla, and B. K. Kaushik, "Potential MRAM Technologies for Low Power SoCs", *SPIN World Scientific Publisher, SCIE*; Vol. 10, No. 04, p. 2050027, 2020.
109. S. Singh, and B. Raj, "Parametric Variation Analysis on Hetero-Junction Vertical t-Shape TFET for Suppressing Ambipolar Conduction", *Indian Journal of Pure and Applied Physics*, Vol. 58, pp. 478–485, 2020.
110. S. S. Soniya, G. Wadhwa, and B. Raj, "Design and Analysis of Dual Source Vertical Tunnel Field Effect Transistor for High Performance", *Transactions on Electrical and Electronics Materials*, Springer, Vol. 21, pp. 74–82, 2019.
111. M. Kaur, N. Gupta, S. Kumar, B. Raj, and A. K. Singh, "RF Performance Analysis of Intercalated Graphene Nanoribbon Based Global Level Interconnects", *Journal of Computational Electronics*, Springer, Vol. 19, pp. 1002–1013, 2020.
112. G. Wadhwa, B. Raj, "Design and Performance Analysis of Junctionless TFET Biosensor for High Sensitivity" *IEEE Nanotechnology*, Vol. 18, pp. 567–574, 2019.
113. J. Singh, and B. Raj, "Enhanced Nonlinear Memristor Model Encapsulating Stochastic Dopant Drift", *JNO*, ASP, 14, 958–963, 2019.

CHAPTER 7

Emerging Nonvolatile Memories for AI Applications

Mandeep Singh, Tarun Chaudhary, and Balwinder Raj

Dr. B.R. Ambedkar National Institute of Technology

CONTENTS

DOI: 10.1201/9781003230113-7

7.1 INTRODUCTION

Artificial intelligence (AI) is, at its most basic level, a technology that allows computers to learn from their experiences, adapt to new inputs, and execute human-like activities. AI is being employed in a variety of fields, such as banking and healthcare. AI has been around for quite some time. It was first explored mathematically and theoretically, and then designed and implemented as software. The AI structure itself does not require hardware architecture because the AI technology is implemented in software and leverages the existing CPU, GPU, and memory system. However, as the use of AI grew, it became important to execute AI not only by CPU and GPU, but also through an AI-dedicated process represented by a neural processing unit [1]. The three issues that AI processors face are the memory wall, energy efficiency, and on-chip memory capacity. Since the 1980s, as Moores law improves within IC fabrication technology, computational power has climbed by 60% per year. However, memory performance, specifically Dynamic Random Access Memory (DRAM), has only grown by 7% each year during the same period. For even more than two decades, the gap among CPU and memory performance has been growing. Like a consequence, data bandwidth is limited in comparison to processing speed. The RAM well-known memory wall may be found here. For decades, CPUs have struggled to overcome the memory barrier. In AI chip architecture, the memory partition is particularly significant since AI computations require far more data than required for most other purposes. There are two basic techniques to dealing with the memory wall issue currently available. One possibility is to increase the data transfer clock speed. The second option is to increase the data transmission width. The first approach is used in consistently high memory, like extremely high Double Data Rate (DDR) memory and High Bandwidth Memory (HBM) memory. The power consumption of AI processors is the key problem. The carbon footprint of training an AI model is more than five times that of training a human. Computing and data transport units are the major sources of power consumption. AI circuits must be able to handle both mathematically and data transmission activities. To use modern IC fabrication technology and lowering capacitance load on data transmission channels are two popular techniques to reducing power consumption, in contrast to algorithm improvement. Fast memory capacity is the third problem for AI processors. On-chip or near-chip memory is a type of fast memory that includes information rapidly without slowing the processor unit. On-chip Static Random Access Memory (SRAM)

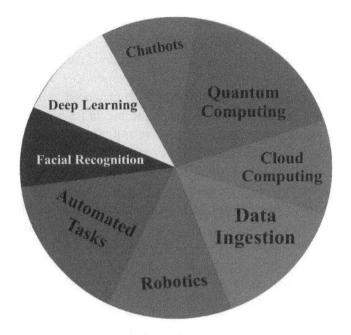

FIGURE 7.1   Artificial intelligence (AI) characteristics.

is the most common kind of fast memory. Fast access time is a benefit of SRAM; however, its size restricts memory capacity [2]. We've seen how AI can give us a glimpse into the future while we're still in the present. It has a wide range of applications. AI is having a long-term influence on practically every sector and individual. AI has worked as a driving force behind developing technologies such as big data and robots, and it will continue to do so for the near future. The dynamics of our work and workplaces will forever alter as we learn more about AI and how it is used more efficiently. Figure 7.1 represents the various characteristics of AI in future like Robotics, Deep Learning, Quantum Computing, Facial Recognitions, Cloud Computing, Data Ingestions, Chatboats, Automatics Tasks, etc.

A modern electronic system always has mainly focused on semiconductor memory as a critical component and backbone [3]. It was observed that potential for utilizing nonvolatile Metal Oxide Semiconductor (MOS) memory device for futuristic circuits. Since then, semiconductor memory has played a key role in the revolution in digital electronics, especially till the 64-bit revolution. Storage systems have progressed from punch cards that hold just few bytes of data to multi-terabyte capacity in considerably less space and power usage. In recent years, the performance of storage systems must be as quick as possible. The most significant issue today is the electronic device structure's limited capacity for ongoing scaling. In embedded flash devices, research is focusing on (1) shrinking device memory cell sizes, (2) minimizing voltage operation, and (3) employing a multi-layer cell to increase the density of states per memory cell. To keep up with the constant scaling, traditional flash devices may need to undergo radical alterations. We go through the fundamentals of flash memory before focusing on the current issues with increasing tunnel dielectric in such devices. Here, a brief description of historical shift that occurs in traditional FG NVM and how it suffers from charge loss when the device's size shrinks. In various research substitutes for the traditional FG memory, it is proposed to use a separate polysilicon-oxide-nitride-oxide-silicon memory. Because of the confined charge, the NC memory is intended to do a good job of preserving it. While simultaneously displaying a discrete charge store node Faster program/erase rates, minimal power consumption, and other great characteristics programming potentials, as well as a high level of durability [4].

7.2 SOLID-STATE MEMORY TECHNOLOGY CLASSIFICATION

The categorization of memory devices is depicted in Figure 7.2. Until now, a single memory was insufficient to do all tasks simultaneously. SRAM is the quickest in general, with a 100 ps "write"/"erase" time, although the 6-transistors-based architecture consumes a large number of wafers area. The one-transistor-one-capacitor (1T1C)-based DRAM is a viable option; yet, the data storage capacity is severely limited owing to leaking capacitors [5–9]. The nonvolatile, expensive 1T flash memory, on the other hand, is ideal for large storage purposes and accounts for the majority of the semiconductor memory industry. However, because of physical constraints, the rapid rise of fundamental technologies has hit a snag in device scalability. In comparison to DRAM, flash memory devices have a high voltage, low-speed performance, as well as weak durability. Now, electronics demands a highly nonvolatile, scalable, low-cost memory technique that is super, moderate, and has a high level of durability and endurance. A need for finding a viable replacement NVM that can meet the study field has widened due to the rising demand for reliability in regular industrial application [10–12]. An advanced innovation is projected to be a high-speed and ultra-low-power, another very expense, flexible device that is extremely reliable and durable as compared with existing basic memories. With the exception of baseline devices, "prototype" memories are those that are prototype test chips which are accessible or are in the early stages of manufacture. The potential alternatives in the prototype categories are ferroelectric

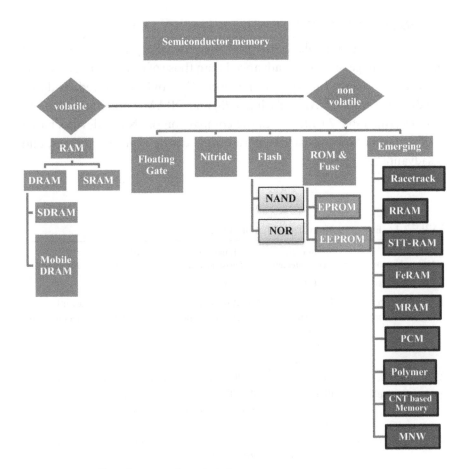

FIGURE 7.2   Classification of semiconductor memory.

random-access memory, phase change memory (PCM), magnetic RAM (MRAM), and spin-transfer-torque RAM (STTRAM). The development of prototype technology is influenced by a number of variables [13–15]. The prototype NVM's efficiency must be superior to, if not identical to, that of existing baseline technology [16–22]. So to a shortage of in-depth knowledge, several of the gadgets on the prototype list still are regarded emerging technology. Novel structural design and new material usage are frequently studied in emerging nonvolatile memory (eNVM) devices. The innovative technique in such devices goes beyond the traditional electrical silicon device manufacturing, which includes quantum mechanical phenomenon, redox reactions, section transitions, spin-states, molecule rearrangement, and other things. Most crucially, the two-terminal eNVM devices offer sufficient ground for the high-density crossbar design to be implemented [23].

7.3 EMERGING NONVOLATILE MEMORY DEVICES

Many devices are available in this category. The processes of eNVM devices are, in general, more advanced than those of basic devices. As storage class memory, a high-performance eNVM can be employed, bridging the distance among NAND flash [24,25] and DRAM storage and memory devices [26]. Table 7.1 illustrates the comparison of eNVM devices based on the number of transistor material used, device type, advantages, and disadvantages.

TABLE 7.1 Emerging Nonvolatile Memory Devices

S. No.	Memory Type	Emerging Ferroelectric	Emerging Ferroelectric	Carbon Nanotube	Nanowire
	Sb (scale)	FeFET	FTJ		
1.	Storage mechanism	Remnant polarization on a ferroelectric dielectric	Giant tunnel electroresistance	Multiple mechanisms	Multiple mechanisms
2.	Cell element	1T	1T1R or 1D1R	1T1R or 1D1R	1T1R or 1D1R
3.	Device type	FET with FE gate insulator	M-FJT semiconductor	Nanotube, carbon	MIS
4.	Material used	PZT	PZT (lead zirconate titanate)	Graphite	Si, Ge, GaAs, ZnO, etc.
5.	Advantages	Excellent endurance, scalability	Large ON/OFF ratio, high scalability	Very small in size, low power consumption	Operate very quickly, high storage capacity, low power consumption
6.	Disadvantages	Large memory size	Low operational speed	The lack of solubility	Low retention time
7.	Applications	Datalogger in portable/ implantable medical devices	Smart meters for its fast write speed and high endurance	High-density next-generation memories	Medical implants in humans, such as artificial skin where the PRM cells could be used

7.4 NANOWIRE-BASED NVM

Nanotubes and semiconductor nanowires have both attracted research-ers' curiosity as possible components for nanoscale electronics and sys-tems. Both materials (i.e. Nanotubes and semiconductor nanowires) are already used to show a variety of field-effect transistors and free electron transistors are examples of these devices, or biologic sensors [27,28]. The nanowire system can be utilized as a platform to research new memory concepts due to its small size and superior control. Alternative memory concepts strive to tackle the major drawbacks of conventional electronic memories, such as DRAM's instability and flash memory's sluggish pro-gramming speed and low endurance [29–35]. Universal memory is the ultimate goal: high-density memory which can be written and retrieved at high rates for an almost infinite number of cycles while maintaining data nonvolatility. The nanowire-based memories are classified accord-ing to the material and its properties. Some emerging nanowire NVMs are shown in Figure 7.3.

In Table 7.2, the comparison of different nanowires are shown on the basis of diameter, length, mobility, and resistivity.

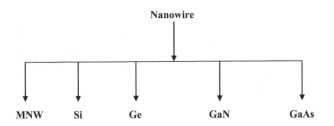

FIGURE 7.3   Types of nanowire.

TABLE 7.2   Comparison of Different Nanowires on the Basis of Parameters

S. No.	Material	Diameter (nm)	Length (μm)	Mobility (cm²/V.s)	Resistivity (Ω cm)	Permittivity (ϵ_r)	Electron Effective Mass (m_{eff})	Reference
1.	Si	<20	>1	30	0.039	11.8	$0.340\,m_0$	[26]
2.	Ge	30–300	100	10.6	10^{-4}	16	$0.180\,m_0$	[36]
3.	GaN	20–40	1	300	10^7–10^3	8.9	$0.370\,m_0$	[37]
4.	InAs	40–50	5	650	5.5×10^{-3}	15.15	$0.153\,m_0$	[38]
5.	ZnO	41	3.2	166	10^{-2}–10^3	9.4	$0.40\,m_0$	[5]

7.4.1 MNW

Mostly in recent two decades, there has been a growing interest in technology devices, as well as hunt for a global data storage system with fast reading or writing rates, increased nonvolatility, and storage efficiency, which has sparked research interest into novel nanoscale materials. A revolutionary transistor design incorporating nanowire memory cells at the molecular level the potential of unprecedentedly tiny storing of information as a substitute for conventional Flash memory technology. The molecular nanowire array (MNW) memory differs from traditional semiconductor memories: in the former, information is stored in a channel of a nanowire transistor that has been modified with redox-active molecule or even by manipulating tiny quantities of charge. It is inefficient and lacks random-access capabilities, in which data which can be read and written at random at each and every bite are aggressively pursued. Nanowire-based memories technique is a strong means to build digital equipment at ultra-small scales because of its sub-lithographic dimension, disordered single-crystalline composition, and distinctive form. Nanowires are almost flawless structures made out of a single crystal tiny shape and ideal horizon that are synthesized by chemical or physical techniques. Redox-active compounds are used to improve the properties the channel of a nanowire transistor. Ultra-high efficiency, low power dissipation, simple fabrication, 3D structure, and multilayer storage are all advantages of the MNW memory, which performs at nanoscale only with a restricted number of electrons in a relative short period of time [39,40]. The schematic design of an MNW memory cell is given in Figure 7.4. Because of

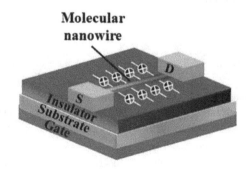

FIGURE 7.4 MNW memory cell structure.

its sub-lithographic size, nanowire-based memory technology is a strong way for assembling electronic/photonic systems at ultra-small levels [5].

7.5 SI NANOWIRE-BASED PCM

Phase-change RAM (PCRAMs) are NVMs that take use of the huge electrical conductivity comparison between crystalline and amorphous stages of phase change materials (PCMs), like Ge2Sb2Te5 (GST) or GeTe chalcogenide glasses. Appropriate annealing of the PCM by regulated electrical pulses causes phase change [41–45]. A reversible, fast, and radiation-resistant transformation is possible [17–19]. A moderately powerful yet brief electrical pulse is used to heat the PCM5 over its melting point, followed by quick cooling, leading to a highly resistant amorphous state. Reduced power consumption was a major problem, particularly during reset procedure, which necessitates high currents (0.5 mA). Figure 7.5 demonstrates a schematic diagram of two possible layouts. The programmable current source inside the single-ended system is one transistor that is turned off during the read period. All these transistors should be active even during programming step in the double-ended approach. The PCM cell acquires high impedance with regard to Power Supply (VDD) and ground when both SNWBTs are turned off, making it accessible for the 'read' circuits for both ends. Yet, the focus of the study has been simulating a single-ended design [26].

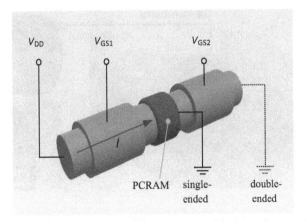

FIGURE 7.5   Schematic setup of SNWBT-PCM [26].

7.6 GE-NW-BASED FET MEMORY

With a standard Field Effect Transistor (FET) setup, flash memory based on inherent Ge Nanowires (NWs) may be created. A solitary Ge core and a heterogeneous Ge oxide shell make up the Ge NWs' core–shell configuration. The memory retention capacity depends on the thickness and structure of a Ge oxide shell, which may be achieved by a basic hardening procedure in air [46–51]. The current method does not require any protective coating or deliberate doping, and it suggests that semiconducting NWs with substantial surface oxide layers might be used to create nanoscale NVMs [36]. To build a Ge NW-based FETs, the lithographic approach specified the Au top electrodes (drain and source, 50 nm), and a representative device is depicted in the scanning electron microscope shown in Figure 7.6.

7.7 GAN NANOWIRE-BASED MEMORY

Owing to its special material features, gallium nitride (GaN), among the numerous semiconductor materials, is ideally suited for optical or advances technological circuits due to its wider energy band gap and quick carrier concentration. Furthermore, due to its radiation hardness, it has the potential to be used in severe situations. Optical and electrical nanoscale devices based on GaN nanowires have been developed and proven promising in recent years. A NVM device is suggested like another future application of GaN nanowires. Over the years, considerable progress has been made in

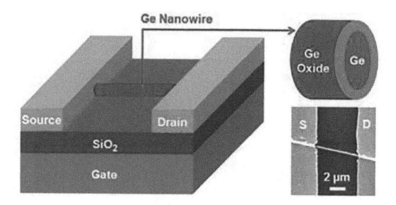

FIGURE 7.6 Proposed device construction of a Ge-NW-based FET memory with a Ge core surrounded by a Ge oxide shell.

the development of re-programmable and NVM technologies. The theory of employing idea of NVM devices was sparked by a FG mechanism in which electrons are trapped inside and released from the FG by significant tunneling [21,22]. Leakage via tiny holes in the dielectric is a severe problem with FG memory devices owing to the complexity of establishing a thin dielectric sheet with no defects. The charge-trapping memory device is yet another sort of memory device. Moreover, with charge-trapping devices, there seems to be an inherent retention difficulty caused by charge leakage from the insulating layer owing to the applied potential. Charge-trapping devices, on the other hand, have an inherent retention difficulty caused by the loss of charges from insulating layer throughout normal conditions, when the applied potential is reverse; caught electrons tends to be freed if they're in deep traps [52–56]. To solve this retention issue, an oxide-nitride-oxide composition was suggested. The addition of an oxide layer on the opposite side of the nitride storage nodes aids in the retention of collected charge [37]. Using a multilayer e-beam resist approach, the air-bridge constructed the gate layer above the source electrode. Figure 7.7a–c shows

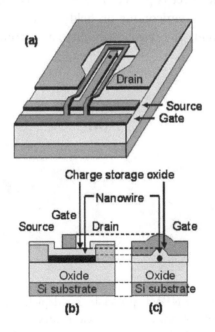

FIGURE 7.7 (a) A GaN nanowire FET with a top-gate is depicted. (b) The cross-section of a nanowire channel is depicted in this diagram. (c) A cross-sectional diagram of a nanowire channel [37].

Scanning Electron Microscope (SEM) views of a nanowire and manufactured devices.

7.8 FEFET-BASED MEMORY

Ferroelectrics are dielectric crystalline having a perovskite structure in general. Because of a deformation of the lattice involving the relative disposition of B^{4+} in each cell, piezoelectric effect occurs when the temperature changes. Just at a certain degree do this ferroelectric behavior arise (Curie temperature, TC) [57–63]. In other terms, by modulating E, P can be switched, and the leftover polarization + Pr and Pr phases are kept in ferroelectric. For Nonvolatile Memory Devices (NVMDs), the monostable state of ferroelectric may be represented as binary data '1' and '0.' As a result, significant efforts have been made to utilize accessible NVMD devices on the basis of the above. In order to take full advantage or benefits of ferroelectric for producing NVMDs, a suitable model is required [64–67]. The capacitor or Ferroelectric Field Effect Transistor (FeFET) is used as the foundation for most memory devices. In the first concept, a thin ferroelectric sheet is placed between two conducting electrodes, while a metal-oxide-semiconductor field-effect transistor (MOSFET) is used in the second. The respective schematic diagrams are shown in Figure 7.8.

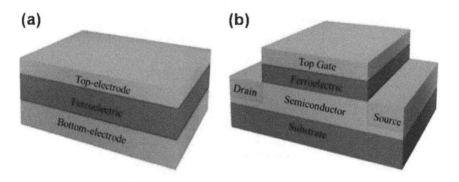

FIGURE 7.8 The existing NVMD principles are depicted in above diagram. (a) A capacitor is made up of two conducting electrodes separated by a thin ferroelectric sheet. (b) The FeFET design that uses ferroelectric instead of MOSFET dielectric.

7.9 MARKET MEMORY TECHNOLOGIES BY APPLICATIONS

In 2010–2014, the globally embedded NVM industry was valued USD 129.9 million. Figure 7.9 presents the information about the increasing prevalence of IoT-based devices and systems in developing nations are credited with the market's rise. The demand for pervasive connectivity demands the rapid implementation of low-cost, low-power solutions capable of secure communication. NVM is a tiny chip that can be employed in a wide range of embedded system purposes [68–75]. It is generally used for data encryption, coding, trimming, authentication, coding, and redundancies in smart cards, SIM cards, microcontrollers, Power management integrated circuits (PMICs), and displays driver ICs [76–84]. Companies are concentrating their efforts on delivering secure eNVMs for Microprocessor Control Unit (MCUs) used in IoT-based products.

7.10 PRODUCT SUGGESTIONS

Because of its widespread use in autos, smart cards, consumer electronics, and industrial applications, eFlash is likely to dominate the product segment [85–91]. The change from eFlash to Ferroelectric Random Access Memory (FRAM) in IoT microcontroller devices, on the other hand, could drive eFlash development in the automobile market. In terms of functionality, endurance, density, and read and write speed, eE^2 PROM is similar to eFlash. Due to the inclusion of the security module, which expands the application area from SIM card, social security card, U-key, and bank card to a range of security ICs, the size of eE^2 PROM

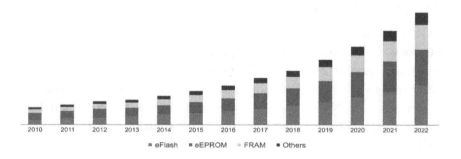

FIGURE 7.9 Market size for different Nonvolatile Semiconductor Memory (NVSM) applications in the electronics industry in 2022.

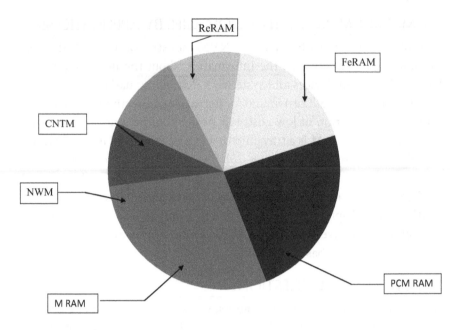

FIGURE 7.10   eNVM market share by product by 2021 (in Million USD).

varies greatly [92–103]. However, various additional products with extremely efficient security technologies, such as RRAM and STT-RAM, CNT Memory, and nanowire-based memory are expected to gradually displace eE^2 PROM over the projection period. Figure 7.10 represents the various types of NVM according to the market demand.

7.11 CONCLUSION

In this chapter we have discussed the various types of nanowire-based memory on the basis of different parameters like diameter, mobility, resistivity, permittivity, etc. The GaN-based memory is the best as compared to other memories, because it consumes less power and less power delay, etc. NVMs have great demand in market and this will lead further semiconductor industry. The work presented in this chapter will be useful for scientific, research, and industry personnel working in this area.

ACKNOWLEDGMENTS

The authors acknowledged Dr. B.R. Ambedkar National Institute of Technology Jalandhar for providing resources to this research work. We would like to express our gratitude to the Department of ECE at NIT

Jalandhar for providing lab space and a supportive research atmosphere for this project. We also thank VLSI research group, Department of Electronics and Communication Engineering, NITTTR Chandigarh, for their interest in this work and useful comments to draft the final version of the chapter.

REFERENCES

1. A. Bhardwaj, P. Kumar, B. Raj, and S. Anand, "Design and Performance Optimization of Doping-Less Vertical Nanowire TFET Using Gate Stack Technique," *Journal of Electronic Materials (JEMS)*, Springer, Vol. 41, No. 7, pp. 4005–4013, 2022.
2. J. Singh, and B. Raj, "Tunnel Current Model of Asymmetric MIM Structure Levying Various Image Forces to Analyze the Characteristics of Filamentary Memristor", *Applied Physics A*, Springer, Vol. 125, No. 3, pp. 203.1 to 203.11, 2019.
3. C. Goyal, J. S. Ubhi, and B. Raj, "Low Leakage Zero Ground Noise Nanoscale Full Adder Using Source Biasing Technique", *Journal of Nanoelectronics and Optoelectronics*, American Scientific Publishers, Vol. 14, pp. 360–370, 2019.
4. G. Singh, R. K. Sarin, and B. Raj, "A Novel Robust Exclusive-OR Function Implementation in QCA Nanotechnology with Energy Dissipation Analysis", *Journal of Computational Electronics*, Springer, Vol. 15, No. 2, pp. 455–465, 2016.
5. A. S. Tomar, V. K. Magraiya, and B. Raj, "Scaling of Access and Data Transistor for High Performance DRAM Cell Design", *Quantum Matter*, Vol. 2, pp. 412–416, 2013.
6. N. Jain, and B. Raj, "Parasitic Capacitance and Resistance Model Development and Optimization of Raised Source/Drain SOI FinFET Structure for Analog Circuit Applications", *Journal of Nanoelectronics and Optoelectronics*, ASP, USA, Vol. 13, pp. 531–539, 2018.
7. S. Singh, S. K. Vishvakarma, and B. Raj, "Analytical Modeling of Split-Gate Junction-Less Transistor for a Biosensor Application", *Sensing and Bio-Sensing*, Elsevier, Vol. 18, pp. 31–36, 2018.
8. M. Gopal, and B. Raj, "Low Power 8T SRAM Cell Design for High Stability Video Applications", *ITSI Transaction on Electrical and Electronics Engineering*, Vol. 1, No. 5, pp. 91–97, 2013.
9. B. Raj, J. Mitra, D. K. Bihani, V. Rangharajan, A. K. Saxena, and S. Dasgupta, "Analysis of Noise Margin, Power and Process Variation for 32 nm FinFET Based 6T SRAM Cell", *Journal of Computer (JCP)*, Academy Publisher, FINLAND, Vol. 5, No. 6, pp. 1–8, 2010.
10. D. Sharma, R. Mehra, and B. Raj, "Comparative Analysis of Photovoltaic Technologies for High Efficiency Solar Cell Design", *Superlattices and Microstructures*, Elsevier, Vol. 153, pp. 106861, 2021.
11. P. Kaur, A. S. Buttar, and B. Raj, "A Comprehensive Analysis of Nanoscale Transistor Based Biosensor: A Review", *Indian Journal of Pure and Applied Physics*, Vol. 59, pp. 304–318, 2021.

12. D. Yadav, B. Raj, and B. Raj, "Design and Simulation of Low Power Microcontroller for IoT Applications", *Journal of Sensor Letters*, ASP, Vol. 18, pp. 401–409, 2020.

13. S. Singh, and B. Raj, "A 2-D Analytical Surface Potential and Drain Current Modeling of Double-Gate Vertical t-Shaped Tunnel FET", *Journal of Computational Electronics*, Springer, Vol. 19, pp. 1154–1163, 2020.

14. J. Singh, and B. Raj, "An Accurate and Generic Window function for Non-linear Memristor Model" *Journal of Computational Electronics*, Springer, Vol. 18, No. 2, pp. 640–647, 2019

15. M. Kaur, N. Gupta, S. Kumar, B. Raj, and A. K. Singh, "Comparative RF and Crosstalk Analysis of Carbon Based Nano Interconnects", *IET Circuits, Devices & Systems*, Vol. 15, No. 6, pp. 493–503, 2021

16. N. Jain, and B. Raj, "Dual-k Spacer Region Variation at the Drain Side of Asymmetric SOI FinFET Structure: Performance Analysis towards the Analog/RF Design Applications", *Journal of Nanoelectronics and Optoelectronics*, American Scientific Publishers, Vol. 14, pp. 349–359, 2019.

17. J. Singh, S. Sharma, B. Raj, and "M. Khosla, "Analysis of Barrier Layer Thickness on Performance of $In_{1-x}Ga_xAs$ Based Gate Stack Cylindrical Gate Nanowire MOSFET", *JNO*, ASP, Vol. 13, pp. 1473–1477, 2018.

18. N. Jain, and B. Raj, "Analysis and Performance Exploration of High-k SOI FinFETs over the Conventional Low-k SOI FinFET toward Analog/ RF Design", *Journal of Semiconductors (JoS)*, IOP Science, Vol. 39, No. 12, pp. 124002-1-7, 2018.

19. C. Goyal, J. S. Ubhi, and B. Raj, "A Reliable Leakage Reduction Technique for Approximate Full Adder with Reduced Ground Bounce Noise", *Journal of Mathematical Problems in Engineering*, Hindawi, Vol. 2018, Article ID 3501041, 16 pages, 2018.

20. Anuradha, J. Singh, B. Raj, and M. Khosla, "Design and Performance Analysis of Nano-scale Memristor-Based Nonvolatile SRAM", *Journal of Sensor Letter*, American Scientific Publishers, Vol. 16, pp. 798–805, 2018.

21. G. Wadhwa, and B. Raj, "Parametric Variation Analysis of Charge-Plasma-Based Dielectric Modulated JLTFET for Biosensor Application", *IEEE Sensor Journal*, Vol. 18, No. 15, pp. 6070–6077, 2018.

22. J. Singh, and B. Raj, "Comparative Analysis of Memristor Models for Memories Design", *JoS*, IoP, Vol. 39, No. 7, pp. 074006-1-12, 2018.

23. T. Wadhera, D. Kakkar, G. Wadhwa, and B. Raj, "Recent Advances and Progress in Development of the Field Effect Transistor Biosensor: A Review" *Journal of Electronic Materials*, Springer, Vol. 48, No. 12, pp. 7635–7646, 2019.

24. N. Kandasamy, F. Ahmad, D. Ajitha, B. Raj, and N. Telagam, "Quantum Dot Cellular Automata Based Scan Flip Flop and Boundary Scan Register", *IETE Journal of Research*, 2020

25. S. K. Sharma, B. Raj, and M. Khosla, "Enhanced Photosensitivity of Highly Spectrum Selective Cylindrical Gate $In_{1-x}Ga_xAs$ Nanowire MOSFET Photodetector", *Modern Physics Letter-B*, Vol. 33, No. 12, p. 1950144, 2019.

26. G. Wadhwa, P. Kamboj, and B. Raj, "Design Optimisation of Junctionless TFET Biosensor for High Sensitivity", *Advances in Natural Sciences: Nanoscience and Nanotechnology*, Vol. 10, No. 7, p. 045001, 2019.

27. J. Singh, and B. Raj, "Design and Investigation of 7T2M NVSARM with Enhanced Stability and Temperature Impact on Store/Restore Energy", *IEEE Transactions on Very Large Scale Integration Systems*, Vol. 27, No. 6, pp. 1322–1328, 2019.

28. A. K. Bhardwaj, S. Gupta, B. Raj, and A. Singh, "Impact of Double Gate Geometry on the Performance of Carbon Nanotube Field Effect Transistor Structures for Low Power Digital Design", *Computational and Theoretical Nanoscience*, ASP, Vol. 16, pp. 1813–1820, 2019.

29. D. Yadav, S. S. Chouhan, S. K. Vishvakarma, and B. Raj, "Application Specific Microcontroller Design for IoT Based WSN", *Sensor Letter*, ASP, Vol. 16, pp. 374–385, 2018.

30. G. Singh, R. K. Sarin, and B. Raj, "Fault-Tolerant Design and Analysis of Quantum-Dot Cellular Automata Based Circuits", *IEEE/IET Circuits, Devices & Systems*, Vol. 12, pp. 638–664, 2018.

31. J. Singh, and B. Raj, "Modeling of Mean Barrier Height Levying Various Image Forces of Metal Insulator Metal Structure to Enhance the Performance of Conductive Filament Based Memristor Model", *IEEE Nanotechnology*, Vol. 17, No. 2, pp. 268–275, 2018.

32. A. Jain, S. Sharma, and B. Raj, "Analysis of Triple Metal Surrounding Gate (TM-SG) III-V Nanowire MOSFET for Photosensing Application", *Opto-Electronics Journal*, Elsevier, Vol. 26, No. 2, pp. 141–148, 2018.

33. A. Jain, S. Sharma, and B. Raj, "Design and Analysis of High Sensitivity Photosensor Using Cylindrical Surrounding Gate MOSFET for Low Power Sensor Applications", *Engineering Science and Technology, an International Journal*, Elsevier's, Vol. 19, No. 4, pp. 1864–1870, 2016.

34. A. Singh, M. Khosla, and B. Raj, "Analysis of Electrostatic Doped Schottky Barrier Carbon Nanotube FET for Low Power Applications," *Journal of Materials Science: Materials in Electronics*, Springer, Vol. 28, pp. 1762–1768, 2017.

35. G. Saiphani Kumar, A. Singh, B. Raj, "Design and Analysis of Gate All Around CNTFET Based SRAM Cell Design", *Journal of Computational Electronics*, Springer, Vol. 17, No.1, pp. 138–145, 2018.

36. P. Bansal, and B. Raj, "Memristor Modeling and Analysis for Linear Dopant Drift Kinetics", *Journal of Nanoengineering and Nanomanufacturing*, American Scientific Publishers, Vol. 6, pp. 1–7, 2016.

37. A. Singh, M. Khosla, and B. Raj, "Circuit Compatible Model for Electrostatic Doped Schottky Barrier CNTFET", *Journal of Electronic Materials*, Springer, Vol. 45, No. 12, pp. 4825–4835, 2016.

38. Ashima, D. Vaithiyanathan, and B. Raj, "Performance Analysis of Charge Plasma Induced Graded Channel Si Nanotube", *Journal of Engineering Research (JER)*, EMSME Special Issue, pp. 146–154, 2021.

39. N. Jain, and B. Raj, "Thermal Stability Analysis and Performance Exploration of Asymmetrical Dual-k Underlap Spacer (ADKUS) SOI FinFET for Security and Privacy Applications", *Indian Journal of Pure & Applied Physics (IJPAP)*, Vol. 57, pp. 352–360, 2019.

40. A. Singh, M. Khosla, and B. Raj, "Design and Analysis of Dynamically Configurable Electrostatic Doped Carbon Nanotube Tunnel FET", *Microelectronics Journal*, Elsevier, Vol. 85, pp. 17–24, 2019.

41. G. P. Singh, B. S. Sohi, and B. Raj, "Material Properties Analysis of Graphene Base Transistor (GBT) for VLSI Analog Circuits", *Indian Journal of Pure & Applied Physics (IJPAP)*, Vol. 55, pp. 896–902, 2017.

42. S. Kumar and B. Raj, "Estimation of Stability and Performance metric for Inward Access Transistor Based 6T SRAM Cell Design using n-type/p-type DMDG-GDOV TFET", *IEEE VLSI Circuits and Systems Letter*, Vol. 3, No. 2, pp. 25–39, 2017.

43. S. Sharma, A. Kumar, M. Pattanaik, and B. Raj, "Forward Body Biased Multimode Multi-Threshold CMOS Technique for Ground Bounce Noise Reduction in Static CMOS Adders", *International Journal of Information and Electronics Engineering*, Vol. 3, No. 3, pp. 567–572, 2013.

44. H. Singh, P. Kumar, and B. Raj, "Performance Analysis of Majority Gate SET Based 1-bit Full Adder", *International Journal of Computer and Communication Engineering (IJCCE)*, IACSIT Press Singapore, ISSN: 2010-3743, Vol. 2, No. 4, pp. 1–6, 2013.

45. A. K. Bhardwaj, S. Gupta, and B. Raj, "Investigation of Parameters for Schottky Barrier (SB) Height for Schottky Barrier Based Carbon Nanotube Field Effect Transistor Device", *Journal of Nanoelectronics and Optoelectronics*, ASP, Vol. 15, pp. 783–791, 2020.

46. P. Bansal, and B. Raj, "Memristor: A Versatile Nonlinear Model for Dopant Drift and Boundary Issues", *JCTN*, American Scientific Publishers, Vol. 14, No. 5, pp. 2319–2325, 2017.

47. N. Jain, and B. Raj, "An Analog and Digital Design Perspective Comprehensive Approach on Fin-FET (Fin-Field Effect Transistor) Technology - A Review", *Reviews in Advanced Sciences and Engineering (RASE)*, ASP, Vol. 5, pp. 1–14, 2016.

48. S. Sharma, B. Raj, and M. Khosla, "Subthreshold Performance of $In_{1-x}Ga_xAs$ Based Dual Metal with Gate Stack Cylindrical/Surrounding Gate Nanowire MOSFET for Low Power Analog Applications", *Journal of Nanoelectronics and Optoelectronics*, American Scientific Publishers, USA, Vol. 12, pp. 171–176, 2017.

49. B. Raj, A. K. Saxena, and S. Dasgupta, "Analytical Modeling for the Estimation of Leakage Current and Subthreshold Swing Factor of Nanoscale Double Gate FinFET Device" *Microelectronics International, UK*, Vol. 26, pp. 53–63, 2009.

50. S. S. Soniya, G. Wadhwa, and B. Raj, "An Analytical Modeling for Dual Source Vertical Tunnel Field Effect Transistor", *International Journal of Recent Technology and Engineering (IJRTE)*, Vol. 8, No. 2, pp. 603–608, 2019.

51. S. Singh, and B. Raj, "Design and Analysis of Heterojunction Vertical T-Shaped Tunnel Field Effect Transistor", *Journal of Electronics Material*, Springer, Vol. 48, No. 10, pp. 6253–6260, 2019.

52. C. Goyal, J. S. Ubhi, and B. Raj, "A Low Leakage CNTFET Based Inexact Full Adder for Low Power Image Processing Applications", *International Journal of Circuit Theory and Applications*, Wiley, Vol. 47, No. 9, pp. 1446–1458, 2019.

53. B. Raj, A. K. Saxena, and S. Dasgupta, "A Compact Drain Current and Threshold Voltage Quantum Mechanical Analytical Modeling for FinFETs", *Journal of Nanoelectronics and Optoelectronics (JNO)*, *USA*, Vol. 3, No. 2, pp. 163–170, 2008.

54. G. Wadhwa, and B. Raj, "An Analytical Modeling of Charge Plasma Based Tunnel Field Effect Transistor with Impacts of Gate Underlap Region", *Superlattices and Microstructures*, Elsevier, Vol. 142, p. 106512, 2020.

55. S. Singh, and B. Raj, "Modeling and Simulation Analysis of SiGe Heterojunction Double Gate Vertical t-Shaped Tunnel FET", *Superlattices and Microstructures*, Elsevier, Vol. 142, p. 106496, 2020.

56. A. Singh, D. K. Saini, D. Agarwal, S. Aggarwal, M. Khosla, and B. Raj, "Modeling and Simulation of Carbon Nanotube Field Effect Transistor and its Circuit Application", *Journal of Semiconductors (JoS)*, IOP Science, Vol. 37, pp. 074001–074006, 2016.

57. N. Jain, and B. Raj, "Device and Circuit Co-Design Perspective Comprehensive Approach on FinFET Technology - A Review", *Journal of Electron Devices*, Vol. 23, No. 1, pp. 1890–1901, 2016.

58. S. Kumar and B. Raj, "Analysis of I_{ON} and Ambipolar Current for Dual-Material Gate-Drain Overlapped DG-TFET", *Journal of Nanoelectronics and Optoelectronics*, American Scientific Publishers, USA, Vol. 11, pp. 323–333, 2016.

59. N. Anjum, T. Bali, and B. Raj, "Design and Simulation of Handwritten Multiscript Character Recognition", *International Journal of Advanced Research in Computer and Communication Engineering*, Vol. 2, No. 7, pp. 2544–2549, 2013.

60. S. Sharma, B. Raj, and M. Khosla, "A Gaussian Approach for Analytical Subthreshold Current Model of Cylindrical Nanowire FET with Quantum Mechanical Effects", *Microelectronics Journal*, Elsevier, Vol. 53, pp. 65–72, 2016.

61. K. Singh, and B. Raj, "Performance and Analysis of Temperature Dependent Multi-Walled Carbon Nanotubes as Global Interconnects at Different Technology Nodes", *Journal of Computational Electronics*, Springer, Vol. 14, No. 2, pp. 469–476, 2015.

62. S. Kumar and B. Raj, "Compact Channel Potential Analytical Modeling of DG-TFET Based on Evanescent–Mode Approach", *Journal of Computational Electronics*, Springer, Vol. 14, No. 2, pp. 820–827, 2015.

63. K. Singh, and B. Raj, "Temperature Dependent Modeling and Performance Evaluation of Multi-Walled CNT and Single-Walled CNT as Global Interconnects", *Journal of Electronic Materials*, Springer, Vol. 44, No. 12, pp. 4825–4835, 2015.

64. V. K. Sharma, M. Pattanaik, and B. Raj, "INDEP Approach for Leakage Reduction in Nanoscale CMOS Circuits", *International Journal of Electronics*, Taylor & Francis, Vol. 102, No. 2, pp. 200–215, 2014.

65. K. Singh, and B. Raj, "Influence of Temperature on MWCNT Bundle, SWCNT Bundle and Copper Interconnects for Nanoscaled Technology Nodes", *Journal of Materials Science: Materials in Electronics*, Springer, Vol. 26, No. 8, pp. 6134–6142, 2015.

66. N. Anjum, T. Bali, and B. Raj, "Design and Simulation of Handwritten Gurumukhi and Devanagri Numerical Recognition", *International Journal of Computer Applications*, Published by Foundation of Computer Science, New York, USA, Vol. 73, No. 12, pp. 16–21, 2013.

67. S. Khandelwal, V. Gupta, B. Raj, and R. D. Gupta, "Process Variability Aware Low Leakage Reliable Nano Scale DG-FinFET SRAM Cell Design Technique", *Journal of Nanoelectronics and Optoelectronics*, Vol. 10, No. 6, pp. 810–817, 2015.

68. V. K. Sharma, M. Pattanaik, and B. Raj, "ONOFIC Approach: Low Power High Speed Nanoscale VLSI Circuits Design", *International Journal of Electronics*, Taylor & Francis, Vol. 101, No. 1, pp. 61–73, 2014.

69. S. Khandelwal, B. Raj, and R. D. Gupta, "FinFET Based 6T SRAM Cell Design: Analysis of Performance Metric, Process Variation and Temperature Effect", *Journal of Computational and Theoretical Nanoscience*, ASP, USA, Vol. 12, pp. 2500–2506, 2015.

70. S. Singh, Y. Shekhar, R. Jagdeep, S. Anurag, and B. Raj, "Impact of HfO_2 in Graded Channel Dual Insulator Double Gate MOSFET", *Journal of Computational and Theoretical Nanoscience*, American Scientific Publishers, Vol. 12, No. 6, pp. 950–953, 2015.

71. V. K. Sharma, M. Pattanaik, and B. Raj, "PVT Variations Aware Low Leakage INDEP Approach for Nanoscale CMOS Circuits", *Microelectronics Reliability*, Elsevier, Vol. 54, pp. 90–99, 2014.

72. B. Raj, A. K. Saxena and S. Dasgupta, "Quantum Mechanical Analytical Modeling of Nanoscale DG FinFET: Evaluation of Potential, Threshold Voltage and Source/Drain Resistance", *Elsevier's Journal of Material Science in Semiconductor Processing*, Elsevier, Vol. 16, No. 4, pp. 1131–1137, 2013.

73. M. Gopal, S. S. D. Prasad, and B. Raj, "8T SRAM Cell Design for Dynamic and Leakage Power Reduction", *International Journal of Computer Applications*, Published by Foundation of Computer Science, New York, USA, Vol. 71, No. 9, pp. 43–48, 2013.

74. M. Pattanaik, B. Raj, S. Sharma, and A. Kumar, "Diode Based Trimode Multi-Threshold CMOS Technique for Ground Bounce Noise Reduction in Static CMOS Adders", *Advanced Materials Research*, Trans Tech Publications, Switzerland, Vol. 548, pp. 885–889, 2012.

75. B. Raj, A. K. Saxena, and S. Dasgupta, "Nanoscale FinFET Based SRAM Cell Design: Analysis of Performance metric, Process variation, Underlapped FinFET and Temperature effect", *IEEE Circuits and System Magazine*, Vol. 11, No. 2, pp. 38–50, 2011.

76. V. K. Sharma, M. Pattanaik, and B. Raj, "Leakage Current ONOFIC Approach for Deep Submicron VLSI Circuit Design", *International Journal of Electrical, Computer, Electronics and Communication Engineering*, World Academy of Sciences, Engineering and Technology, Vol. 7, No. 4, pp. 239–244, 2013.

77. T. Chawla, M. Khosla, and B. Raj, "Design and simulation of Triple metal Double-gate Germanium on Insulator Vertical Tunnel Field Effect Transistor", *Microelectronics Journal*, Elsevier, Vol. 114, pp. 105125, 2021.

78. P. Kaur, S. S. Gill, and B. Raj, "Comparative Analysis of OFETs Materials and Devices for Sensor Applications", *Journal of Silicon*, Springer, Vol. 14, pp. 4463–4471, 2022.

79. S. K. Sharma, P. Kumar, B. Raj, and B. Raj, "In$_{1-x}$Ga$_x$As Double Metal Gate-Stacking Cylindrical Nanowire MOSFET for Highly Sensitive Photo detector", *Journal of Silicon*, Springer, Vol. 14, pp. 3535–3541, 2022.

80. B. Raj, A. K. Saxena, and S. Dasgupta, "Analytical Modeling of Quasi Planar Nanoscale Double Gate FinFET with Source/Drain Resistance and Field Dependent Carrier Mobility: A Quantum Mechanical Study", *Journal of Computer (JCP)*, Academy Publisher, FINLAND, Vol. 4, No. 9, pp. 1–8, 2009.

81. S. Bhushan, S. Khandelwal, and B. Raj, "Analyzing Different Mode FinFET Based Memory Cell at Different Power Supply for Leakage Reduction", Seventh International Conference on Bio-Inspired Computing: Theories and Application, (BIC-TA 2012), *Advances in Intelligent Systems and Computing*, Vol. 202, pp. 89–100, 2013.

82. J. Singh, and B. Raj, "Temperature Dependent Analytical Modeling and Simulations of Nanoscale Memristor", *Engineering Science and Technology, an International Journal*, Elsevier's, Vol. 21, pp. 862–868, 2018.

83. S. Singh, S. Bala, B. Raj, and B. Raj, "Improved Sensitivity of Dielectric Modulated Junctionless Transistor for Nanoscale Biosensor Design", *Sensor Letter*, ASP, Vol. 18, pp. 328–333, 2020.

84. V. Kumar, S. K. Vishvakarma, and B. Raj, "Design and Performance Analysis of ASIC for IoT Applications", *Sensor Letter*, ASP, Vol. 18, pp. 31–38, 2020.

85. A. Jaiswal, R. K. Sarin, B. Raj, and S. Sukhija, "A Novel Circular Slotted Microstrip-fed Patch Antenna with Three Triangle Shape Defected Ground Structure for Multiband Applications", *Advanced Electromagnetic (AEM)*, Vol. 7, No. 3, pp. 56–63, 2018.

86. G. Wadhwa, and B Raj, "Label Free Detection of Biomolecules Using Charge-Plasma-Based Gate Underlap Dielectric Modulated Junctionless TFET", *Journal of Electronic Materials (JEMS)*, Springer, Vol. 47, No. 8, pp. 4683–4693, 2018.

87. G. Singh, R. K. Sarin, and B. Raj, "Design and Performance Analysis of a New Efficient Coplanar Quantum-Dot Cellular Automata Adder", *Indian Journal of Pure & Applied Physics (IJPAP)*, Vol. 55, pp. 97–103, 2017.

88. A. Singh, M. Khosla, and B. Raj, "Design and Analysis of Electrostatic Doped Schottky Barrier CNTFET Based Low Power SRAM", *International Journal of Electronics and Communications, (AEÜ)*, Elsevier, Vol. 80, pp. 67–72, 2017.

89. P. Kaur, V. Pandey, and B. Raj, "Comparative Study of Efficient Design, Control and Monitoring of Solar Power Using IoT", *Sensor Letter*, ASP, Vol. 18, pp. 419–426, 2020.

90. G. Wadhwa, P. Kamboj, J. Singh, B. Raj, "Design and Investigation of Junctionless DGTFET for Biological Molecule Recognition", *Transactions on Electrical and Electronic Materials*, Springer, Vol. 22, pp. 282–289, 2020

91. T. Chawla, M. Khosla, and B. Raj, "Optimization of Double-gate Dual material GeOI-Vertical TFET for VLSI Circuit Design", *IEEE VLSI Circuits and Systems Letter*, Vol. 6, No. 2, pp. 13–25, 2020.

92. S. K. Verma, S. Singh, G. Wadhwa and B. Raj, "Detection of Biomolecules using Charge-Plasma Based Gate Underlap Dielectric Modulated Dopingless TFET", *Transactions on Electrical and Electronic Materials (TEEM)*, Springer, Vol. 21, pp. 528–535, 2020.

93. N. Jain, and B. Raj, "Impact of Underlap Spacer Region Variation on Electrostatic and Analog/RF Performance of Symmetrical High-k SOI FinFET at 20 nm Channel Length", *Journal of Semiconductors (JoS)*, IOP Science, Vol. 38, No. 12, p. 122002, 2017.

94. S. Singh, and B. Raj, "Analytical Modeling and Simulation Analysis of T-Shaped III-V Heterojunction Vertical T-FET", *Superlattices and Microstructures*, Elsevier, Vol. 147, pp. 106717, 2020.

95. G. Singh, R. K. Sarin, and B. Raj, "Design and Analysis of Area Efficient QCA Based Reversible Logic Gates", *Journal of Microprocessors and Microsystems*, Elsevier, Vol. 52, pp. 59–68, 2017.

96. A. Singh, M. Khosla, and B. Raj, "Compact Model for Ballistic Single Wall CNTFET under Quantum Capacitance Limit", *Journal of Semiconductors (JoS)*, IOP Science, Vol. 37, pp. 104001–104008, 2016.

97. S. Singh, M. Khosla, G. Wadhwa, and B. Raj, "Design and Analysis of Double-Gate Junctionless Vertical TFET for Gas Sensing Applications", *Applied Physics A*, Springer, Vol. 127, No. 16, pp. 725–732, 2021.

98. I. Singh, B. Raj, M. Khosla, and B. K. Kaushik, "Potential MRAM Technologies for Low Power SoCs", *SPIN World Scientific Publisher, SCIE*; Vol. 10, No. 04, p. 2050027, 2020.

99. S. Singh, and B. Raj, "Parametric Variation Analysis on Hetero-Junction Vertical t-Shape TFET for Suppressing Ambipolar Conduction", *Indian Journal of Pure and Applied Physics*, Vol. 58, pp. 478–485, 2020.

100. S. S. Soniya, G. Wadhwa, and B. Raj, "Design and Analysis of Dual Source Vertical Tunnel Field Effect Transistor for High Performance", *Transactions on Electrical and Electronics Materials*, Springer, Vol. 21, pp. 74–82, 2019.

101. M. Kaur, N. Gupta, S. Kumar, B. Raj, and A. K. Singh, "RF Performance Analysis of Intercalated Graphene Nanoribbon Based Global Level Interconnects", *Journal of Computational Electronics*, Springer, Vol. 19, pp. 1002–1013, 2020.

102. G. Wadhwa, B. Raj, "Design and Performance Analysis of Junctionless TFET Biosensor for High Sensitivity" *IEEE Nanotechnology*, Vol. 18, pp. 567–574, 2019.

103. J. Singh, and B. Raj, "Enhanced Nonlinear Memristor Model Encapsulating Stochastic Dopant Drift", *JNO*, ASP, 14, 958–963, 2019.

CHAPTER 8

Intelligent Irrigation Systems

Parveen Kumar

Dr. B.R. Ambedkar National Institute of Technology

Balwant Raj

Panjab University SSG Regional Centre

Sanjeev Kumar Sharma and Balwinder Raj

Dr. B.R. Ambedkar National Institute of Technology

CONTENTS

DOI: 10.1201/9781003230113-8

8.1 INTRODUCTION

In the current scenario, the reduction of water and electricity consumption and its wastage is a major problem, which is faced by all of us due to the carelessness of the authorities, water operators, or unawareness of the farmers, which results in wastage of electricity as well as water. Agriculture is the predominant activity in the world for the production of vegetables, foods, fruits, and other essential items, which are used by human beings to sustain their lives. Worldwide, agriculture uses a huge amount of water (~85%) and electricity for cultivation and increases the demand for electricity and fresh water with the increase in population [1–4]. The most of the farmers are uses the traditional manual method for watering, cultivating plants and switching of water pumps which occupy a lot of time, manpower and unable to prevents their fields from environmental change in temperature [5–7]. In the agricultural system, there is a need for change in cultivation methods for saving water and electricity and preventing the plants from environmental impacts. The designed system overcomes the abovesaid problems and provides a suitable intelligent irrigation system for automatic plant watering, temperature monitoring for the safety of plants, and saving of electricity and water through wireless techniques such as global-system-for-mobile-communication (GSM) at low cost. In the present times, most of the people are using GSM-based mobile phones. With the advancement of technology in the past decades, a new concept called wireless switching has become established and through this concept people have been trying to control and secure their devices remotely by using the GSM technique [8]. The intelligent irrigation system controls water and electricity wastage through various methods and techniques all over the world [9–13]. So, it motivates us to design a system for intelligent irrigation system, which provides wireless access for agriculture works such as watering of plants, switching of water pump, and safety of plants using temperature and moisture sensors through SMS [14–22]. Figure 8.1 shows the block description of an intelligent irrigation system. The block diagram consists of three units, namely, processing unit (intelligent microcontroller), input unit (moisture sensor, temperature sensor, analog to digital converter, GSM Modem, and Plant Area), and output unit (relay driver, water pump, indicators, liquid crystal display, GSM modem, and user's handset). The processing unit is the heart of the whole

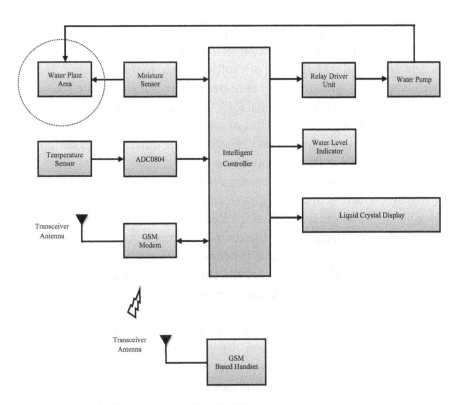

FIGURE 8.1 Block description of an intelligent irrigation system.

system, which is as intelligent controller (IC). It can be any controller such as Atmel microcontroller (AT89S52), AVR Controller, Ardiuno, Phillips (P89v51RD2), Resberry pie, or any other processing and controlling device; it depends upon the requirement and budget of the product. The input unit gives the input to the system through moisture sensor followed by their comparator circuitry, temperature sensor (LM35), and analog to digital converter (ADC0804) for the conversion of analog signal to digital form and GSM modem for receive messages from the user [23–30].

The output unit contains relay and its driver unit, which is used to perform the switching action of water pump, light-emitting diode (LED) indicator to show the status of water level or moisture level of soil, liquid crystal display (LCD) to display the current status of water pump and temperature, and GSM modem to send the message to the user.

8.2 DESIGN AND IMPLEMENTATION

The complete design and implementation of an intelligent irrigation system is the combination of hardware unit and software unit. The hardware unit is further divided into two sections like water planting section and another is the temperature monitoring section, which is discussed in a later section. The implementation of the system is performed through schematic design with the help of a software unit. In the schematic design, the components are virtually connected as per the required circuit diagram with the help of professional ISIS 7 Proteus designing and simulation software X [31–36]. The properties of every component can be varied during simulation and components can also change during circuit designing, which is available in the Proteous library.

After completion of the schematic design, simulation is performed and virtually verified in the circuit performance on Proteus with controller Hex file, which is generated through Keil complier and written in embedded C programming [37–42]. The complete software code has been generated in Keil complier and it also generates the Hex file for burning of the microcontroller, which is used at the time of physical as well as virtual verification. The complete schematic design of an intelligent irrigation system is shown in Figure 8.2.

The GSM modem (SIM300) acts as an intermediate between users/farmers and the designed system, which provides the wireless environment through SMS. As GSM modem receives the message, microcontroller extracts the command automatically and turns ON/OFF water pump. The moisture sensor is used to detect moisture level of the plant area and sends the signal to IC for further action and glows the corresponding indicators as per the level moisture level of the soil [43–48]. The IC will automatically turn OFF the water pump if the water plant area is full or moisture level of soil is higher, which is indicated by the Red LED. The relay driver unit contains a PNP and NPN transistor, which act as a Darlington pair and generates LOW output if it receives LOW input and HIGH output if it receives HIGH input. The relay is a switching device, which turns ON or OFF the water pump as per instructions given by the IC [49–56]. The microcontroller automatically generates a SMS to the farmer's handset through the GSM module to notify the status of the water pump, current temperature, and water level of the plant area. The detailed configuration of the designed system is given as:

8.2.1 Water Planting Section

In this session, automatic plant watering takes place. In the start, a SMS (acts as the password) is sent through the user's handset for system initialization. The system will be initialized only if the received password is matched with the stored password, otherwise it will be still in the off state. If the system starts, the input of the session is taken from the moisture

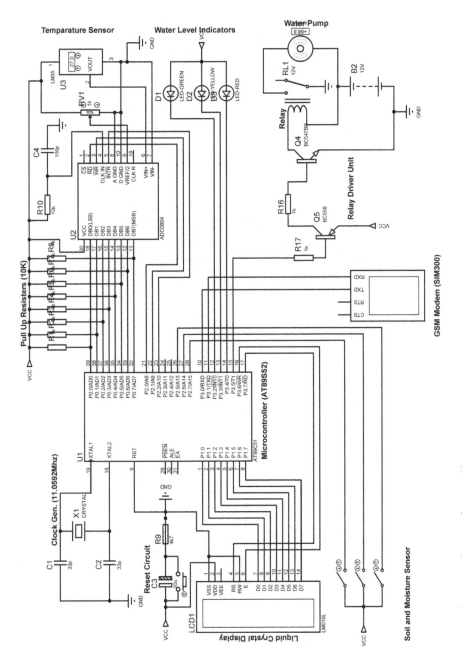

FIGURE 8.2   Schematic design of an intelligent irrigation system.

sensor, which is installed in the plant area to check the moisture level of soil. The received signal is passed to the intelligent microcontroller for further processing followed by comparator circuitry of the moisture sensor [57–63]. The microcontroller decodes the received input from moisture sensor and executes the instructions as per the hex code in the read only memory (ROM) of the microcontroller. If the moisture level is low then the IC automatically ON the water pump for water planting as well as given the indication through Green LED and middle level of moisture indicated by yellow LED and Higher moisture level indicated by Red LED as discussed earlier in Section 8.1. The flow chart of water planting session is illustrated in Figure 8.3.

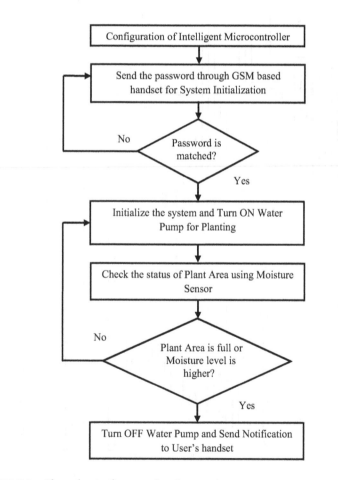

FIGURE 8.3   Flow chart of water planting session.

If the current moisture level is higher and RED is ON, then the water pump automatically turns off and a text message is generated to the user's handset for the current status of the pump through the GSM modem. The overall processing of this work is performed by IC (AT89S52) and schematic has been designed as shown in Figure 8.4. The Proteous tool has been used for the circuit designing of the water planting system.

If the current moisture level is higher and RED is ON, then the water pump automatically turns off and a text message is generated to the user's handset regarding the current status of the pump through the GSM [64–70]. The water pump is driven by relay and its driver circuit, which is the Darlington pair of transistors which gives LOW output if it receives LOW input and HIGH output if receives HIGH input. As per the schematic diagram, the positive supply is directly given to the water pump and negative supply is given through the relay. The relay is the automatic switch, which turns on the water pump by receiving LOW input from the Darlington pair, which acts as relay driver circuit and turns off the water pump by receiving HIGH input [71–75].

8.2.2 Temperature Monitoring Section

In this session, the temperature monitoring has been performed to prevent the plants from external undesired environmental effects in terms of temperature. The system will start through the user's handset by sending an accurate SMS, which act as the password for system initialization. If the received password is matched with stored data, then the system will be ON [76–81]. The input of the session is taken from the temperature sensor (LM35), which is used to measure the environmental temperature and pass the signal to the analog to digital converter (ADC) for further processing. The flow chart of the temperature monitoring session is illustrated by Figure 8.5.

The received signal from ADC is passed to the intelligent microcontroller and the corresponding value of temperature is displayed by the LCD as well as sent as an alert message to the user's handset by decoding the stored software code in the ROM of the microcontroller [82–87].

If the temperature level is lower or higher than the desired temperature for the plants, the microcontroller automatically sends an alert message to the user's handset for covering of plants, which provides safety to growing or grown plants on the agricultural land. The schematic has been designed for temperature monitoring session as shown in Figure 8.6.

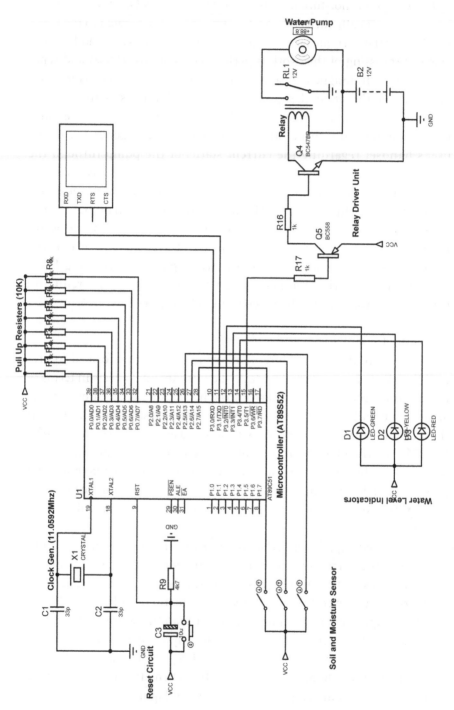

FIGURE 8.4   Schematic of water planting session.

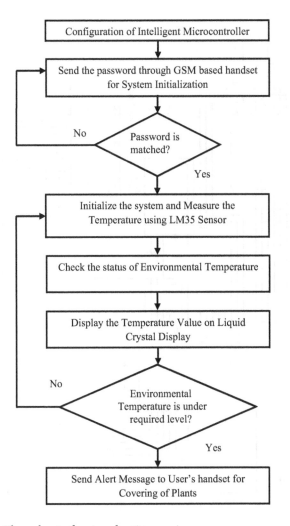

FIGURE 8.5 Flow chart of water planting session.

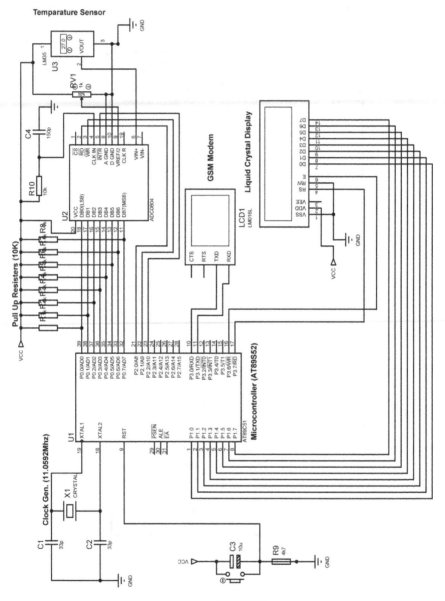

FIGURE 8.6   Schematic of water planting session along with LCD Display.

8.3 HARDWARE COMPONENTS DESCRIPTION

The completer hardware description of the intelligent irrigation system has been discussed in this session, which consists of microcontroller, GSM modem, relay and its driver unit, moisture sensor, temperature sensor, analog to digital converter, water pump, and power supply [88–93]. The complete hardware component descriptions are given in the following sessions:

8.3.1 Microcontroller (AT89S52)

The main processing unit of the designed system is Atmel 8-bit microcontroller (AT89S52). A microcontroller consists of random access memory (RAM = 128bytes), ROM (4Kbyte), EEPROM, serial COM port (1), microprocessor, interrupts (8), and peripheral ports (4) on a single chip itself and is considered as a computer on a chip. The pin description of AT89S52 microcontroller is shown in Figure 8.7.

The microcontroller (AT89S52) has four input/output ports (Port 0, Port 1, Port 2, and Port 3), with each port containing 8 bits and the total number of input/output pins is 32 [94–98]. It supports parallel programming (PP), in application programming (IAP), and two 16-bits of timer/

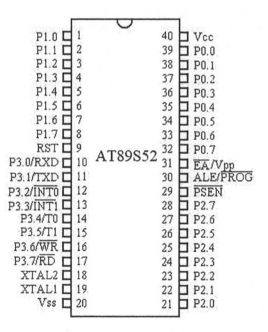

FIGURE 8.7 Pin description of the microcontroller.

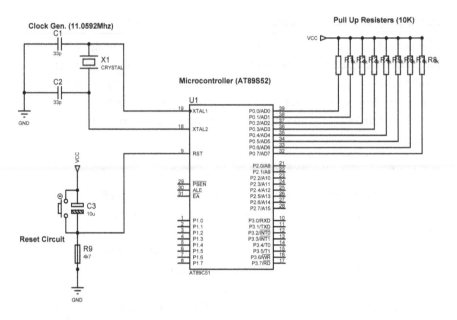

FIGURE 8.8   Basic circuitry of the microcontroller.

counters and operates on +5V dc supply. The basic circuitry of the micro-controller is shown in Figure 8.8.

The port 0 is not directly taken as input or output port until pull-up or pull-down registers cannot be connected to it as shown in Figure 8.8. In the pull-up and pull-down configuration one side of all registers are connected to Vcc (+5V) supply and ground terminal (GND) respectively.

8.3.1.1 Reset Circuit

The pin number 9 of the microcontroller is the reset pin. Initially, it is a low input pin and active on high pulse. When the high input is applied to this pin through external reset circuitry, the microcontroller will be reset and all activities that are currently being executed will be terminated. The reset circuitry consists of a serial combination of a capacitor (10 μF) and resister (R = 10 k) and parallel reset switch with C as shown in Figure 8.9.

8.3.1.2 Clock Generator

The AT89S52 has an on-chip oscillator but it also requires external clock generator circuit for its operation and it is connected to XTAL1 (pin no. 19) and XTAL2 (pin no. 20) of the microcontroller [99–101]. The clock frequency of the AT89S52 microcontroller is 11.0592 MHz (~=12 MHz), so we need to connect the quartz crystal oscillator having

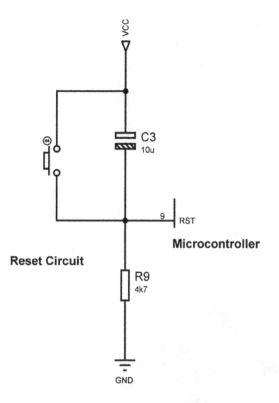

FIGURE 8.9 Reset circuitry of the microcontroller.

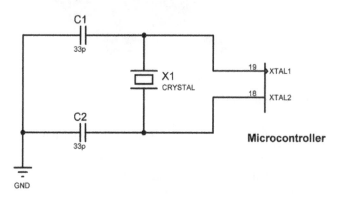

FIGURE 8.10 Clock generator for microcontroller.

the same value or not more than 12 MHz. The circuitry for clock generator is shown in Figure 8.10, which contains one crystal oscillator (11.0592 MHz) and two capacitors (33 pF).

8.3.2 GSM Modem (SIM300)

The GSM modem (SIM300) acts as an intermediary between users/farmers and the designed system, which provides a wireless environment through SMS. The SIM300 uses the AT commands to send or receive the SMS message. The format of the message is predefined as per the datasheet of GSM (SIM300). GSM module can either send or receive SMS through universal-asynchronous-receiver/transmitter (UART) with the help of installed subscriber identity module (SIM) on the GSM modem. The structure of the GSM modem is shown in Figure 8.11.

The serial baud rate of SIM300 is adjustable with 1200 to 115,200 bits per second (bps) and the default baud rate of SIM300 is 9600 bps. Its operating voltage is 7–15V, 1.5–2.0A DC. The operation of the GSM module is performed by AT commands. Table 8.1 shows the AT commands of the GSM Module (SIM300).

FIGURE 8.11   GSM modem (SIM300).

TABLE 8.1   AT Commands of GSM Module (SIM300)

AT Command	Uses
AT+CMGF	Message Mode
AT+CMGS	Message Send
AT+CMGR	Message Receive
AT+CCLK	Set Data and Time of RTC
AT+CALARM	Set Alarm Time
ATA	Answer the Incoming Call
AT+CNMI	Set Baud Rate
AT+CPOWD	Power Down

8.3.3 Relay and Its Driver Unit

The switching action is performed by the relay driver unit, which contains relay and its drivers. The relay driver performs as D flip flop through transistors (PNP and NPN) and biasing resisters as shown in Figure 8.12. The relay is a switching device, which operates automatically by receiving a signal from the microcontroller through its driver circuit and turning ON or OFF the water pumps. The operating voltage of the relay is +12V DC supply.

8.3.4 Moisture Sensor

The moisture sensor is used to measure the volumetric water content in soil. The relation between the measured property and soil moisture must be calibrated and may vary depending on environmental factors such as soil type, temperature, or electric conductivity. Reflected microwave radiation is affected by the soil moisture and is used for remote sensing in hydrology and agriculture. These sensors are usually referred to as soil water potential sensors and include tension meters and gypsum blocks. Figure 8.13 shows the moisture sensor.

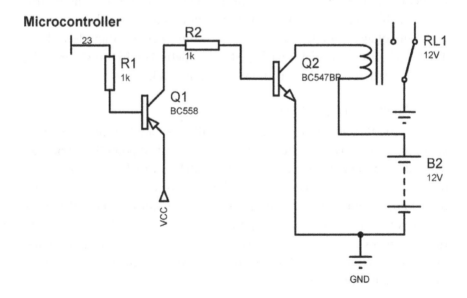

FIGURE 8.12   Relay and its driver circuit.

FIGURE 8.13   Moisture sensor.

8.3.5 Temperature Sensor

The LM35 series are precision integrated-circuit temperature sensors, whose output voltage is linearly proportional to the Celsius (Centigrade) temperature. The LM35 thus has an advantage over linear temperature sensors calibrated in °Kelvin, as the user is not required to subtract a large constant voltage from its output to obtain convenient Centigrade scaling. The LM35 series is available packaged in hermetic TO-46 transistor packages. The structure of LM35 is shown in Figure 8.14.

8.3.6 Analog to Digital Converter

The ADC080X (shown in Figure 8.15) family are CMOS 8-Bit, successive approximation A/D converters, which use a modified potentiometric ladder and are designed to operate with the 8080A control bus via three-state outputs. These converters appear to the processor as memory locations or I/O ports, and hence no interfacing logic is required. The differential analog voltage input has good common mode rejection and permits offsetting the analog zero-input voltage value. In addition, the voltage reference input can be adjusted to allow encoding any smaller analog voltage span to the full 8 bits of resolution.

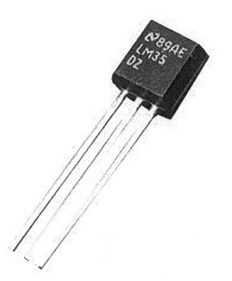

FIGURE 8.14   Temperature sensor.

FIGURE 8.15   Analog to digital converter.

8.3.7 Power Supply

In this session, circuit of the power supply has been discussed in detail. It is used to convert the alternating current (AC) into direct current (DC). The power supply contains a step-down transformer (0–12V), a bridge rectifier including four 1N4008 diodes, three capacitors (C1 = 100 µF, C2 = 100 µF,

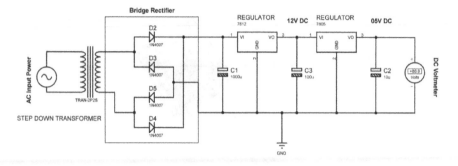

FIGURE 8.16   Power supply circuitry.

and C3 = 10 µF), and two voltage regulators (7812 and 7805). The input AC supply is given to the transfer's primary side and out secondary is given to the bridge rectifier circuit, which contains four diodes. The diodes are taking care of the control action, which clips the negative portion of the applied input supply to the rectifier circuit, because the diode acts as a clipper circuit. The circuit diagram of power supply is given in Figure 8.16.

The output of the rectifier circuit is given to the regulator, which regulates the input value to desired values such as +12V DC and +5V DC. The capacitors work as a pie filter and are connected to the positive output DC supply with respect to the ground terminal.

8.3.7.1 Transformer
In the power supply circuit, a step-down transformer has been used to step down the 250V AC to 12V AC. A transformer is an electrical device that transfers energy between two circuits/windings. The transformer action has been performed through electromagnetic induction. It commonly consists of two windings of wires around the core. The primary winding of wires is more than the secondary winding, which act as step-down transfer as shown in Figure 8.17.

8.3.7.2 Diode
The diode is a two-terminal electronic device such as anode and cathode. The main property of the diode is that it conducts electric current only in one direction, when it is forward biased. In forward-biased condition, the cathode is connected to the negative supply and the anode is connected to the positive supply voltage. The basic structures of diodes are illustrated in Figure 8.18. The diodes have a variety of applications like rectifiers, voltage regulators, switches, signal modulators and mixers, oscillators, signal limiters, and demodulators.

8.3.7.3 Voltage Regulators

The voltage regulator is an integrated circuit which maintains the output voltage at a constant value. The voltage source in the rectifier circuit may be fluctuating and would not give the fixed voltage output.

To overcome the problem of fluctuation of voltage, linear fixed voltage regulators are used—7812, 7805, 7912, etc. as shown in Figure 8.19.

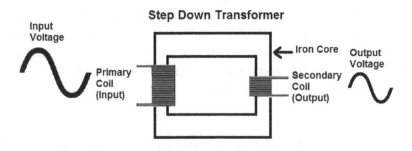

FIGURE 8.17   Step-down transformer.

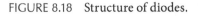

FIGURE 8.18   Structure of diodes.

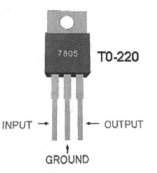

FIGURE 8.19   Voltage regulator.

8.4 CONCLUSION

The intelligent irrigation system is designed and implemented to remotely control with the help of GSM technology. The designed system has been providing an auto plant watering system by taking the input from the moisture sensor and temperature monitoring system with the help of temperature sensor for agricultural work. And, with the features of auto plant watering, the system also saves water as well as electricity. It also provides an alert message to the farmers for the safety of their fields and current status of the moisture level of the soil. The intelligent irrigation system is a successfully designed low cost, auto executed, and remotely controlled solution to prevent the wastage of electricity and water, and to ensure the safety of plants in the agricultural area.

REFERENCES

1. C. Goyal, J. S. Ubhi, and B. Raj, "Low Leakage Zero Ground Noise Nanoscale Full Adder Using Source Biasing Technique", *Journal of Nanoelectronics and Optoelectronics*, American Scientific Publishers, Vol. 14, pp. 360–370, 2019.
2. G. Singh, R. K. Sarin, and B. Raj, "A Novel Robust Exclusive-OR Function Implementation in QCA Nanotechnology with Energy Dissipation Analysis", *Journal of Computational Electronics*, Springer, Vol. 15, No. 2, pp. 455–465, 2016.
3. T. Wadhera, D. Kakkar, G. Wadhwa, and B. Raj, " Recent Advances and Progress in Development of the Field Effect Transistor Biosensor: A Review" *Journal of Electronic Materials*, Springer, Vol. 48, No. 12, pp. 7635–7646, 2019.
4. G. Wadhwa, P. Kamboj, and B. Raj, "Design Optimisation of Junctionless TFET Biosensor for High Sensitivity", *Advances in Natural Sciences: Nanoscience and Nanotechnology*, Vol. 10, No. 7, p. 045001, 2019.
5. P. Bansal, and B. Raj, "Memristor Modeling and Analysis for Linear Dopant Drift Kinetics", *Journal of Nanoengineering and Nanomanufacturing*, American Scientific Publishers, Vol. 6, pp. 1–7, 2016.
6. A. Singh, M. Khosla, and B. Raj, "Circuit Compatible Model for Electrostatic Doped Schottky Barrier CNTFET," *Journal of Electronic Materials*, Springer, Vol. 45, No. 12, pp. 4825–4835, 2016.
7. Ashima, D. Vaithiyanathan, and B. Raj, "Performance Analysis of Charge Plasma induced Graded Channel Si nanotube", *Journal of Engineering Research (JER)*, EMSME Special Issue, pp. 146–154, 2021.
8. A. S. Tomar, V. K. Magraiya, and B. Raj, "Scaling of Access and Data Transistor for High Performance DRAM Cell Design", *Quantum Matter*, Vol. 2, pp. 412–416, 2013.
9. N. Jain, and B. Raj, "Parasitic Capacitance and Resistance Model Development and Optimization of Raised Source/Drain SOI FinFET Structure for Analog Circuit Applications", *Journal of Nanoelectronics and Optoelectronins*, ASP, USA, Vol. 13, pp. 531–539, 2018.

10. S. Singh, S. K. Vishvakarma, and B. Raj, "Analytical Modeling of Split-Gate Junction-Less Transistor for a Biosensor Application", *Sensing and Bio-Sensing*, Elsevier, Vol. 18, pp. 31–36, 2018.

11. M. Gopal, and B. Raj, "Low Power 8T SRAM Cell Design for High Stability Video Applications", *ITSI Transaction on Electrical and Electronics Engineering*, Vol. 1, No. 5, pp. 91–97, 2013.

12. B. Raj, J. Mitra, D. K. Bihani, V. Rangharajan, A. K. Saxena, and S. Dasgupta, "Analysis of Noise Margin, Power and Process Variation for 32 nm FinFET Based 6T SRAM Cell", *Journal of Computer (JCP)*, Academy Publisher, FINLAND, Vol. 5, No. 6, 2010.

13. D. Sharma, R. Mehra, and B. Raj, "Comparative Analysis of Photovoltaic Technologies for High Efficiency Solar Cell Design", *Superlattices and Microstructures*, Elsevier, Vol. 153, pp. 106861, 2021.

14. P. Kaur, A. S. Buttar, and B. Raj, "A Comprehensive Analysis of Nanoscale Transistor Based Biosensor: A Review", *Indian Journal of Pure and Applied Physics*, Vol. 59, pp. 304–318, 2021.

15. D. Yadav, B. Raj, and B. Raj, "Design and Simulation of Low Power Microcontroller for IoT Applications", *Journal of Sensor Letters*, ASP, Vol. 18, pp. 401–409, 2020.

16. S. Singh, and B. Raj, "A 2-D Analytical Surface Potential and Drain current Modeling of Double-Gate Vertical t-Shaped Tunnel FET", *Journal of Computational Electronics*, Springer, Vol. 19, pp. 1154–1163, 2020.

17. J. Singh, and B. Raj, "An Accurate and Generic Window function for Non-linear Memristor Model" *Journal of Computational Electronics*, Springer, Vol. 18, No. 2, pp. 640–647, 2019.

18. M. Kaur, N. Gupta, S. Kumar, B. Raj, and A. K. Singh, "Comparative RF and Crosstalk Analysis of Carbon Based Nano Interconnects", *IET Circuits, Devices & Systems*, Vol. 15, No. 6, pp. 493–503, 2021.

19. N. Kandasamy, F. Ahmad, D. Ajitha, B. Raj, and N. Telagam, "Quantum Dot Cellular Automata Based Scan Flip Flop and Boundary Scan Register", *IETE Journal of Research*, 2020.

20. S. K. Sharma, B. Raj, and M. Khosla, "Enhanced Photosensivity of Highly Spectrum Selective Cylindrical Gate $In_{1-x}Ga_xAs$ Nanowire MOSFET Photodetector", *Modern Physics Letter-B*, Vol. 33, No. 12, p. 1950144, 2019.

21. J. Singh, and B. Raj, "Design and Investigation of 7T2M NVSARM with Enhanced Stability and Temperature Impact on Store/Restore Energy", *IEEE Transactions on Very Large Scale Integration Systems*, Vol. 27, No. 6, pp. 1322–1328, 2019.

22. A. K. Bhardwaj, S. Gupta, B. Raj, and A. Singh, "Impact of Double Gate Geometry on the Performance of Carbon Nanotube Field Effect Transistor Structures for Low Power Digital Design", *Computational and Theoretical Nanoscience*, ASP, Vol. 16, pp. 1813–1820, 2019.

23. N. Jain, and B. Raj, "Thermal Stability Analysis and Performance Exploration of Asymmetrical Dual-k Underlap Spacer (ADKUS) SOI FinFET for Security and Privacy Applications", *Indian Journal of Pure & Applied Physics (IJPAP)*, Vol. 57, pp. 352–360, 2019.

24. A. Singh, M. Khosla, and B. Raj, "Design and Analysis of Dynamically Configurable Electrostatic Doped Carbon Nanotube Tunnel FET", *Microelectronics Journal*, Elsevier, Vol. 85, pp. 17–24, 2019.

25. N. Jain, and B. Raj, "Dual-k Spacer Region Variation at the Drain Side of Asymmetric SOI FinFET Structure: Performance Analysis towards the Analog/RF Design Applications", *Journal of Nanoelectronics and Optoelectronics*, American Scientific Publishers, Vol. 14, pp. 349–359, 2019.

26. J. Singh, S. Sharma, B. Raj, and M. Khosla, "Analysis of Barrier Layer Thickness on Performance of $In_{1-x}Ga_xAs$ Based Gate Stack Cylindrical Gate Nanowire MOSFET", *JNO*, ASP, Vol. 13, pp. 1473–1477, 2018.

27. N. Jain, and B. Raj, "Analysis and Performance Exploration of High-k SOI FinFETs over the Conventional Low-k SOI FinFET toward Analog/RF Design", *Journal of Semiconductors (JoS)*, IOP Science, Vol. 39, No. 12, pp. 124002-1-7, 2018.

28. C. Goyal, J. S. Ubhi, and B. Raj, "A Reliable Leakage Reduction Technique for Approximate Full Adder with Reduced Ground Bounce Noise", *Journal of Mathematical Problems in Engineering*, Hindawi, Vol. 2018, Article ID 3501041, 16 pages, 2018.

29. Anuradha, J. Singh, B. Raj, and M. Khosla, "Design and Performance Analysis of Nano-scale Memristor-Based Nonvolatile SRAM", *Journal of Sensor Letter*, American Scientific Publishers, Vol. 16, pp. 798–805, 2018.

30. G. Wadhwa, and B. Raj, "Parametric Variation Analysis of Charge-Plasma-Based Dielectric Modulated JLTFET for Biosensor Application", *IEEE Sensor Journal*, Vol. 18, No. 15, pp. 6070–6077, 2018.

31. J. Singh, and B. Raj, "Comparative Analysis of Memristor Models for Memories Design", *JoS*, IoP, Vol. 39, No. 7, pp. 074006-1-12, 2018.

32. D. Yadav, S. S. Chouhan, S. K. Vishvakarma, and B. Raj, "Application Specific Microcontroller Design for IoT Based WSN", *Sensor Letter*, ASP, Vol. 16, pp. 374–385, 2018.

33. G. Singh, R. K. Sarin, and B. Raj, "Fault-Tolerant Design and Analysis of Quantum-Dot Cellular Automata Based Circuits", *IEEE/IET Circuits, Devices & Systems*, Vol. 12, pp. 638–664, 2018.

34. J. Singh, and B. Raj, "Modeling of Mean Barrier Height Levying Various Image Forces of Metal Insulator Metal Structure to Enhance the Performance of Conductive Filament Based Memristor Model", *IEEE Nanotechnology*, Vol. 17, No. 2, pp. 268–275, 2018.

35. A. Jain, S. Sharma, and B. Raj, "Analysis of Triple Metal Surrounding Gate (TM-SG) III-V Nanowire MOSFET for Photosensing Application", *Opto-Electronics Journal*, Elsevier, Vol. 26, No. 2, pp. 141–148, 2018.

36. A. Jain, S. Sharma, and B. Raj, "Design and Analysis of High Sensitivity Photosensor Using Cylindrical Surrounding Gate MOSFET for Low Power Sensor Applications", *Engineering Science and Technology, an International Journal*, Elsevier's, Vol. 19, No. 4, pp. 1864–1870, 2016.

37. A. Singh, M. Khosla, and B. Raj, "Analysis of Electrostatic Doped Schottky Barrier Carbon Nanotube FET for Low Power Applications," *Journal of Materials Science: Materials in Electronics*, Springer, Vol. 28, pp. 1762–1768, 2017.

38. G. Saiphani Kumar, A. Singh, B. Raj, "Design and Analysis of Gate All Around CNTFET Based SRAM Cell Design", *Journal of Computational Electronics*, Springer, Vol. 17, No.1, pp. 138–145, 2018.

39. G. P. Singh, B. S. Sohi, and B. Raj, "Material Properties Analysis of Graphene Base Transistor (GBT) for VLSI Analog Circuits", *Indian Journal of Pure & Applied Physics (IJPAP)*, Vol. 55, pp. 896–902, 2017.

40. S. Kumar and B. Raj, "Estimation of Stability and Performance Metric for Inward Access Transistor Based 6T SRAM Cell Design Using n-type/p-type DMDG-GDOV TFET", *IEEE VLSI Circuits and Systems Letter*, Vol. 3, No. 2, pp. 25–39, 2017.

41. S. Sharma, A. Kumar, M. Pattanaik, and B. Raj, "Forward Body Biased Multimode Multi-Threshold CMOS Technique for Ground Bounce Noise Reduction in Static CMOS Adders", *International Journal of Information and Electronics Engineering*, Vol. 3, No. 3, pp. 567–572, 2013.

42. H. Singh, P. Kumar, and B. Raj, "Performance Analysis of Majority Gate SET Based 1-bit Full Adder", *International Journal of Computer and Communication Engineering (IJCCE)*, IACSIT Press Singapore, ISSN: 2010-3743, Vol. 2, No. 4, pp. 567–572, 2013.

43. A. K. Bhardwaj, S. Gupta, and B. Raj, "Investigation of Parameters for Schottky Barrier (SB) Height for Schottky Barrier Based Carbon Nanotube Field Effect Transistor Device", *Journal of Nanoelectronics and Optoelectronics*, ASP, Vol. 15, pp. 783–791, 2020.

44. P. Bansal, and B. Raj, "Memristor: A Versatile Nonlinear Model for Dopant Drift and Boundary Issues", *JCTN*, American Scientific Publishers, Vol. 14, No. 5, pp. 2319–2325, 2017.

45. N. Jain, and B. Raj, "An Analog and Digital Design Perspective Comprehensive Approach on Fin-FET (Fin-Field Effect Transistor) Technology - A Review", *Reviews in Advanced Sciences and Engineering (RASE)*, ASP, Vol. 5, pp. 1–14, 2016.

46. S. Sharma, B. Raj, and M. Khosla, "Subthreshold Performance of $In_{1-x}Ga_xAs$ Based Dual Metal with Gate Stack Cylindrical/Surrounding Gate Nanowire MOSFET for Low Power Analog Applications", *Journal of Nanoelectronics and Optoelectronics*, American Scientific Publishers, USA, Vol. 12, pp. 171–176, 2017.

47. B. Raj, A. K. Saxena, and S. Dasgupta, "Analytical Modeling for the Estimation of Leakage Current and Subthreshold Swing Factor of Nanoscale Double Gate FinFET Device" *Microelectronics International, UK*, Vol. 26, pp. 53–63, 2009.

48. S. S. Soniya, G. Wadhwa, and B. Raj, "An Analytical Modeling for Dual Source Vertical Tunnel Field Effect Transistor", *International Journal of Recent Technology and Engineering (IJRTE)*, Vol. 8, No. 2, pp. 603–608, 2019.

49. S. Singh, and B. Raj, "Design and Analysis of Hetrojunction Vertical T-Shaped Tunnel Field Effect Transistor", *Journal of Electronics Material*, Springer, Vol. 48, No. 10, pp. 6253–6260, 2019.

50. C. Goyal, J. S. Ubhi, and B. Raj, "A Low Leakage CNTFET Based Inexact Full Adder for Low Power Image Processing Applications", *International Journal of Circuit Theory and Applications*, Wiley, Vol. 47, No. 9, pp. 1446–1458, 2019.

51. B. Raj, A. K. Saxena, and S. Dasgupta, "A Compact Drain Current and Threshold Voltage Quantum Mechanical Analytical Modeling for FinFETs", *Journal of Nanoelectronics and Optoelectronics (JNO), USA*, Vol. 3, No. 2, pp. 163–170, 2008.

52. G. Wadhwa, and B. Raj, "An Analytical Modeling of Charge Plasma Based Tunnel Field Effect Transistor with Impacts of Gate Underlap Region", *Superlattices and Microstructures*, Elsevier, Vol. 142, p. 106512, 2020.

53. S. Singh, and B. Raj, "Modeling and Simulation Analysis of SiGe Hetrojunction Double GateVertical t-Shaped Tunnel FET", *Superlattices and Microstructures*, Elsevier, Vol. 142, p. 106496, 2020.

54. A. Singh, D. K. Saini, D. Agarwal, S. Aggarwal, M. Khosla, and B. Raj, "Modeling and Simulation of Carbon Nanotube Field Effect Transistor and Its Circuit Application", *Journal of Semiconductors (JoS)*, IOP Science, Vol. 37, pp. 074001–074006, 2016.

55. N. Jain, and B. Raj, "Device and Circuit Co-Design Perspective Comprehensive Approach on FinFET Technology - A Review", *Journal of Electron Devices*, Vol. 23, No. 1, pp. 1890–1901, 2016.

56. S. Kumar and B. Raj, "Analysis of I_{ON} and Ambipolar Current for Dual-Material Gate-Drain Overlapped DG-TFET", *Journal of Nanoelectronics and Optoelectronics*, American Scientific Publishers, USA, Vol. 11, pp. 323–333, 2016.

57. N. Anjum, T. Bali, and B. Raj, "Design and Simulation of Handwritten Multiscript Character Recognition", *International Journal of Advanced Research in Computer and Communication Engineering*, Vol. 2, No. 7, pp. 2544–2549, 2013.

58. S. Sharma, B. Raj, and M. Khosla, "A Gaussian Approach for Analytical Subthreshold Current Model of Cylindrical Nanowire FET with Quantum Mechanical Effects", *Microelectronics Journal*, Elsevier, Vol. 53, pp. 65–72, 2016.

59. K. Singh, and B. Raj, "Performance and Analysis of Temperature Dependent Multi-Walled Carbon Nanotubes as Global Interconnects at Different Technology Nodes", *Journal of Computational Electronics*, Springer, Vol. 14, No. 2, pp. 469–476, 2015.

60. S. Kumar and B. Raj, "Compact Channel Potential Analytical Modeling of DG-TFET Based on Evanescent–Mode Approach", *Journal of Computational Electronics*, Springer, Vol. 14, No. 2, pp. 820–827, 2015.

61. K. Singh, and B. Raj, "Temperature Dependent Modeling and Performance Evaluation of Multi-Walled CNT and Single-Walled CNT as Global Interconnects", *Journal of Electronic Materials*, Springer, Vol. 44, No. 12, pp. 4825–4835, 2015.

62. V. K. Sharma, M. Pattanaik, and B. Raj, "INDEP Approach for Leakage Reduction in Nanoscale CMOS Circuits", *International Journal of Electronics*, Taylor & Francis, Vol. 102, No. 2, pp. 200–215, 2014.

63. K. Singh, and B. Raj, "Influence of Temperature on MWCNT Bundle, SWCNT Bundle and Copper Interconnects for Nanoscaled Technology Nodes", *Journal of Materials Science: Materials in Electronics*, Springer, Vol. 26, No. 8, pp. 6134–6142, 2015.

64. N. Anjum, T. Bali, and B. Raj, "Design and Simulation of Handwritten Gurumukhi and Devanagri Numerical Recognition", *International Journal of Computer Applications*, Published by Foundation of Computer Science, New York, USA, Vol. 73, No. 12, pp. 16–21, 2013.

65. S. Khandelwal, V. Gupta, B. Raj, and R. D. Gupta, "Process Variability Aware Low Leakage Reliable Nano Scale DG-FinFET SRAM Cell Design Technique", *Journal of Nanoelectronics and Optoelectronics*, Vol. 10, No. 6, pp. 810–817, 2015.

66. V. K. Sharma, M. Pattanaik, and B. Raj, "ONOFIC Approach: Low Power High Speed Nanoscale VLSI Circuits Design", *International Journal of Electronics*, Taylor & Francis, Vol. 101, No. 1, pp. 61–73, 2014.

67. S. Khandelwal, B. Raj, and R. D. Gupta, "FinFET Based 6T SRAM Cell Design: Analysis of Performance Metric, Process Variation and Temperature Effect", *Journal of Computational and Theoretical Nanoscience*, ASP, USA, Vol. 12, pp. 2500–2506, 2015.

68. S. Singh, Y. Shekhar, R. Jagdeep, S. Anurag, and B. Raj, "Impact of HfO_2 in Graded Channel Dual Insulator Double Gate MOSFET", *Journal of Computational and Theoretical Nanoscience*, American Scientific Publishers, Vol. 12, No. 6, pp. 950–953, 2015.

69. V. K. Sharma, M. Pattanaik, and B. Raj, "PVT Variations Aware Low Leakage INDEP Approach for Nanoscale CMOS Circuits", *Microelectronics Reliability*, Elsevier, Vol. 54, pp. 90–99, 2014.

70. B. Raj, A. K. Saxena and S. Dasgupta, "Quantum Mechanical Analytical Modeling of Nanoscale DG FinFET: Evaluation of Potential, Threshold Voltage and Source/Drain Resistance", *Elsevier's Journal of Material Science in Semiconductor Processing*, Elsevier, Vol. 16, No. 4, pp. 1131–1137, 2013.

71. M. Gopal, S. S. D. Prasad, and B. Raj, "8T SRAM Cell Design for Dynamic and Leakage Power Reduction", *International Journal of Computer Applications*, Published by Foundation of Computer Science, New York, USA, Vol. 71, No. 9, pp. 43–48, 2013.

72. M. Pattanaik, B. Raj, S. Sharma, and A. Kumar, "Diode Based Trimode Multi-Threshold CMOS Technique for Ground Bounce Noise Reduction in Static CMOS Adders", *Advanced Materials Research*, Trans Tech Publications, Switzerland, Vol. 548, pp. 885–889, 2012.

73. B. Raj, A. K. Saxena, and S. Dasgupta, "Nanoscale FinFET Based SRAM Cell Design: Analysis of Performance Metric, Process Variation, Underlapped FinFET and Temperature Effect", *IEEE Circuits and System Magazine*, Vol. 11, No. 2, pp. 38–50, 2011.

74. V. K. Sharma, M. Pattanaik, and B. Raj, "Leakage Current ONOFIC Approach for Deep Submicron VLSI Circuit Design", *International Journal of Electrical, Computer, Electronics and Communication Engineering*, World Academy of Sciences, Engineering and Technology, Vol. 7, No. 4, pp. 239–244, 2013.

75. T. Chawla, M. Khosla, and B. Raj, "Design and Simulation of Triple Metal Double-Gate Germanium on Insulator Vertical Tunnel Field Effect Transistor", *Microelectronics Journal*, Elsevier, Vol. 114, p. 105125, 2021.

76. P. Kaur, S. S. Gill, and B. Raj, "Comparative Analysis of OFETs Materials and Devices for Sensor Applications", *Journal of Silicon*, Springer, Vol. 14, pp. 4463–4471, 2022.

77. S. K. Sharma, P. Kumar, B. Raj, and B. Raj, "In$_{1-x}$Ga$_x$As Double Metal Gate-Stacking Cylindrical Nanowire MOSFET for Highly Sensitive Photo detector", *Journal of Silicon*, Springer, Vol. 14, pp. 3535–3541, 2022.

78. B. Raj, A. K. Saxena, and S. Dasgupta, "Analytical Modeling of Quasi Planar Nanoscale Double Gate FinFET with Source/Drain Resistance and Field Dependent Carrier Mobility: A Quantum Mechanical Study", *Journal of Computer (JCP)*, Academy Publisher, FINLAND, Vol. 4, No. 9, pp. 1–8, 2009.

79. S. Bhushan, S. Khandelwal, and B. Raj, "Analyzing Different Mode FinFET Based Memory Cell at Different Power Supply for Leakage Reduction", Seventh International Conference on Bio-Inspired Computing: Theories and Application, (BIC-TA 2012), *Advances in Intelligent Systems and Computing*, Vol. 202, pp. 89–100, 2013.

80. J. Singh, and B. Raj, "Temperature Dependent Analytical Modeling and Simulations of Nanoscale Memristor", *Engineering Science and Technology, an International Journal*, Elsevier's, Vol. 21, pp. 862–868, 2018.

81. S. Singh, S. Bala, B. Raj, and B. Raj, "Improved Sensitivity of Dielectric Modulated Junctionless Transistor for Nanoscale Biosensor Design", *Sensor Letter*, ASP, Vol. 18, pp. 328–333, 2020

82. V. Kumar, S. K. Vishvakarma, and B. Raj, "Design and Performance Analysis of ASIC for IoT Applications", *Sensor Letter*, ASP, Vol. 18, pp. 31–38, 2020.

83. A. Jaiswal, R. K. Sarin, B. Raj, and S. Sukhija, "A Novel Circular Slotted Microstrip-fed Patch Antenna with Three Triangle Shape Defected Ground Structure for Multiband Applications", *Advanced Electromagnetic (AEM)*, Vol. 7, No. 3, pp. 56–63, 2018.

84. G. Wadhwa, and B Raj, "Label Free Detection of Biomolecules Using Charge-Plasma-Based Gate Underlap Dielectric Modulated Junctionless TFET", *Journal of Electronic Materials (JEMS)*, Springer, Vol. 47, No. 8, pp. 4683–4693, 2018.

85. G. Singh, R. K. Sarin, and B. Raj, "Design and Performance Analysis of a New Efficient Coplanar Quantum-Dot Cellular Automata Adder", *Indian Journal of Pure & Applied Physics (IJPAP)*, Vol. 55, pp. 97–103, 2017.

86. P. Kaur, V. Pandey, and B. Raj, "Comparative Study of Efficient Design, Control and Monitoring of Solar Power Using IoT", *Sensor Letter*, ASP, Vol. 18, pp. 419–426, 2020.

87. G. Wadhwa, P. Kamboj, J. Singh, B. Raj, "Design and Investigation of Junctionless DGTFET for Biological Molecule Recognition", *Transactions on Electrical and Electronic Materials*, Springer, Vol. 22, pp. 282–289, 2020.

88. G. Singh, R. K. Sarin, and B. Raj, "Design and Analysis of Area Efficient QCA Based Reversible Logic Gates", *Journal of Microprocessors and Microsystems*, Elsevier, Vol. 52, pp. 59–68, 2017.

89. A. Singh, M. Khosla, and B. Raj, "Compact Model for Ballistic Single Wall CNTFET under Quantum Capacitance Limit", *Journal of Semiconductors (JoS)*, IOP Science, Vol. 37, pp. 104001–104008, 2016.

90. S. Singh, M. Khosla, G. Wadhwa, and B. Raj, "Design and Analysis of Double-Gate Junctionless Vertical TFET for Gas Sensing Applications", *Applied Physics A*, Springer, Vol. 127, No. 16, 2021.

91. I. Singh, B. Raj, M. Khosla, and B. K. Kaushik, "Potential MRAM Technologies for Low Power SoCs", SPIN World Scientific Publisher, SCIE; Vol. 10, No. 04, p. 2050027, 2020.

92. S. Singh, and B. Raj, "Parametric Variation Analysis on Hetero-Junction Vertical t-Shape TFET for Supressing Ambipolar Conduction", *Indian Journal of Pure and Applied Physics*, Vol. 58, pp. 478–485, 2020.

93. S. S. Soniya, G. Wadhwa, and B. Raj, "Design and Analysis of Dual Source Vertical Tunnel Field Effect Transistor for High Performance", *Transactions on Electrical and Electronics Materials*, Springer, Vol. 21, pp. 74–82, 2019

94. M. Kaur, N. Gupta, S. Kumar, B. Raj, and A. K. Singh, "RF Performance Analysis of Intercalated Graphene Nanoribbon Based Global Level Interconnects", *Journal of Computational Electronics*, Springer, Vol. 19, pp. 1002–1013, 2020.

95. G. Wadhwa, B. Raj, "Design and Performance Analysis of Junctionless TFET Biosensor for High Sensitivity" *IEEE Nanotechnology*, Vol. 18, pp. 567–574, 2019.

96. J. Singh, and B. Raj, "Enhanced Nonlinear Memristor Model Encapsulating Stochastic Dopant Drift", *JNO*, ASP, 14, 958–963, 2019.

97. A. Singh, M. Khosla, and B. Raj, "Design and Analysis of Electrostatic Doped Schottky Barrier CNTFET Based Low Power SRAM", *International Journal of Electronics and Communications, (AEÜ)*, Elsevier, Vol. 80, pp. 67–72, 2017.

98. T. Chawla, M. Khosla, and B. Raj, "Optimization of Double-gate Dual Material GeOI-Vertical TFET for VLSI Circuit Design", *IEEE VLSI Circuits and Systems Letter*, Vol. 6, No. 2, pp. 13–25, 2020.

99. S. K. Verma, S. Singh, G. Wadhwa and B. Raj, "Detection of Biomolecules Using Charge-Plasma based Gate Underlap Dielectric Modulated Dopingless TFET", *Transactions on Electrical and Electronic Materials (TEEM)*, Springer, Vol. 21, pp. 528–535, 2020.

100. N. Jain, and B. Raj, "Impact of Underlap Spacer Region Variation on Electrostatic and Analog/RF Performance of Symmetrical High-k SOI FinFET at 20 nm Channel Length", *Journal of Semiconductors (JoS)*, IOP Science, Vol. 38, No. 12, p. 122002, 2017.

101. S. Singh, and B. Raj, "Analytical Modeling and Simulation Analysis of T-Shaped III-V Heterojunction Vertical T-FET", *Superlattices and Microstructures*, Elsevier, Vol. 147, p. 106717, 2020.

CHAPTER 9

Reversible Logic Gates Using Quantum Dot Cellular Automata (QCA) Nanotechnology

Vijay Kumar Sharma

Shri Mata Vaishno Devi University

CONTENTS

9.1 INTRODUCTION

The current electronic circuits are facing the issue of power dissipation, especially for portable devices. QCA nanotechnology overcomes the issue of large power dissipation. Power dissipation can further be decreased using reversible gates. The large energy dissipation limits the growth of the nanoelectronics devices [1]. Reversible computing reduces this large energy dissipation. Irreversible function leads to information loss and energy dissipation [2]. As per Bennett's observation, reversible gate contains zero energy dissipation [3]. The advances in semiconductor technology need reduction in feature size, while designing in CMOS technology. QCA nanotechnology is an effective option for the CMOS technology in

DOI: 10.1201/9781003230113-9

nanoscaled circuits [4–6]. Lent has generated the theory of QCA cells and its applications. QCA nanotechnology is one of the emerging technologies, which is completely developed by Lent [7]. QCA technology has its basic component known as quantum cell. QCA cell is the essential element used in QCA-based technology [8]. Each cell is of a small size and uses a square shape. Two electrons are residing in a square-shaped cell [9]. A cell has four quantum dots at the corners [10]. Figure 9.1 shows a QCA cell.

The electrons are located diagonally, and tunnel through the vacant quantum dots [11]. The electrons stop to flow due to high barrier difference between the end-to-end QCA cells. This diagonal arrangement of electrons within a cell is due to Columbic repulsion force. The polarization 0 and 1 values are showing the binary equivalents, "1" and "0," respectively. Clock pulse is vital for the accurate working of the QCA technology. It helps the electrons to movet inside the cell [12]. Movement of electrons takes place when the clock is applied [13]. Four zones form a clock pulse. The zones are having a regular phase shift. The clock pulse is shown in Figure 9.2. Each zone includes four phases: switch, hold, release, and relax.

Inter-dot barrier is rising in the switch phase, and the cell starts polarizing. QCA cell begins without polarization, and becomes polarized [14]. The QCA clock is used for powering the automation, and monitoring the

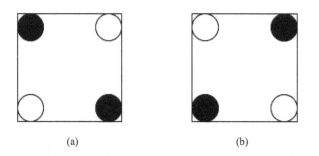

(a)   (b)

FIGURE 9.1   QCA cell representing (a) binary "0" and (b) binary "1."

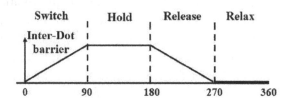

FIGURE 9.2   QCA clock and zones.

movement of data [15]. Polarization is maintained by cell in hold phase as the state of cell remains the same, whereas the potential barrier is high. The QCA cell decreases its inter-dot barrier during the release phase. This state leads to unpolarized cells. The inter-dot barrier remains lowered in the relax phase [16]. Flow of information from input to output involves no electric current between the cells. It results in less power dissipation of the circuit. In CMOS technology, the clock is mostly used in sequential circuits, whereas while using QCA-based technology, the clock is used in both combinational as well as in sequential circuits. In this technology, the clock provides power as well as switching to the circuits [17].

In QCA technology, the signal is transferred from one end to another end using the QCA wire, and a chain of inverters (diagonal QCA wire). The interaction of electrons with their neighboring cells takes place, which results in transfer of the effect of polarization from one cell to its neighboring cells [18]. Cells are arranged in series whether in horizontal or vertical position to form a QCA wire [19]. The input cell is also known as driver cell. The QCA wire is shown in Figure 9.3.

If cells are arranged in horizontal plane in series form, then whatever is the digital logic of input cell, complete array of cells settle to that digital value, thus forming a QCA wire. Inverter chain contains QCA cells that are rotated by 45° from the normal 90°cells [20]. The arrangement of QCA cells is such that each cell has opposite polarization of their neighboring cells. An important gate in QCA is NOT or inverter gate [21]. An inverter gate inverts the input signal that is applied. If input exhibits logic low, then output will be at logic high, and similarly for the other input logic. Figure 9.4 shows the QCA-based inverter gate [22].

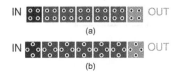

FIGURE 9.3   QCA wires: (a) normal QCA wire and (b) diagonal QCA wire.

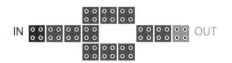

FIGURE 9.4   QCA inverter gate.

Inverter and majority gate are the prime logic gates in QCA nanotech-nology. Designers can implement any logical function using these two basic gates [23,24].

9.2 REVERSIBLE GATES

Static and dynamic power dissipations are commonly discussed issues in the nanoscaled region. But, Landauer found that information loss is also a key issue. The information loss can be neglected using the revers-ibility idea. The reversible concept deals with equal number of inputs and outputs, which is known as the one-to-one mapping process. The number of inputs is decided by the applications. Hence, for making a reversible computation, designers must use the same number of outputs, irrespective of its functionality [25]. Many researchers have developed many kinds of reversible gates, which are based on the reversibility computation [26–28].

A reversible gate, known as Toffoli gate, is shown in Figure 9.5. Toffoli gate is a 3 × 3 gate; it has three inputs (A, B, C) and three outputs (P, Q, R). The input–output relationships for the Toffoli gate are presented in Eqs. (9.1–9.3).

$$P = A \tag{9.1}$$

$$Q = B \tag{9.2}$$

$$R = AB \oplus C \tag{9.3}$$

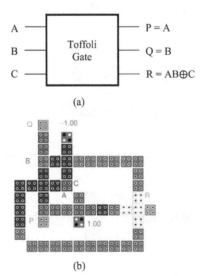

(a)

(b)

FIGURE 9.5   A Toffoli gate: (a) block diagram and (b) QCA design [29].

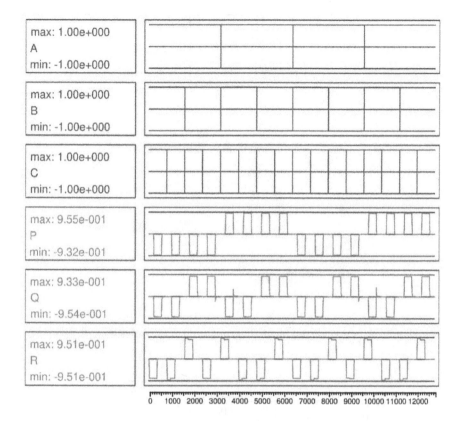

FIGURE 9.6   Simulation of the Toffoli gate [29].

The inputs A, and B are propagating exactly the same to the outputs. The block diagram for Toffoli gate is shown in Figure 9.5a. A QCA implementation for the Toffoli gate is shown in Figure 9.5b [29].

The simulation result for the Toffoli gate is given in Figure 9.6.

The Toffoli gate as presented in Ref. [29] uses 54 QCA cells, occupies 0.06 μm² of area, and uses four clocks.

The block diagram and QCA design for the other reversible gate known as Peres gate are shown in Figure 9.7a and 9.7b, respectively [29]. The Peres gate is also a 3 × 3 type gate. Here, only input A is propagating to the output. The input–output relationships for the Peres gate are presented in Eqs. (9.4–9.6).

$$P = A \tag{9.4}$$

$$Q = A \oplus B \tag{9.5}$$

$$R = AB \oplus C \tag{9.6}$$

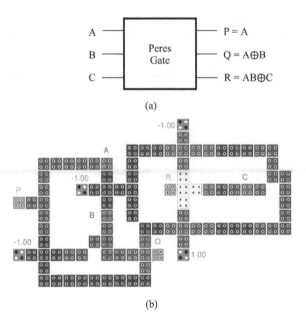

(a)

(b)

FIGURE 9.7   A Peres gate: (a) block diagram and (b) QCA design [29].

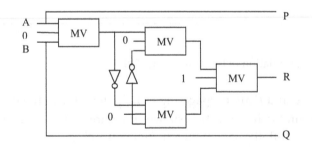

FIGURE 9.8   Toffoli gate using MV representation [30].

The input *A* is propagating exactly the same to the output *P*.

The presented Peres gate applies 98 QCA cells, occupies 0.13 μm² area, and uses four clocks.

A schematic for Toffoli gate using the majority voter (MV) approach is presented in Figure 9.8 [30].

There are four MVs in a Toffoli gate [30]. AND operation is performed by a MV in the Toffoli gate. Two NOT operations are required for the XOR operation. *P* and *Q* outputs are the propagating outputs. A Toffoli gate is shown in Figure 9.9 using MV's theory [30].

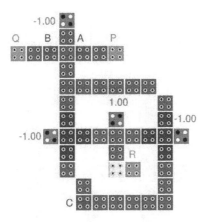

FIGURE 9.9   Toffoli gate designed in Ref. [30].

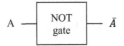

FIGURE 9.10   Block diagram of NOT gate [31].

The Toffoli gate can be utilized as a universal logic gate to implement the other Boolean functions. The Toffoli gate acts as NOT, AND, OR, NAND, XOR gates by assigning the accurate input combinations [30]. The Boolean functions for the different logic gates using the Toffoli gate are presented in Eqs. (9.7–9.11).

$$\text{NOT}(A) = \text{Toffoli}(A,1,1) \qquad (9.7)$$

$$\text{AND}(A,B) = \text{Toffoli}(A,B,0) \qquad (9.8)$$

$$\text{NAND}(A,B) = \text{Toffoli}(A,B,1) \qquad (9.9)$$

$$\text{OR}(A,B) = \text{Toffoli}(A,B,0) \qquad (9.10)$$

$$\text{EXOR}(A,C) = \text{Toffoli}(A,1,C) \qquad (9.11)$$

NOT gate is also a reversible gate. It is a 1×1 gate, which acts as a fundamental logic gate [31]. The block diagram of NOT gate is given in Figure 9.10.

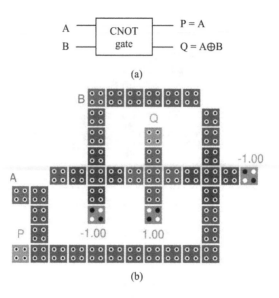

(a)

(b)

FIGURE 9.11   CNOT gate: (a) block diagram representation and (b) QCA design [31].

Another reversible gate is controlled NOT (CNOT) gate. CNOT is a 2 × 2 type gate. Most of the time, the CNOT gate is called as the Feynman gate. The block diagram representation and QCA design for CNOT gate are illustrated in Figure 9.11 [31].

The advanced version of the CNOT gate is double Feynman gate. It is a 3 × 3 type gate. It is more capable to compute the large number of Boolean function as compared to the Feynman gate. The block diagram representation and a QCA design of double Feynman gate are provided in Figure 9.12 [31].

The other important reversible gate is the Fredkin gate. It is also a 3 × 3 type gate [32,33]. The input–output relationships for the Fredkin gate are presented in Eqs. (9.12–9.14).

$$P = A \tag{9.12}$$

$$Q = \bar{A}B + AC \tag{9.13}$$

$$R = AB + \bar{A}C \tag{9.14}$$

The block diagram representation and QCA design for the Fredkin gate is given in Figure 9.13 [31].

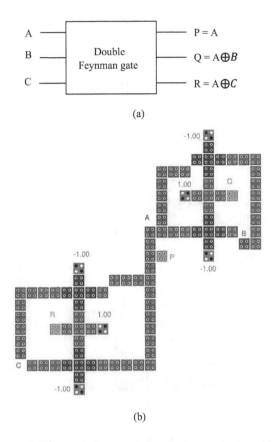

(a)

(b)

FIGURE 9.12 Double Feynman gate: (a) block diagram representation and (b) QCA design [31].

The other reversible gate is the BJN gate. It is also a 3 × 3 type gate. The block diagram representation and QCA design for the BJN gate is shown in Figure 9.14 [31].

MCL is a 3×3 type reversible gate. The block diagram representation and QCA design for the MCL gate is depicted in Figure 9.15 [31].

A Fredkin gate was designed using majority gates [34]. The schematic arrangement and QCA design for the Fredkin gate using majority (Maj) gates is shown in Figure 9.16 [34].

Another QCA implementation of the Fredkin gate is designed in Figure 9.17 [35].

A Peres gate consists two XOR and one AND operations. A Peres gate is designed using these two operations [36]. The schematic arrangement and QCA design for the Peres gate are illustrated in Figure 9.18 [36].

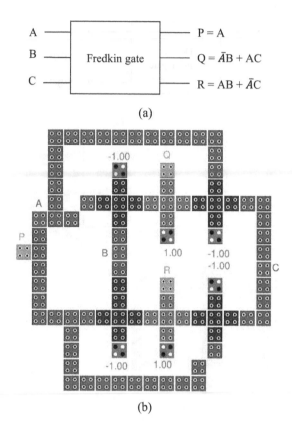

(a)

(b)

FIGURE 9.13 Fredkin gate: (a) block diagram representation and (b) QCA design [31].

ALU is a key module to design different logic circuits. It can perform various logical and arithmetic operations. A significant ALU can be designed using reversible gates. Arithmetic and logical operations can be optimized using the reversible gate. But, the select lines, garbage outputs, cost, and delays must be reduced, while designing the circuits. QCA-based different reversible ALU have been designed in literature [37–43].

A reversible ALU was designed using reversible multiplexers [38]. Arithmetic and logical components of ALU are designed separately. The implementation contains a single layer and rotated cells for the crossings. It includes 9 constant inputs and 15 garbage outputs.

Fredkin and Toffoli gates are utilized for designing single bit reversible ALU [39]. Multilayer crossing has been used in this design. This design contains the garbage outputs.

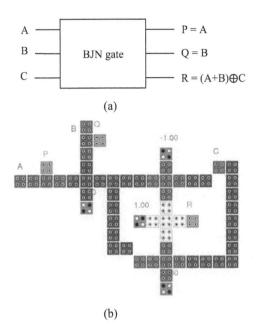

(a)

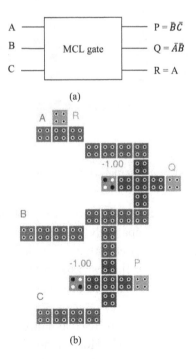

(b)

FIGURE 9.14 BJN gate: (a) block diagram representation and (b) QCA design [31].

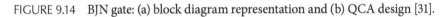

(a)

(b)

FIGURE 9.15 MCL gate: (a) block diagram representation and (b) QCA design [31].

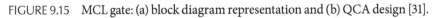

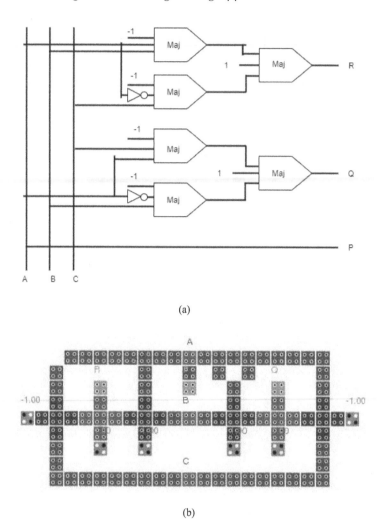

(a)

(b)

FIGURE 9.16   Fredkin gate: (a) schematic representation and (b) QCA design [34].

A reversible universal gate (RUG) is used to complete the arithmetic, and logical operations, separately [40,41]. It causes a reversible ALU
design. QCA design shown in Ref. [40] uses single layer, with rotated cells,
whereas QCA design in Ref. [41] doesn't use rotated cells, but it uses cross
wires. This QCA design performs 16 arithmetic and logical operations
[44–47].

A 4 × 4 type reversible gate can be used as a building block for ALU, and
this gate is known as Naghibzadeh–Hoshmand Gate (NHG) [42]. NHG is
implemented using multilayer crossing, and performs 16 arithmetic and
logical operations.

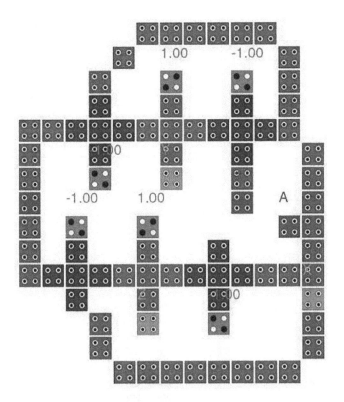

FIGURE 9.17   A QCA implementation of Fredkin gate [35].

KMD Gate1, KMD Gate2, KMD Gate3, and KMD Gate4 are the four other reversible gates [43]. These gates are applied to design the reversible ALU using two different approaches. Only KMD gates are applied in the first approach, while KMD, Toffoli, and Fredkin gates are used in the second approach.

Fredkin and HNG gates can be used to design an ALU [37]. HNG is a 4 × 4 type gate. The block diagram representation of HNG gate is illustrated in Figure 9.19.

QCA-based reversible gates such as Feynman (CNOT), Toffoli, and Fredkin have many logic implementations [48–54]. The schematic design of a Feynman gate is provided in Figure 9.20, where M shows the majority gate [48].

Various numbers of reversible gates are used for different applications, and make the design more efficient [55–60]. The designing of the reversible gates is still an emerging topic using the QCA technology, and the research is ongoing to obtain an optimized design. This is done to develop

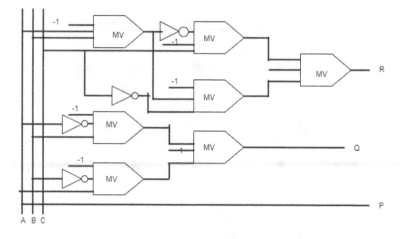

(a)

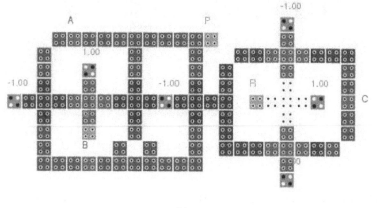

(b)

FIGURE 9.18   A Peres gate: (a) schematic arrangement and (b) QCA design [36].

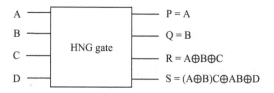

FIGURE 9.19   Block diagram representation of HNG gate [37].

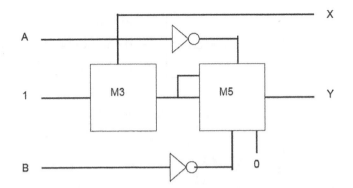

FIGURE 9.20   Schematic diagram of a Feynman reversible gate [48].

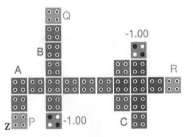

FIGURE 9.21   QCA layout for a Toffoli gate [61].

ultra-low-size devices having ultra-low-power dissipation. If these two targets are achieved, then it is possible to use the resultant design for various applications, and make it possible to implement the designs practically. The Toffoli gate is one of the oldest reversible gates. Figure 9.21 represents a QCA layout for the Toffoli gate [61]. This design uses only 24 cells, an area of 0.0226 µm², and has a latency of 0.50 clock cycles. This design uses a single layer and is therefore easy to implement.

RQG is a 3 × 3 type reversible gate, having three inputs (A, B, C) and three outputs (P, Q, R). The schematic diagram and QCA design for RQG gate are shown in Figure 9.22 [62].

Many logic circuits have been designed using reversible gates, especially for low-power design [63–67]. A new QCA-based design for the Feynman gate is given in Figure 9.23 [63].

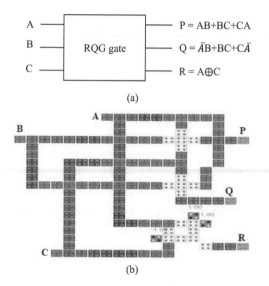

FIGURE 9.22 RQG gate: (a) block diagram representation and (b) QCA design [62].

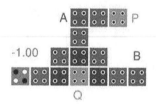

FIGURE 9.23 A new QCA-based Feynman gate [63].

This Feynman gate consists of only 14 cells, occupies an area of 0.011 µm² area, and has a latency of two clocks.

A new QCA design for the Toffoli gate is shown in Figure 9.24 [63].

The Toffoli gate consists of only 20 cells, occupies an area of 0.021 µm², and has a delay of two clocks. Inversion of the input can be performed by a controllable inverter, and it is a combinational digital circuit. The QCA layout of a controllable NOT (CNOT) gate is given in Figure 9.25 [68].

This CNOT gate occupies an area of 0.0196 µm² and has a delay of 0.75 clocks.

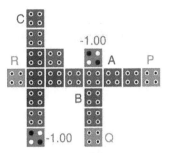

FIGURE 9.24   QCA design of a Toffoli gate [63].

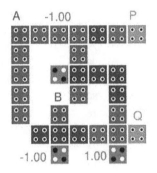

FIGURE 9.25   QCA design for a CNOT gate [68].

9.3 PERFORMANCE COMPARISON

This section compares the different available reversible gates in QCA nanotechnology. Table 9.1 shows the comparison among the various reversible gates. Some of the reversible gates use the three-input XOR gate [69–71]. They gained the least number of QCA cells, and cover a minimum area without using any wire crossing. Different designers and different QCA layouts have been designed for the different reversible gates. They have targeted the least number of QCA cells and clock phases.

The QCA designer is the software used for the simulation of QCA-based circuits. It is used for the simulation and verification of QCA-based designs [73–76].

TABLE 9.1   Comparison of Different Reversible Gates in QCA Technology

Reversible Gate	Cell Count	Area (μm²)	Clock
Toffoli [29]	54	0.06	4
Peres [29]	98	0.13	4
Toffoli [30]	45	0.04	4
NOT [31]	4	NA	1
CNOT [31]	49	0.06	3
Feynman [31]	53	0.07	3
Double Feynman [31]	93	0.19	3
Toffoli [31]	57	0.06	3
Fredkin [31]	97	0.10	3
Peres [31]	117	0.18	3
BJN [31]	58	0.09	4
MCL [31]	36	0.05	2
Fredkin [34]	93	0.09	3
Fredkin [35]	79	0.07	3
Peres [36]	99	0.10	4
Fredkin [37]	100	0.12	4
HNG [37]	80	0.12	3
Feynman [72]	16	0.02	2
Feynman [48]	32	NA	3
Toffoli [61]	24	0.02	1
Feynman [63]	14	0.01	2
Toffoli [63]	20	0.02	2
CNOT [68]	28	0.02	3

9.4 CONCLUSION

The reversible gate is the best choice as compared to the irreversible gate. It offers no information loss, thereby having negligible power dissipation. Different reversible gates using QCA technology are available in the literature. Few designs consist of both constant inputs and garbage outputs, whereas few designs use only garbage outputs to make the circuit reversible. Most of the circuits used a single layer, as it is difficult to fabricate multilayer-based circuits. Design of reversible gates made up of minimum number of cells, occupying less area as compared to the normal designs. Designers always try to minimize the constant inputs and garbage outputs because these are used only for making the design reversible. Most of the reversible gate designs don't require rotated cells [77–88].

REFERENCES

1. C. S. Lent, M. Liu, and Y. Lu, "Bennett Clocking of Quantum-Dot Cellular Automata and the Limits to Binary Logic Scaling", *Nanotechnology*, Vol. 17, No. 16, p. 4240, 2006.
2. R. Landauer, "Irreversibility and Heat Generation in the Computing Process", *IBM Journal of Research and Development*, Vol. 5, No. 3, pp. 183–191, 1961.
3. C. Bennett, "Logical Reversibility of Computation", *Maxwell's Demon: Entropy, Information, Computing*, pp. 197–204, 1973.
4. S. F. Naz, S. Riyaz, and V. K. Sharma, "A Review of QCA Nanotechnology as an Alternate to CMOS", *Current Nanoscience*, Vol. 18, No. 1, pp. 18–30, 2022.
5. V. K. Sharma, "CNTFET Circuit-Based Wide Fan-In Domino Logic for Low Power Applications", *Journal of Circuits, Systems and Computers*, Vol. 31, No. 2, p. 2250036, 2022.
6. V. K. Sharma, "Optimal Design for 1: 2^n Demultiplexer using QCA Nanotechnology with Energy Dissipation Analysis", *International Journal of Numerical Modelling: Electronic Networks, Devices and Fields*, Vol. 34, No. 6, pp. e2907, 2021.
7. V. K. Sharma, "Optimal Design for Digital Comparator Using QCA Nanotechnology with Energy Estimation", *International Journal of Numerical Modelling: Electronic Networks, Devices and Fields*, Vol. 34, No. 2, p. e2822, 2021.
8. J. Singh, and B. Raj, "Design and Investigation of 7T2M NVSARM with Enhanced Stability and Temperature Impact on Store/Restore Energy", *IEEE Transactions on Very Large Scale Integration Systems*, Vol. 27, No. 6, pp. 1322–1328, 2019.
9. A. K. Bhardwaj, S. Gupta, B. Raj, and A. Singh, "Impact of Double Gate Geometry on the Performance of Carbon Nanotube Field Effect Transistor Structures for Low Power Digital Design", *Computational and Theoretical Nanoscience*, ASP, Vol. 16, pp. 1813–1820, 2019
10. N. Jain, and B. Raj, "Thermal Stability Analysis and Performance Exploration of Asymmetrical Dual-k Underlap Spacer (ADKUS) SOI FinFET for Security and Privacy Applications", *Indian Journal of Pure & Applied Physics (IJPAP)*, Vol. 57, pp. 352–360, 2019.
11. A. Singh, M. Khosla, and B. Raj, "Design and Analysis of Dynamically Configurable Electrostatic Doped Carbon Nanotube Tunnel FET", *Microelectronics Journal*, Elesvier, Vol. 85, pp. 17–24, 2019.
12. N. Jain, and B. Raj, "Dual-k Spacer Region Variation at the Drain Side of Asymmetric SOI FinFET Structure: Performance Analysis towards the Analog/RF Design Applications", *Journal of Nanoelectronics and Optoelectronics*, American Scientific Publishers, Vol. 14, pp. 349–359, 2019.
13. J. Singh, S. Sharma, B. Raj, and M. Khosla, "Analysis of Barrier Layer Thickness on Performance of $In_{1-x}Ga_xAs$ Based Gate Stack Cylindrical Gate Nanowire MOSFET", *JNO*, ASP, Vol. 13, pp. 1473–1477, 2018.

14. N. Jain, and B. Raj, "Analysis and Performance Exploration of High-k SOI FinFETs over the Conventional Low-k SOI FinFET toward Analog/RF Design", *Journal of Semiconductors (JoS)*, IOP Science, Vol. 39, No. 12, pp. 124002-1-7, 2018.

15. C. Goyal, J. S. Ubhi, and B. Raj, "A Reliable Leakage Reduction Technique for Approximate Full Adder with Reduced Ground Bounce Noise", *Journal of Mathematical Problems in Engineering*, Hindawi, Vol. 2018, Article ID 3501041, 16 pages, 2018.

16. Anuradha, J. Singh, B. Raj, and M. Khosla, "Design and Performance Analysis of Nano-Scale Memristor-Based Nonvolatile SRAM", *Journal of Sensor Letter*, American Scientific Publishers, Vol. 16, pp. 798–805, 2018.

17. G. Wadhwa, and B. Raj, "Parametric Variation Analysis of Charge-Plasma-based Dielectric Modulated JLTFET for Biosensor Application", *IEEE Sensor Journal*, Vol. 18, No. 15, 2018.

18. J. Singh, and B. Raj, "Comparative Analysis of Memristor Models for Memories Design", *JoS*, IoP, Vol. 39, No. 7, pp. 074006-1-12, 2018.

19. D. Yadav, S. S. Chouhan, S. K. Vishvakarma, and B. Raj, "Application Specific Microcontroller Design for IoT Based WSN", *Sensor Letter*, ASP, Vol. 16, pp. 374–385, 2018.

20. G. Singh, R. K. Sarin, and B. Raj, "Fault-Tolerant Design and Analysis of Quantum-Dot Cellular Automata Based Circuits", *IEEE/IET Circuits, Devices & Systems*, Vol. 12, pp. 638–664, 2018.

21. J. Singh, and B. Raj, "Modeling of Mean Barrier Height Levying Various Image Forces of Metal Insulator Metal Structure to Enhance the Performance of Conductive Filament Based Memristor Model", *IEEE Nanotechnology*, Vol. 17, No. 2, pp. 268–275, 2018.

22. A. Jain, S. Sharma, and B. Raj, "Analysis of Triple Metal Surrounding Gate (TM-SG) III-V Nanowire MOSFET for Photosensing Application", *Opto-Electronics Journal*, Elsevier, Vol. 26, No. 2, pp. 141–148, 2018.

23. A. Jain, S. Sharma, and B. Raj, "Design and Analysis of High Sensitivity Photosensor Using Cylindrical Surrounding Gate MOSFET for Low Power Sensor Applications", *Engineering Science and Technology, an International Journal*, Elsevier's, Vol. 19, No. 4, pp. 1864–1870, 2016.

24. A. Singh, M. Khosla, and B. Raj, "Analysis of Electrostatic Doped Schottky Barrier Carbon Nanotube FET for Low Power Applications," *Journal of Materials Science: Materials in Electronics*, Springer, Vol. 28, pp. 1762–1768, 2017.

25. G. Saiphani Kumar, A. Singh, B. Raj, "Design and Analysis of Gate All around CNTFET Based SRAM Cell Design", *Journal of Computational Electronics*, Springer, Vol. 17, No.1, pp. 138–145, 2018.

26. G. P. Singh, B. S. Sohi, and B. Raj, "Material Properties Analysis of Graphene Base Transistor (GBT) for VLSI Analog Circuits", *Indian Journal of Pure & Applied Physics (IJPAP)*, Vol. 55, pp. 896–902, 2017.

27. S. Kumar and B. Raj, "Estimation of Stability and Performance Metric for Inward Access Transistor Based 6T SRAM Cell Design Using n-type/p-type DMDG-GDOV TFET", *IEEE VLSI Circuits and Systems Letter*, Vol. 3, No. 2, pp. 25–39, 2017.

28. S. Sharma, A. Kumar, M. Pattanaik, and B. Raj, "Forward Body Biased Multimode Multi-Threshold CMOS Technique for Ground Bounce Noise Reduction in Static CMOS Adders", *International Journal of Information and Electronics Engineering*, Vol. 3, No. 3, pp. 567–572, 2013.

29. H. Singh, P. Kumar, and B. Raj, "Performance Analysis of Majority Gate SET Based 1-bit Full Adder", *International Journal of Computer and Communication Engineering (IJCCE)*, IACSIT Press Singapore, ISSN: 2010-3743, Vol. 2, No. 4, pp. 2933–2940, 2013.

30. A. K. Bhardwaj, S. Gupta, and B. Raj, "Investigation of Parameters for Schottky Barrier (SB) Height for Schottky Barrier Based Carbon Nanotube Field Effect Transistor Device", *Journal of Nanoelectronics and Optoelectronics*, ASP, Vol. 15, pp. 783–791, 2020.

31. P. Bansal, and B. Raj, "Memristor: A Versatile Nonlinear Model for Dopant Drift and Boundary Issues", *JCTN*, American Scientific Publishers, Vol. 14, No. 5, pp. 2319–2325, 2017.

32. N. Jain, and B. Raj, "An Analog and Digital Design Perspective Comprehensive Approach on Fin-FET (Fin-Field Effect Transistor) Technology - A Review", *Reviews in Advanced Sciences and Engineering (RASE)*, ASP, Vol. 5, pp. 1–14, 2016.

33. S. Sharma, B. Raj, and M. Khosla, "Subthreshold Performance of $In_{1-x}Ga_xAs$ Based Dual Metal with Gate Stack Cylindrical/Surrounding Gate Nanowire MOSFET for Low Power Analog Applications", *Journal of Nanoelectronics and Optoelectronics*, American Scientific Publishers, USA, Vol. 12, pp. 171–176, 2017.

34. B. Raj, A. K. Saxena, and S. Dasgupta, "Analytical Modeling for the Estimation of Leakage Current and Subthreshold Swing Factor of Nanoscale Double Gate FinFET Device" *Microelectronics International, UK*, Vol. 26, pp. 53–63, 2009.

35. S. S. Soniya, G. Wadhwa, and B. Raj, "An Analytical Modeling for Dual Source Vertical Tunnel Field Effect Transistor", *International Journal of Recent Technology and Engineering (IJRTE)*, Vol. 8, No. 2, pp. 603–610, 2019.

36. S. Singh, and B. Raj, "Design and Analysis of Hetrojunction Vertical T-Shaped Tunnel Field Effect Transistor", *Journal of Electronics Material*, Springer, Vol. 48, No. 10, pp. 6253–6260, 2019.

37. C. Goyal, J. S. Ubhi, and B. Raj, "A Low Leakage CNTFET Based Inexact Full Adder for Low Power Image Processing Applications", *International Journal of Circuit Theory and Applications*, Wiley, Vol. 47, No. 9, pp. 1446–1458, 2019.

38. B. Raj, A. K. Saxena, and S. Dasgupta, "A Compact Drain Current and Threshold Voltage Quantum Mechanical Analytical Modeling for FinFETs", *Journal of Nanoelectronics and Optoelectronics (JNO), USA*, Vol. 3, No. 2, pp. 163–170, 2008.

39. G. Wadhwa, and B. Raj, "An Analytical Modeling of Charge Plasma Based Tunnel Field Effect Transistor with Impacts of Gate Underlap Region", *Superlattices and Microstructures*, Elsevier, Vol. 142, p. 106512, 2020.

40. S. Singh, and B. Raj, "Modeling and Simulation Analysis of SiGe Hetrojunction Double GateVertical t-Shaped Tunnel FET", *Superlattices and Microstructures*, Elsevier, Vol. 142, p. 106496, 2020.

41. A. Singh, D. K. Saini, D. Agarwal, S. Aggarwal, M. Khosla, and B. Raj, "Modeling and Simulation of Carbon Nanotube Field Effect Transistor and Its Circuit Application", *Journal of Semiconductors (JoS)*, IOP Science, Vol. 37, pp. 074001–074006, 2016.

42. N. Jain, and B. Raj, "Device and Circuit Co-Design Perspective Comprehensive Approach on FinFET Technology - A Review", *Journal of Electron Devices*, Vol. 23, No. 1, pp. 1890–1901, 2016.

43. S. Kumar and B. Raj, "Analysis of I_{ON} and Ambipolar Current for Dual-Material Gate-Drain Overlapped DG-TFET", *Journal of Nanoelectronics and Optoelectronics*, American Scientific Publishers, USA, Vol. 11, pp. 323–333, 2016.

44. S. S. Soniya, G. Wadhwa, and B. Raj, "Design and Analysis of Dual Source Vertical Tunnel Field Effect Transistor for High Performance", *Transactions on Electrical and Electronics Materials*, Springer, Vol. 21, pp. 74–82, 2019.

45. M. Kaur, N. Gupta, S. Kumar, B. Raj, and A. K. Singh, "RF Performance Analysis of Intercalated Graphene Nanoribbon Based Global Level Interconnects", *Journal of Computational Electronics*, Springer, Vol. 19, pp. 1002–1013, 2020.

46. G. Wadhwa, B. Raj, "Design and Performance Analysis of Junctionless TFET Biosensor for High Sensitivity" *IEEE Nanotechnology*, Vol. 18, pp. 567–574, 2019.

47. J. Singh, and B. Raj, "Enhanced Nonlinear Memristor Model Encapsulating Stochastic Dopant Drift", *JNO*, ASP, 14, 958–963, 2019.

48. N. Anjum, T. Bali, and B. Raj, "Design and Simulation of Handwritten Multiscript Character Recognition", *International Journal of Advanced Research in Computer and Communication Engineering*, Vol. 2, No. 7, pp. 2544–2549, 2013.

49. S. Sharma, B. Raj, and M. Khosla, "A Gaussian Approach for Analytical Subthreshold Current Model of Cylindrical Nanowire FET with Quantum Mechanical Effects", *Microelectronics Journal*, Elsevier, Vol. 53, pp. 65–72, 2016.

50. K. Singh, and B. Raj, "Performance and Analysis of Temperature Dependent Multi-Walled Carbon Nanotubes as Global Interconnects at Different Technology Nodes", *Journal of Computational Electronics*, Springer, Vol. 14, No. 2, pp. 469–476, 2015.

51. S. Kumar and B. Raj, "Compact Channel Potential Analytical Modeling of DG-TFET Based on Evanescent–Mode Approach", *Journal of Computational Electronics*, Springer, Vol. 14, No. 2, pp. 820–827, 2015.

52. K. Singh, and B. Raj, "Temperature Dependent Modeling and Performance Evaluation of Multi-Walled CNT and Single-Walled CNT as Global Interconnects", *Journal of Electronic Materials*, Springer, Vol. 44, No. 12, pp. 4825–4835, 2015.

53. V. K. Sharma, M. Pattanaik, and B. Raj, "INDEP Approach for Leakage Reduction in Nanoscale CMOS Circuits", *International Journal of Electronics*, Taylor & Francis, Vol. 102, No. 2, pp. 200–215, 2014.

54. K. Singh, and B. Raj, "Influence of Temperature on MWCNT Bundle, SWCNT Bundle and Copper Interconnects for Nanoscaled Technology Nodes", *Journal of Materials Science: Materials in Electronics*, Springer, Vol. 26, No. 8, pp. 6134–6142, 2015.

55. N. Anjum, T. Bali, and B. Raj, "Design and Simulation of Handwritten Gurumukhi and Devanagri Numerical Recognition", *International Journal of Computer Applications*, Published by Foundation of Computer Science, New York, USA, Vol. 73, No. 12, pp. 16–21, 2013.

56. S. Khandelwal, V. Gupta, B. Raj, and R. D. Gupta, "Process Variability Aware Low Leakage Reliable Nano Scale DG-FinFET SRAM Cell Design Technique", *Journal of Nanoelectronics and Optoelectronics*, Vol. 10, No. 6, pp. 810–817, 2015.

57. V. K. Sharma, M. Pattanaik, and B. Raj, "ONOFIC Approach: Low Power High Speed Nanoscale VLSI Circuits Design", *International Journal of Electronics*, Taylor & Francis, Vol. 101, No. 1, pp. 61–73, 2014.

58. S. Khandelwal, B. Raj, and R. D. Gupta, "FinFET Based 6T SRAM Cell Design: Analysis of Performance Metric, Process Variation and Temperature Effect", *Journal of Computational and Theoretical Nanoscience*, ASP, USA, Vol. 12, pp. 2500–2506, 2015.

59. S. Singh, Y. Shekhar, R. Jagdeep, S. Anurag, and B. Raj, "Impact of HfO$_2$ in Graded Channel Dual Insulator Double Gate MOSFET", *Journal of Computational and Theoretical Nanoscience*, American Scientific Publishers, Vol. 12, No. 6, pp. 950–953, 2015.

60. V. K. Sharma, M. Pattanaik, and B. Raj, "PVT Variations Aware Low Leakage INDEP Approach for Nanoscale CMOS Circuits", *Microelectronics Reliability*, Elsevier, Vol. 54, pp. 90–99, 2014.

61. B. Raj, A. K. Saxena and S. Dasgupta, "Quantum Mechanical Analytical Modeling of Nanoscale DG FinFET: Evaluation of Potential, Threshold Voltage and Source/Drain Resistance", *Elsevier's Journal of Material Science in Semiconductor Processing*, Elsevier, Vol. 16, No. 4, pp. 1131–1137, 2013.

62. M. Gopal, S. S. D. Prasad, and B. Raj, "8T SRAM Cell Design for Dynamic and Leakage Power Reduction", *International Journal of Computer Applications*, Published by Foundation of Computer Science, New York, USA, Vol. 71, No. 9, pp. 43–48, 2013.

63. M. Pattanaik, B. Raj, S. Sharma, and A. Kumar, "Diode Based Trimode Multi-Threshold CMOS Technique for Ground Bounce Noise Reduction in Static CMOS Adders", *Advanced Materials Research*, Trans Tech Publications, Switzerland, Vol. 548, pp. 885–889, 2012.

64. B. Raj, A. K. Saxena, and S. Dasgupta, "Nanoscale FinFET Based SRAM Cell Design: Analysis of Performance Metric, Process Variation, Underlapped FinFET and Temperature effect", *IEEE Circuits and System Magazine*, Vol. 11, No. 2, pp. 38–50, 2011.

65. V. K. Sharma, M. Pattanaik, and B. Raj, "Leakage Current ONOFIC Approach for Deep Submicron VLSI Circuit Design", *International Journal of Electrical, Computer, Electronics and Communication Engineering*, World Academy of Sciences, Engineering and Technology, Vol. 7, No. 4, pp. 239–244, 2013.

66. T. Chawla, M. Khosla, and B. Raj, "Design and Simulation of Triple Metal Double-Gate Germanium on Insulator Vertical Tunnel Field Effect Transistor", *Microelectronics Journal*, Elsevier, Vol. 114, p. 105125, 2021.

67. P. Kaur, S. S. Gill, and B. Raj, "Comparative Analysis of OFETs Materials and Devices for Sensor Applications", *Journal of Silicon*, Springer, Vol. 14, pp. 4463–4471, 2022.

68. S. K. Sharma, P. Kumar, B. Raj, and B. Raj, "In$_{1-x}$Ga$_x$As Double Metal Gate-Stacking Cylindrical Nanowire MOSFET for Highly Sensitive Photo detector", *Journal of Silicon*, Springer, Vol. 14, pp. 3535–3541, 2022.

69. B. Raj, A. K. Saxena, and S. Dasgupta, "Analytical Modeling of Quasi Planar Nanoscale Double Gate FinFET with Source/Drain Resistance and Field Dependent Carrier Mobility: A Quantum Mechanical Study", *Journal of Computer (JCP)*, Academy Publisher, FINLAND, Vol. 4, No. 9, pp. 1–8, 2009.

70. S. Bhushan, S. Khandelwal, and B. Raj, "Analyzing Different Mode FinFET Based Memory Cell at Different Power Supply for Leakage Reduction", Seventh International Conference on Bio-Inspired Computing: Theories and Application, (BIC-TA 2012), *Advances in Intelligent Systems and Computing*, Vol. 202, pp. 89–100, 2013.

71. I. Singh, B. Raj, M. Khosla, and B. K. Kaushik, "Potential MRAM Technologies for Low Power SoCs", SPIN World Scientific Publisher, SCIE; Vol. 10, No. 04, p. 2050027, 2020.

72. S. Singh, and B. Raj, "Parametric Variation Analysis on Hetero-Junction Vertical t-Shape TFET for Supressing Ambipolar Conduction", *Indian Journal of Pure and Applied Physics*, Vol. 58, pp. 478–485, 2020.

73. A. Singh, M. Khosla, and B. Raj, "Design and Analysis of Electrostatic Doped Schottky Barrier CNTFET Based Low Power SRAM", *International Journal of Electronics and Communications, (AEÜ)*, Elsevier, Vol. 80, pp. 67–72, 2017.

74. T. Chawla, M. Khosla, and B. Raj, "Optimization of Double-Gate Dual Material GeOI-Vertical TFET for VLSI Circuit Design", *IEEE VLSI Circuits and Systems Letter*, Vol. 6, No. 2, pp. 13–25, 2020.

75. S. K. Verma, S. Singh, G. Wadhwa and B. Raj, "Detection of Biomolecules Using Charge-Plasma Based Gate Underlap Dielectric Modulated Dopingless TFET", *Transactions on Electrical and Electronic Materials (TEEM)*, Springer, Vol. 21, pp. 528–535, 2020.

76. N. Jain, and B. Raj, "Impact of Underlap Spacer Region Variation on Electrostatic and Analog/RF Performance of Symmetrical High-k SOI FinFET at 20 nm Channel Length", *Journal of Semiconductors (JoS)*, IOP Science, Vol. 38, No. 12, p. 122002, 2017.

77. S. Singh, and B. Raj, "Analytical Modeling and Simulation Analysis of T-Shaped III-V Heterojunction Vertical T-FET", *Superlattices and Microstructures*, Elsevier, Vol. 147, p. 106717, 2020.

78. J. Singh, and B. Raj, "Temperature Dependent Analytical Modeling and Simulations of Nanoscale Memristor", *Engineering Science and Technology, an International Journal*, Elsevier's, Vol. 21, pp. 862–868, 2018.

79. S. Singh, S. Bala, B. Raj, and B. Raj, "Improved Sensitivity of Dielectric Modulated Junctionless Transistor for Nanoscale Biosensor Design", *Sensor Letter*, ASP, Vol. 18, pp. 328–333, 2020.
80. V. Kumar, S. K. Vishvakarma, and B. Raj, "Design and Performance Analysis of ASIC for IoT Applications", *Sensor Letter*, ASP, Vol. 18, pp. 31–38, 2020.
81. A. Jaiswal, R. K. Sarin, B. Raj, and S. Sukhija, "A Novel Circular Slotted Microstrip-fed Patch Antenna with Three Triangle Shape Defected Ground Structure for Multiband Applications", *Advanced Electromagnetic (AEM)*, Vol. 7, No. 3, pp. 56–63, 2018.
82. G. Wadhwa, and B Raj, "Label Free Detection of Biomolecules using Charge-Plasma-Based Gate Underlap Dielectric Modulated Junctionless TFET", *Journal of Electronic Materials (JEMS)*, Springer, Vol. 47, No. 8, pp. 4683–4693, 2018.
83. G. Singh, R. K. Sarin, and B. Raj, "Design and Performance Analysis of a New Efficient Coplanar Quantum-Dot Cellular Automata Adder", *Indian Journal of Pure & Applied Physics (IJPAP)*, Vol. 55, pp. 97–103, 2017.
84. P. Kaur, V. Pandey, and B. Raj, "Comparative Study of Efficient Design, Control and Monitoring of Solar Power Using IoT", *Sensor Letter*, ASP, Vol. 18, pp. 419–426, 2020.
85. G. Wadhwa, P. Kamboj, J. Singh, B. Raj, "Design and Investigation of Junctionless DGTFET for Biological Molecule Recognition", *Transactions on Electrical and Electronic Materials*, Springer, Vol. 22, pp. 282–289, 2020.
86. G. Singh, R. K. Sarin, and B. Raj, "Design and Analysis of Area Efficient QCA Based Reversible Logic Gates", *Journal of Microprocessors and Microsystems*, Elsevier, Vol. 52, pp. 59–68, 2017
87. A. Singh, M. Khosla, and B. Raj, "Compact Model for Ballistic Single Wall CNTFET under Quantum Capacitance Limit", *Journal of Semiconductors (JoS)*, IOP Science, Vol. 37, pp. 104001–104008, 2016.
88. S. Singh, M. Khosla, G. Wadhwa, and B. Raj, "Design and Analysis of Double-Gate Junctionless Vertical TFET for Gas Sensing Applications", *Applied Physics A*, Springer, Vol. 127, No. 16, pp. 725–732, 2021.